The Trade Lifecycle

For other titles in the Wiley Finance series
please see www.wiley.com/finance

The Trade Lifecycle

*Behind the Scenes of the
Trading Process*

Robert Baker

A John Wiley and Sons, Ltd., Publication

This edition first published 2010
© 2010 John Wiley & Sons, Ltd

Registered office
John Wiley & Sons Ltd, The Atrium, Southern Gate, Chichester, West Sussex, PO19 8SQ, United Kingdom

For details of our global editorial offices, for customer services and for information about how to apply for
permission to reuse the copyright material in this book please see our website at www.wiley.com.

Library of Congress Cataloging-in-Publication Data

Baker, Robert.
   The trade lifecycle : behind the scenes of the trading process / Robert Baker.
      p. cm.
   ISBN 978-0-470-68591-4
1. Commodity exchanges. 2. Commercial products. 3. Risk. I. Title.
HG6046.B323 2010
332.64–dc22   2010003322

A catalogue record for this book is available from the British Library.

ISBN 978-0-470-68591-4

Set in 10/12pt Times by Aptara Inc., New Delhi, India
Printed in Great Britain by CPI Antony Rowe, Chippenham, Wiltshire

To the memory of my dear mother

Contents

Preface   xxiii

Author's Note   xxv

Acknowledgements   xxvii

PART I PRODUCTS AND THE BACKGROUND TO TRADING   **1**

1 Trading   **3**
    1.1   How and why do people trade?   3
    1.2   Factors affecting trade   3
    1.3   Market participants   3
        1.3.1   Producer   4
        1.3.2   Consumer   4
        1.3.3   Speculator   4
        1.3.4   Market maker   4
    1.4   Means by which trades are transacted   4
        1.4.1   Brokers   4
        1.4.2   Exchanges   5
        1.4.3   Over-the-counter   5
    1.5   When is a trade live?   6
    1.6   Consequences of trading   6
    1.7   Trading in the financial services industry   6
        1.7.1   Two types of trading policy   7
        1.7.2   Why does a financial entity trade?   7
    1.8   What do we mean by a trade?   9
    1.9   Who works on the trade and when?   9
    1.10   Summary   10

2 Risk   **11**
    2.1   Introduction   11
    2.2   Risk is inevitable   11
    2.3   Quantifying risk   11

2.4	Methods of dealing with risk	12
	2.4.1 Ignore	12
	2.4.2 Minimise	12
	2.4.3 Avoid	12
	2.4.4 Remove	13
2.5	Managing risk	13
2.6	Problems of unforeseen risk	13
2.7	Summary	13

3 Asset Classes   **15**
3.1	Interest rates	15
	3.1.1 Deposit	15
	3.1.2 Future	15
	3.1.3 Swap	15
	3.1.4 Tradeflow issues	17
3.2	Foreign exchange (FX)	17
	3.2.1 Spot	17
	3.2.2 Futures and forwards	17
	3.2.3 Swaps	17
	3.2.4 Baskets	18
	3.2.5 Tradeflow issues	18
3.3	Equity	19
	3.3.1 Synthetic equities (index)	19
	3.3.2 Lifecycle issues pertinent to equity trades	19
3.4	Bonds and credit	20
	3.4.1 Bonds	20
	3.4.2 Other credit risk bearing instruments	24
3.5	Commodities	27
	3.5.1 What are commodities?	27
	3.5.2 Agricultural commodities	27
	3.5.3 Examples of animal products	27
	3.5.4 Energy	28
	3.5.5 Precious metals	28
	3.5.6 Industrial metals	28
	3.5.7 OTC commodities	28
	3.5.8 Localised nature of production	28
	3.5.9 Time lag	28
	3.5.10 Utility of commodities	29
	3.5.11 Precious metals as a currency	29
	3.5.12 Physical settlement	29
	3.5.13 Other tradeflow issues	29
3.6	Trading across asset classes	30
3.7	Summary	30

4 Derivatives, Structures and Hybrids   **31**
| 4.1 | What is a derivative? | 31 |
| 4.2 | Linear | 31 |

    4.3   Nonlinear   31
          4.3.1   Trade process issues relating to options   33
          4.3.2   Exercise   33
          4.3.3   Optionality   33
          4.3.4   Leverage   33
    4.4   Some option terminology   35
    4.5   Option valuation   35
    4.6   Exotic options   36
          4.6.1   Issues with exotics   37
    4.7   Structures and hybrids   37
    4.8   Importance of simpler products   38
    4.9   Trade matrix   39
    4.10 Summary   39

5   Credit Derivatives   **41**
    5.1   Introduction   41
    5.2   CDS   41
    5.3   CLN   42
    5.4   CDO   43
          5.4.1   CDO reference pool   44
          5.4.2   Static and managed CDOs   45
          5.4.3   CDO pricing methodology   46
          5.4.4   Other terminology   47
    5.5   Data relating to CDOs   48
          5.5.1   Reference pool data   48
          5.5.2   Tranche data   49
          5.5.3   CDO deal details   49
    5.6   Practical aspects of CDO management   49
          5.6.1   What is happening?   49
          5.6.2   What has happened?   50
          5.6.3   What is likely to happen and what is the worst that can happen?   51
          5.6.4   What opportunities do I have?   51
          5.6.5   Reporting   52
          5.6.6   Limits   52
          5.6.7   Alerts   53
    5.7   Practical aspects of CDO valuation   53
    5.8   Why are credit derivatives different?   54
    5.9   Summary   56

6   Liquidity, Price and Leverage   **57**
    6.1   Liquidity   57
          6.1.1   Two types of trading   57
          6.1.2   What is liquidity?   57
          6.1.3   Asset liquidity   57
          6.1.4   Measuring liquidity   57
          6.1.5   Risks associated with liquidity   58

6.2   Price   58
      6.2.1   Over-the-counter price   58
      6.2.2   Exchange price   58
      6.2.3   Broker price   59
      6.2.4   What can we infer from price?   59
      6.2.5   Cost of unwind   59
      6.2.6   Volumes   59
6.3   Leverage   60
      6.3.1   Advantages of leverage   60
      6.3.2   Disadvantages of leverage   61
      6.3.3   Measurement of leverage   61
      6.3.4   Current market position   61
      6.3.5   Time   62
      6.3.6   Asset class   62
      6.3.7   Monitoring of leverage   62
      6.3.8   Summary   62

PART II   THE TRADE LIFECYCLE   63

7   Anatomy of a Trade   65
    7.1   The underlying   65
    7.2   General   65
    7.3   Economic   66
    7.4   Sales   66
    7.5   Legal   66
    7.6   Booking   66
    7.7   Counterparty   67
    7.8   Timeline   67
          7.8.1   Dates relating to a trade   67
          7.8.2   Fixed cash or asset exchange dates   67
          7.8.3   Unknown cash or asset exchange dates   67
          7.8.4   Example   67

8   Lifecycle   69
    8.1   Pre Execution   69
          8.1.1   Provisional trades   69
          8.1.2   Orders   70
    8.2   Execution and booking   71
          8.2.1   Execution   71
          8.2.2   Booking   71
    8.3   Confirmation   72
          8.3.1   Matching   73
          8.3.2   Confirmation   73
    8.4   Post booking   74
          8.4.1   Trade scrutiny   74
          8.4.2   Enrichment   75

	8.4.3	Cashflows	75
	8.4.4	Fees and duties	75
	8.4.5	Error reporting	75
8.5	Settlement		75
	8.5.1	The importance of settlement	76
	8.5.2	Settlement instructions	76
	8.5.3	Custodian	76
	8.5.4	Cash or physical	76
	8.5.5	Cash	76
	8.5.6	Documentation	76
	8.5.7	Physical commodity	77
	8.5.8	Cash settlement of commodities	77
	8.5.9	Nostro accounts	77
	8.5.10	Risks	77
	8.5.11	Advantage of quick settlement	78
	8.5.12	Multiple settlement dates	78
	8.5.13	Breaks	79
8.6	Overnight		79
	8.6.1	Individual trade and aggregation with other trades	79
	8.6.2	Date and time	79
	8.6.3	Internal and external trade dates	80
	8.6.4	Deciding time for end of day	80
	8.6.5	End of day roll	80
	8.6.6	Overnight processes	81
	8.6.7	Pre overnight checks	81
	8.6.8	Amalgamation between systems	81
	8.6.9	Stale data	82
8.7	Changes during lifetime		82
	8.7.1	Dividends	82
	8.7.2	Coupons	83
	8.7.3	Other corporate actions	83
	8.7.4	Changes as a result of market data	83
	8.7.5	Counterparty changes	84
	8.7.6	Collateral	84
	8.7.7	Changes to the trade	85
	8.7.8	Management of changes	86
	8.7.9	Risks	86
8.8	Reporting during lifetime		86
8.9	Exercise		87
	8.9.1	Exercise date	87
	8.9.2	When to exercise	87
	8.9.3	Cash or physical	87
	8.9.4	Exercise as a process	87
	8.9.5	Fugit	88
	8.9.6	Risks associated with exercise	88
8.10	Maturity		88
	8.10.1	Final settlement date	88

8.11   Example trade   89
       8.11.1   The trade lifecycle   89
8.12   Summary   91

9   Cashflows and Asset Holdings   **93**
9.1   Introduction   93
9.2   Holdings   94
9.3   Value of holding   95
9.4   Reconciliation   96
9.5   Consolidated reporting   97
9.6   Realised and unrealised P&L   97
9.7   Diversification   97
9.8   Bank within a bank   98
9.9   Custody of securities   98
       9.9.1   Registered securities   98
       9.9.2   Bearer securities   98
       9.9.3   Use of custodians   99
9.10   Risks   99
9.11   Summary   99

10   Risk Management   **101**
10.1   Traders   101
       10.1.1   Desirable exposure   101
       10.1.2   Undesirable exposure   101
10.2   Risk control   101
10.3   Trading management   102
10.4   Senior management   102
10.5   How do risks arise?   102
       10.5.1   Spot trades   102
       10.5.2   Futures and forwards   102
       10.5.3   Options   103
       10.5.4   Exposures to fixed or float income streams   103
       10.5.5   Exposure to debt   103
       10.5.6   Exposure to group of products   103
10.6   Different reasons for trades   103
10.7   Hedging   103
10.8   What happens when the trader is not around?   104
       10.8.1   Availability of other traders   104
       10.8.2   Stop and limit orders   104
10.9   Types of risk   105
       10.9.1   Delta   105
       10.9.2   Gamma   105
       10.9.3   Vega (sometimes known as kappa)   105
       10.9.4   Rho   105
       10.9.5   Theta   106
       10.9.6   Additional risks for credit products   106
       10.9.7   Default risk (or jump to default)   106

          10.9.8   Recovery rate   106
          10.9.9   Correlation risk   106
          10.9.10   Risks in general   106
          10.9.11   Dreaming ahead   107
   10.10   Trading strategies   107
          10.10.1   Front book   107
          10.10.2   Back book   107
   10.11   Hedging strategies   108
          10.11.1   Delta hedging   108
          10.11.2   Stop-loss hedging   108
   10.12   Summary   109

11 **Market Risk Control**   **111**
   11.1   Various methodologies   111
          11.1.1   Scenario analysis   111
          11.1.2   Value at Risk (VaR)   112
          11.1.3   Instantaneous measures of risk (sensitivity analysis) 113
   11.2   Need for risk   114
   11.3   Allocation of risk   114
   11.4   Monitoring of market risk   115
   11.5   Controlling the risk   115
   11.6   Responsibilities of the market risk control department   116
   11.7   Limitations of market risk departments   116
          11.7.1   Everything correlated   117
          11.7.2   The tails   117
          11.7.3   The human factor   117
          11.7.4   Balanced approach   117
   11.8   Regulatory requirements   117
          11.8.1   Basel II   117
          11.8.2   Capital Adequacy Ratio (CAR)   118
   11.9   Summary   118

12 **Counterparty Risk Control**   **119**
   12.1   Reasons for non fulfilment of obligations   119
   12.2   Consequences of counterparty default   119
   12.3   Counterparty risk over time   120
   12.4   How to measure the risk   120
          12.4.1   Expected loss   121
          12.4.2   Credit exposure   121
          12.4.3   Potential future exposure (PFE)   122
          12.4.4   Netting   122
          12.4.5   Back-to-back   123
   12.5   Imposing limits   123
   12.6   Who is the counterparty?   124
   12.7   Collateral   124
          12.7.1   Example of a collateral agreement   124
          12.7.2   Advantages of collateral in general   124

12.8   Activities of the counterparty risk control department   125
   12.8.1   Set policies for estimating exposure   125
   12.8.2   Assign limits based on credit worthiness   125
   12.8.3   Measure exposure   125
   12.8.4   Deal with breaches   126
   12.8.5   Policies for new trade types   126
   12.8.6   Maintain legal data   126
   12.8.7   Managing margin payments and receipts   126
   12.8.8   Interface with management   127
12.9   What are the risks involved in analysing credit risk?   127
   12.9.1   Correlation between counterparties   127
   12.9.2   Added complication of credit risk   127
   12.9.3   Insufficient consideration of counterparty risk   127
   12.9.4   Sudden counterparty changes   127
12.10   Payment systems   128
12.11   Summary   129

13   Accounting   131
13.1   Balance sheet   131
   13.1.1   Fixed assets   131
   13.1.2   Investments   131
   13.1.3   Cash   131
   13.1.4   Debtors   132
   13.1.5   Creditors   132
   13.1.6   Capital   132
   13.1.7   Profit and loss   132
   13.1.8   Events that affect balance sheet items   132
13.2   Profit and loss account   133
   13.2.1   Introduction   133
   13.2.2   Realised   134
   13.2.3   Unrealised   134
   13.2.4   Accrued   134
   13.2.5   Incidental   134
   13.2.6   Worked example   134
   13.2.7   Individual trades   135
   13.2.8   Who is responsible for producing P&L?   136
   13.2.9   Risks associated with reporting P&L   136
13.3   Financial reports for hedge funds and asset managers   137
   13.3.1   Overview   137
   13.3.2   Fees   137
   13.3.3   Reports   137

14   P&L Attribution   139
14.1   Benefits   139
   14.1.1   Catches mistakes   139
   14.1.2   Reconciliation   139
   14.1.3   Better understanding of the trades and the market   139

14.2   The process   140
        14.2.1   Market movements   140
        14.2.2   Theta   140
        14.2.3   Unexplained   142
14.3   Example   142
14.4   Summary   143

PART III   SYSTEMS AND PROCEDURES   145

15   **People**   147
      15.1   Traders   147
      15.2   Trading assistants   148
      15.3   Structurers   148
      15.4   Sales   149
      15.5   Researchers   149
      15.6   Middle office (product control)   149
              15.6.1   Trade   149
              15.6.2   Data   149
              15.6.3   Implementing trade changes   150
              15.6.4   Reporting   150
              15.6.5   Valuation   150
              15.6.6   Responsibility   150
              15.6.7   Liaison   150
              15.6.8   Processes   151
              15.6.9   Security   151
              15.6.10   End of day   151
              15.6.11   End of month   151
              15.6.12   Summary   152
      15.7   Back office (operations)   152
      15.8   Quantitative analyst   152
              15.8.1   Short-term pricing   153
              15.8.2   Long-term model development   153
              15.8.3   Tools of the trade   153
              15.8.4   Role of quantitative analysts   154
      15.9   Information technology   154
              15.9.1   Front-line support   155
              15.9.2   Infrastructure   155
              15.9.3   Architects   155
              15.9.4   Programmers   156
              15.9.5   Project managers   156
              15.9.6   IT operators   157
              15.9.7   Testers   157
      15.10   Legal   158
      15.11   Model validation   158
      15.12   Market risk control department   159
      15.13   Counterparty risk control department   159
      15.14   Finance   159

15.15   Internal audit   160
   15.15.1   Routine checks   160
   15.15.2   Thorough audit of one area   160
15.16   Compliance   160
   15.16.1   Due diligence   161
   15.16.2   External regulation   161
   15.16.3   Staff training   161
15.17   Trading manager   161
15.18   Management   162
   15.18.1   Balance   162
   15.18.2   Board of directors   162
15.19   Human risks   162
   15.19.1   Too much knowledge in one person   162
   15.19.2   Not enough knowledge   162
   15.19.3   The wrong people   163
   15.19.4   Not enough investment in people   163
   15.19.5   Incentive   163
   15.19.6   Short-term thinking   164
   15.19.7   Conflicts and tensions   164
   15.19.8   Communication   165
15.20   Summary   166

16   Developing Processes for New Products (and Improving Processes for Existing Products)   **167**
16.1   What is a process?   167
16.2   The status quo   167
16.3   How processes evolve   167
16.4   Inventory of current systems   169
16.5   Coping with change   170
16.6   Improving the situation   171
   16.6.1   What would the ideal set of processes be?   171
   16.6.2   Understanding the current processes   171
16.7   Inertia   173
16.8   Summary   174

17   New Products   **175**
17.1   Origin of new products   175
17.2   Trial basis   176
   17.2.1   Why trial?   176
   17.2.2   Features of the trial   176
   17.2.3   Advantages of the trial   176
17.3   New trade checklist   177
   17.3.1   Management approval   177
   17.3.2   Legal and regulatory approval   177
   17.3.3   Trading limits   177
   17.3.4   Risk control limits   178

17.3.5 Models   178
17.3.6 Trade lifecycle processes   178
17.3.7 Middle office can book and mark the products   178
17.4 New product evolution   178
17.5 Risks   179
17.6 Summary   179

18 Systems   **181**
18.1 What makes a good system?   181
18.2 IT procurement   182
18.3 System stakeholders   182
18.4 The IT team   183
18.5 Timeline of a project   184
18.6 Project management   185
18.7 The IT divide   185
18.8 Techniques and issues related to IT   186
18.9 Systems architecture   191
       18.9.1 User interface   191
       18.9.2 Business logic   191
       18.9.3 Data repository   192
       18.9.4 Example   192
18.10 Different types of development   193
       18.10.1 Rapid application development (RAD)   193
       18.10.2 Dedicated IT team for a business function or area   193
       18.10.3 Independent IT division   193
       18.10.4 General comments   194
18.11 Buy versus build   195
18.12 Software vendors   196
18.13 Performance   196
       18.13.1 Hardware constraints   197
       18.13.2 Grid computing   197
18.14 Project estimation   197
18.15 General thoughts on IT   199
18.16 Summary   199

19 Testing   **201**
19.1 What is testing?   201
19.2 Why is testing important?   201
19.3 Who does testing?   202
19.4 When should testing be done?   203
19.5 What are the types of testing?   203
       19.5.1 Stages of testing   203
       19.5.2 Testing types   204
19.6 Fault logging   205
       19.6.1 Types of fault   205
       19.6.2 Workaround   205

	19.6.3	Priority	205
	19.6.4	Area	206
	19.6.5	Fault description	206
19.7	Risks		206
19.8	Summary		207

20 Data — **209**

20.1	Common characteristics		209
20.2	Database		209
20.3	Types of data		209
	20.3.1	Why does type of data matter?	210
20.4	Bid/offer spread		210
20.5	Curves and surfaces		211
20.6	Sets of market data		213
	20.6.1	Business usage of market data sets	214
20.7	Back testing		216
20.8	How can data go wrong?		216
	20.8.1	Techniques for dealing with bad data	217
	20.8.2	When to fix bad data	218
20.9	Typical data sources		218
20.10	How to cope with corrections to data		219
20.11	Data integrity		220
	20.11.1	Importance of data integrity	220
20.12	The business risks of data		221
	20.12.1	Putting too much faith in data	221
	20.12.2	Not reacting to data	221
	20.12.3	Coping when data not there	221
	20.12.4	Ensuring authentic data	222
20.13	Summary		222

21 Reports — **223**

21.1	Introduction		223
21.2	What makes a good report?		223
21.3	Reporting requirements		223
	21.3.1	Readership	223
	21.3.2	Content	224
	21.3.3	Presentation	224
	21.3.4	External readership	224
	21.3.5	Habit	225
	21.3.6	Distribution	225
	21.3.7	Timing	225
	21.3.8	Accuracy	226
	21.3.9	Raw reporting	226
	21.3.10	Configuration	226
	21.3.11	Dynamic	227
	21.3.12	Frame of reference	228
	21.3.13	The problem of multiple dimensions	228

21.4   When things go wrong   228
21.5   Redundancy   229
21.6   Control   229
21.7   Enhancement   230
21.8   Security   230
21.9   Risks   230
21.10   Summary   230

22   Calculation   231
22.1   What does the calculation process actually do?   231
        22.1.1   Example from outside the financial world   231
        22.1.2   Valuation of one trade   232
        22.1.3   Why not use mark-to-market?   232
        22.1.4   Other reasons why having a calculation engine is useful   234
        22.1.5   Why not rely solely on calculation engines?   235
        22.1.6   Compromise   235
        22.1.7   The model   236
22.2   The calculation itself   236
        22.2.1   Conversion to reporting currency   237
        22.2.2   Unknown cashflows   238
        22.2.3   Other dependencies   238
        22.2.4   Monte Carlo   239
22.3   Sensitivity analysis   239
22.4   Bootstrapping   240
22.5   Calculation of dates   241
22.6   Calibration to market   242
22.7   Testing   242
22.8   Integrating a model within a full system   243
22.9   Risks associated with the valuation process   243
22.10   Summary   243

23   Mathematical Model and Systems Validation   245
        Geoff Chaplin
23.1   Testing procedures   245
23.2   Implementation and documentation   247
23.3   Summary   247

24   Regulatory, Legal and Compliance   249
24.1   Regulatory requirements   249
        24.1.1   Registration   249
        24.1.2   Reporting   250
        24.1.3   Inspections   250
        24.1.4   Personal registration   250
24.2   Legal   250
24.3   Compliance   251
        24.3.1   Money laundering   251
        24.3.2   Insider trading   252

24.4   Risks   252
       24.4.1   Closure   252
       24.4.2   Penalties and prosecution   252
       24.4.3   Litigation   252
       24.4.4   Costs   253
       24.4.5   Reputational risk   253
       24.4.6   Advisory risk   253
24.5   Summary   253

25   Business Continuity Planning   255
25.1   What is business continuity planning?   255
25.2   Why is it important?   255
25.3   Types of disaster   255
25.4   How does it work?   256
25.5   Risks associated with BCP   257
25.6   Summary   257

PART IV   WHAT CAN GO WRONG, THE CREDIT CRISIS   **259**

26   Credit Derivatives and the Crisis of 2007   261
       Robert Reoch
26.1   Background   261
       26.1.1   SIVs   261
       26.1.2   Market liquidity   262
26.2   The events of mid-2007   263
       26.2.1   Subprime mortgages   263
       26.2.2   Investor impact   264
       26.2.3   Bank impact   265
       26.2.4   The failure of Lehman Brothers and the bailout of AIG   265
26.3   Issues to be addressed   266
       26.3.1   A different rating agency process   266
       26.3.2   Standardised nomenclature for credit ratings   267
       26.3.3   Keeping a percentage of originated risk on balance sheet 268
       26.3.4   Undrawn credit facility capital charge   268
       26.3.5   The future of CDOs   268
       26.3.6   Mitigating the negative impact of mark-to-market   269
26.4   Summary   269

Appendix: Summary of Risks   271
       General comment – unforeseen risk   271
       Operational risk (in the trade lifecycle)   271
       Human risks   273
       Market risk control   274
       Counterparty risk control   275
       Cashflow   275
       Data   276
       Reporting   276

New products   277
Legal and regulatory   277
Testing   277
Business continuity planning (BCP)   278
Valuation and model approval   278
Management   278
Documentation   279
Front office   279
Research   279
IT and systems   279
Effective control and support   280

Recommended Reading   **281**

Index   **283**

Preface

Trading has evolved from a humble apple grower wanting a stable price for his produce come harvest time, to a complex and exciting industry comprising a significant share of the global economy.

Trading is the fundamental activity of investment banks, hedge funds, pension funds and many other financial companies. There is no better way to understand the workings of a financial entity than to follow the progress of a trade through its lifecycle and all the activities performed upon it.

This book will dissect a trade into its components, track it from conception to maturity and describe the *raison d'être* of the business functions of a financial entity all arising from the processing of a trade. Having seen the full path of a trade, the reader will gain a more complete view of the world of finance which will answer some fundamental questions such as why, what and how do people trade.

Derivatives are complex variations of standard trades. By contrast and comparison with the lifecycle of standard trades the reader will glean a better understanding of these often misunderstood financial instruments.

Credit derivatives are another important set of products in our post credit crunch world. How do these instruments work and where do they differ from their non credit counterparts? This book has a special section devoted to them.

Together with the trade itself, the book will explore essential activities such as booking, confirmation, settlement, risk management, legal obligations, finance, and control functions such as credit, market risk and auditing. Almost every person working in an investment bank or hedge fund has a large part of their work connected to the lifecycle of a trade. It is the glue by which all the departments are bound and the aggregated success or failure of each trade determines the survival and growth of the entire organisation.

The various approaches to systems for the management of trade lifecycles are illustrated. The essential raw material to the measure of any trade is data and the book looks at what data is needed and by whom and how to cope with missing or unreliable data.

WHY THIS BOOK?

Many volumes have been written on the business side of trading and related activities such as market risk management. Although particular areas of the processes behind trading have been explained, I have not found the complete lifecycle of a trade fully described in one book. I feel a thorough end-to-end guide would be of interest to:

- anyone seeking work in the financial services industry;
- people already in the industry who want to see how their work fits into the organisation as a whole;
- those with an interest in the activities of a financial entity. They could include clients, academics, pension holders and people making investments of all sizes;
- people selling products and services to the financial sector such as software vendors.

The importance of the financial sector to the world economy has been brought into focus by many recent events: the credit crunch, the collapse of companies such as Lehman Brothers and a recession affecting most countries across the world. The result has been a demand for better inspection and regulation of trading activities. No longer is it sufficient for firms to return profits, they have to convince investors, shareholders and regulators that they are employing due diligence and managing risks.

In writing about the trading process, my aim is to reveal all areas subject to potential risk. Once a risk is known, it can be monitored and managed even if the eventual decision is not to take action – forewarned is forearmed.

Although any financial entity engaged in trading activities will have already arrived at a set of processes spanning the trade lifecycle, these are not always performed in an optimal fashion; they may have evolved more by historical accident than by design. A careful reappraisal of the *entire* trading processes can lead to:

- a reduction in risks
- exposure of weaknesses
- lower operating costs
- elimination of wastage
- better overall awareness leading to more confidence in the trading process.

I hope that this book might encourage all participants in the trade lifecycle to look again at their activities and those of their colleagues and see where improvements can be made to reduce risk and enhance the reputation of a battered industry.

Gaining employment in the financial sector is becoming increasingly competitive. It is no longer sufficient to have the skills and experience in one business function. Applicants must demonstrate an understanding of where they fit into the organisation and have the ability to communicate with other business functions – every activity in the trade lifecycle being connected to others. This book is written with a view to helping this understanding.

I have tried to make the book a readable progression through all the important activities and components of the trade lifecycle. Detailed explanations are given where necessary, but the book is intended as a comprehensive overview and therefore I have avoided too much detail where it might hinder the reader's ability to see the full picture.

Any mistakes are mine. All views expressed are entirely my own.

Author's Note

This book is divided into four parts. The first part is entitled **"Products and the background to trading"**. It starts with a chapter on trading giving an overview of trading in general as well as that related to the financial services industry. The next chapter is a background to risk which is another important theme of the book. We then look into specific trades by examining asset classes, derivative products and a special chapter on credit derivatives. Part I concludes with a look at three important aspects of trading – liquidity, price and leverage.

Part II is **"The trade lifecycle"**. It starts with an anatomy of the trade which is the core element of the lifecycle. Then the lifecycle is analysed in detail followed by a chapter on cashflows and asset holdings which are directly influenced by the lifecycle. We then move on to four methods of direct monitoring of trades throughout their lifetime: risk management, market risk control, counterparty risk control and accounting. The part concludes with a discussion of P&L attribution.

Part III, **"Systems and procedures"** begins with a full description of the business functions in the lifecycle and the people who run the systems and procedures. The next chapter examines the notion of business processes followed by a chapter devoted to incorporating new products into the lifecycle. The chapter on systems illustrates the key role played by information technology followed by testing. The following three chapters on data, reports and calculation examine the scope of business processes – what goes in, what comes out and what happens in between. Next is a chapter on validation of mathematical models and systems. The concluding chapters look at overall procedures connected to legal and regulatory issues and business continuity planning for disasters.

Part IV, **"What can go wrong, the credit crisis"** discusses the events of the well-known crisis of 2007.

Finally the appendix summarises the risks arising from the trade lifecycle.

Acknowledgements

I would like to thank my colleague Geoff Chaplin (of Reoch Credit Partners LLP) for his tremendous help and guidance in bringing this book into existence and for writing one chapter of the book. My appreciation also to Robert Reoch (also of Reoch Credit Partners LLP) for writing a chapter and always being available to answer questions.

I would also like to thank the following for giving up their time and sharing their considerable professional knowledge with me:

Desmond Dundon
Frank Rodriguez
Gerald Gordon
James Hart
Jerry De Melo
Joshua Brady
Richard Lumley
Tim Gledhill.

Special thanks to my sister Mandy for her diligence in checking the whole book for grammar and readability.

This book would not have been possible without the help of Pete Baker, Aimée Dibbens, Karen Weller, Lori Boulton, Louise Holden and many more at the publishers John Wiley & Sons.

Finally I thank my wife Nechama for her constant love and support, my children for reminding me what is important in life and my father for all his advice and guidance.

Part I
Products and the Background to Trading

1

Trading

1.1 HOW AND WHY DO PEOPLE TRADE?

People engage in trade primarily for one or more of the following reasons:

We require more or less of a product: we go shopping because we need things. The same is true of financial products. One person buys something that another person has in surplus and is prepared to sell.

To make profit: if someone anticipates that he can buy for less than he can sell and has the ability to hold a product long enough to take advantage of the price differential, he trades.

To remove risk: sometimes we need protection. We are worried that future events may cause our position to deteriorate and we therefore buy or sell to reduce our risk. The ship is safe, fully loaded in port today, but how will it fare exposed to the open sea tomorrow?

1.2 FACTORS AFFECTING TRADE

Product appetite: everybody wants to buy as cheaply as possible, but some people have a greater need for a product and will be willing to pay more for it. Our appetite for a product will determine the price at which we buy. Conversely, our desire to divest ourselves of a product will affect the price at which we are prepared to sell.

Risk appetite: risk is not necessarily an undesirable concept. Different people and organisations have a different attitude to risk. Some people make money by owning and managing risk. They are prepared to service other people's desire to reduce risk. Many trades arise because some people will pay money to reduce risk and others will accept money for taking on risk.

Exposure: whenever a trade occurs, both counterparts have each increased and reduced their exposure to something. For example, if Company A buys yen and sells euros to Company B, then A has increased its exposure to yen and decreased its exposure to euros and B has done the opposite (see Table 1.1).

The EUR–JPY foreign exchange transaction has resulted in the trading of one exposure for another.

Even when something is bought for money, the seller has increased his exposure to the currency of the money he receives. Someone living in New York and trading in dollars does not consider receiving more dollars as a risk because he is not exposed to changes in exchange rates. But in international commerce most market participants do worry about exposure to all currencies including their domestic currency which may attract less deposit interest than an alternative, making holding money in that currency less attractive.

1.3 MARKET PARTICIPANTS

We use the example of a forward trade to illustrate various market participants. Other trades such as spot trades (immediate buy and sell) and options (rights to buy and sell in the future) have similar participation.

Table 1.1

Item	Exposure for buyer (Company A)	Exposure for seller (Company B)
EUR	Increased	Decreased
JPY	Decreased	Increased

1.3.1   Producer

Imagine an apple grower owning a number of orchards. His product sells once a year and his entire income is dependent upon the size and price of his harvest. He can take steps to maximise his crop but he can do little to predict or control the price. He would rather have a fixed and known price for his produce than be subject to the vagaries of the market price at harvest time. How does he achieve a fixed price? He enters into a forward trade with a speculator obliging him to supply a fixed quantity of apples in return for a guaranteed price. He has now removed price uncertainty (or risk) and can concentrate on producing enough apples to meet his obligation.

1.3.2   Consumer

A cider manufacturer requires a certain supply of apples in six months' time. He is willing to pay more than the current market value to guarantee fresh stock is available when it is useful to him. His desire is to reduce his exposure to fluctuation of supply.

1.3.3   Speculator

A speculator takes a view on the likely direction of price change. If he sees a future shortage of apples, he will buy forward contracts now and hope to take advantage of his ability to supply later. He will take the opposite position and sell forward contracts if he forecasts a future glut. He is a risk taker, prepared to take advantage of other market participants' desire to reduce their level of risk.

1.3.4   Market maker

The market maker brings together buyers and sellers. He creates a market where it might be difficult for them to trade directly. He doesn't require the produce himself, nor does he have a view on the direction of price change; he is the middleman. He makes the market more efficient and helps to ensure prices reflect supply and demand.

1.4   MEANS BY WHICH TRADES ARE TRANSACTED

1.4.1   Brokers

Individuals and small financial entities cannot always get direct access to market makers. This may be due to their unknown credit worthiness, their small volume of trading or their specialised nature. They must rely on brokers to transact their trades. A broker, in return for a commission, will act on their behalf to execute a transaction at a given price or at the best possible price.

Sales departments of investment banks also have a broking function. Customers of the bank may request orders for financial instruments which the sales force transacts on their behalf either at their own bank or using its contacts with other banks.

1.4.2   Exchanges

An organised trading exchange is a safe and reliable place to trade. Prices are published, there is a plentiful supply of all products covered by the exchange and counterparty risk is virtually eliminated. There is a set of products traded, each one is well-defined, eliminating legal risk and liquidity is maintained by the guarantee of a market in each of the products.

Market participants buy or sell a product with the exchange taking the other side of the trade. Members of the exchange ensure that the exchange has sufficient funds to cover any transaction and the members themselves are vetted to ensure they behave according to the rules of the exchange. Examples of exchanges are:

- London Metal Exchange
- Chicago Mercantile Exchange
- New York Stock Exchange.

It is increasingly common for trading to be conducted electronically. Most exchanges have moved beyond open outcry, where participants shout out or visually indicate their requirements and prices. Electronic exchanges work by having participants sending in orders and setting prices across a network of computers connected to the main exchange which publishes all the information simultaneously to all subscribers. This creates a virtual market place: the traders can operate from their own locations without ever meeting their counterparts.

Breaches of security are a greater risk to electronic exchanges – it is essential that the participants are bona fide members of the exchange and that their details, prices and orders are kept secure. There is also communication risk where a computer or network fails in the central exchange or in one location, preventing some or all members from having access to the market data.

1.4.3   Over-the-counter

Exchange trades are limited to:

- members of the exchange
- certain sets of defined products
- times when the exchange is open.

If trading is required without these restrictions, it has to be done directly between the counterparties. This is known as over-the-counter (OTC) trading. There is increased flexibility because the counterparties can agree to any trade at any time but the absence of an exchange carries greater risks. Nowadays, much OTC trading is covered by regulation to ensure, inter alia, that both counterparties are competent and knowledgeable enough to trade, and understand the risks entailed.

1.5   WHEN IS A TRADE LIVE?

A trade is live between the time of execution and the time of maturity. Final delivery may sometimes occur after the maturity date, in which case although the trade has no value at maturity, it does still bear the risk of non delivery. Even when a trade has matured it may still feature in trade processes, such as for compilation of trading statistics, lookback analysis, auditing or due to outstanding litigation.

1.6   CONSEQUENCES OF TRADING

Once a trade has been executed, there will be at least one exchange of cash or assets at some future time ranging from within a few hours or days for spot trades, to many years for trades such as swaps, to unlimited periods for perpetual bonds. (Assets here include cash.)

Apart from exchanging cash or assets, the trade itself has value while it is still live. So all processes and risk analysis must work with both the cash or asset exchanges and the intrinsic trade.

The buyer and seller are holding different sides of the same trade. Although at execution the price they agreed was the same for both, the value of each side of the trade may vary over time.

Here is an example that shows how a trade has two independent sides that result in intrinsic value and exchange of cash.

> On 11 January X buys a future contract from Y in EUR/JPY where he will in six months pay one million EUR and receive 137.88 million JPY (that is a 6m future at 137.88).
> On 11 April, the three-month future price is 140. X holds but Y buys a three-month future from Z.
> On 11 July, both futures settle.
> X pays EUR 1m and receives JPY 137.88m.
> Y receives EUR 1m from X, pays JPY 137.88m to X.
> Y pays EUR 1m to Z and receives JPY 140m from Z.
> Z receives EUR 1m and pays JPY 140m.

So instead of Y buying a new trade (the three-month future), he could simply have sold his side of the original (six-month future) trade with X to Z. The fair price of the sale would be the amount of yen that would result in a value of JPY 2.12 million (140 − 137.88) on 11 July.

We see that through the life of a trade it has past, current and future cash or asset exchanges and it has intrinsic value. Concomitant with these exchanges are their associated risks and processes.

In financial terms, a trade converts potential to actual profit and loss with every exchange of cash or assets.

1.7   TRADING IN THE FINANCIAL SERVICES INDUSTRY

So far we have discussed some of the general issues of trading. Now we will focus on trading within the financial services industry. This includes investment banks, hedge funds, pension funds, brokers, exchanges and any other professional organisations engaged in financial trading. We exclude from this list retail banking services and private investments.

Market makers in a financial institution are sometimes referred to as "front book" traders and typically their "open" positions are held for a maximum of three months – often very much less. In contrast, the risk takers or speculators are often called "back book" traders or the "prop desk" and they may hold positions to maturity of the transaction (though they can also be very short-term traders).

1.7.1 Two types of trading policy

Where a trade is completed very soon after execution with a single exchange of cash or assets (a spot trade), there is no policy required for how to treat it. The only course of action is to accept the change in cash or assets caused by the trade. However, where the trade remains in existence for a period of time, there are two policies that can be adopted.

One is to buy with a view **to holding a trade to its maturity;** the other is to buy with the expectation of **resale before maturity**. Sometimes it is unknown at the time of purchase which policy will be adopted. At other times, changes in market conditions may force the purchaser to alter his course of action. Most trading participants in the financial services industry engage in buy and resell before maturity, whereas private individuals apply both policies. To a large extent the decision is dependent upon:

- the reason for entering into the trade;
- the view on direction of market conditions which affect the value of the trade;
- the possibility of resale – is there a potential buyer willing to buy it before maturity?

1.7.2 Why does a financial entity trade?

We divide our discussion into the principal types of financial entities.

1.7.2.1 Investment banks

These institutions have a large customer base. Some of these customers are drawn from the retail banking arm usually connected to major banks. Due to their size they can offer a range of financial services and draw on expert advice in many different fields. They benefit from economies of scale and because they trade in large volumes, enjoy lower bid/offer spreads making their trading cheaper. They are sometimes referred to as the "sell side" of the industry because they are supplying products for the market place. Investment banks are active in trading activities in order to:

1. Service their clients: The clients come to the bank with requirements that are satisfied by trading. The bank can either act as the middleman or broker to execute trades on behalf of the client who has no access to counterparties or it can trade directly with the client and either absorb the trade or deal an equal and opposite trade (known as back-to-back) in the market place, making a profit by enjoying lower trade costs.

2. Proprietary trading: Most investment banks have proprietary (or "prop") desks with the aim of using the bank's resources to make profit. The financial knowledge and skills base within the bank should enable it to understand the complexities of trades and take a realistic view on the future direction of the market in order to generate revenue for the bank.

3. Offset risks: By engaging in a range of financial activities, the bank may have substantial holdings in various assets. These could expose the bank to risk if the market price moves against them. Therefore much of the trading of investment banks is to offset these risks.
Examples:

- too much holding in a risky foreign currency – trade into less risky or domicile currency;
- too much exposure to a particular corporate debt such as holding a large number of bonds – buy credit protection by way of credit default swaps.

4. Broaden their client base: Just as a shop selling sports equipment might decide to appeal to more customers or better service its existing customers by expanding into sports clothing, so an investment bank might trade in new areas or products to provide a better service to its clients. The bank will constantly review its current service in the light of:

- what the competition is providing;
- what clients are requesting;
- what are likely profit-making ventures in the future.

Some trades done by the bank do not make money or might even lose money, but are justified to attract new business or to service important clients.

The image of a bank is very important. The product of banking is money, from which it cannot distinguish itself (it can't provide better banknotes than its competitor!) so the diversity and quality of its services are the means by which it seeks competitive advantage.

1.7.2.2   Hedge funds

Hedge funds are established to make profits for their investors. In return, the fund managers usually get paid an annual fee plus a percentage of any profits made. The funds are generally constructed to adopt a particular trading strategy. All other risks and exposures that occur as a by-product of following that strategy are offset or hedged. Hedge funds are like the consumers in the financial industry and therefore known as being on the "buy side". They engage in trading in order to pursue their strategy and manage their risks.

1.7.2.3   Pension funds and other asset managers

Asset management is a generic group of financial companies of which pension funds are the most well-known. They trade for very similar reasons to hedge funds. They want to maximise the return on the assets they hold for their clients or employees. They usually take a long-term view and are more risk-averse.

1.7.2.4   Brokers

Brokers facilitate trades by bringing together buyers and sellers. They do not take upon themselves positions or trade risks. They do, however, require many of the trading processes described in the trade lifecycle section of this book with the additional complication of having two counterparties on every trade (one purchaser, one vendor).

1.8   WHAT DO WE MEAN BY A TRADE?

A trade can be a single transaction or a collection of transactions that are associated together for some reason. In this book, we use the former definition.

A trade is an agreement between two counterparts to exchange something for something else. This book will concentrate on financial trades, which means those involving financial instruments.

Examples of financial trades are:

- 1000 barrels of West Texas intermediate crude oil for USD 6015;
- 1000 Royal Bank of Scotland ordinary shares for GBP 33.50;
- LIBOR floating rate for 5 years for 35 basis points per quarter;
- GBP 1 million for JPY 151 million in 6 months' time.

There are many reasons why a trader might transact such trades. To take advantage of expected price rises one would buy (or sell for expected falls). If a large change in price was expected (volatility) but the direction was unknown there are trading strategies (involving call and put options – see Chapter 4) to profit from such a situation. Some trading is motivated by the expected shape of future prices known as the term structure or curve of an asset such as WTI crude oil.

In addition trades are often transacted as hedges to limit exposure to changes in market conditions caused by other trades. We examine hedging in Chapter 10.

The trading parties must agree:

- what each side is committed to supplying;
- when the agreement takes effect;
- how the transfer is to be arranged;
- under what legal jurisdiction the trade is being conducted.

A trade is in essence a legally binding agreement creating an obligation on both sides. It is important to consider that from the point of agreement, the trade exists. If one side reneges on the trade and nothing is actually transacted, the other side will have legal recourse to compensation.

Trading has benefits and risks. It is an everyday activity we sometimes take for granted, but a transacted trade requires processes to be undertaken from conception to expiry. We will examine the journey of a trade and its components and in doing so will explore the activities of a financial entity engaged in trading.

Trading encompasses many types of trades. Some are standardised with very few differences from a regular template. They are traded in high volumes and require little formal documentation. For example, buying a share in an exchange-listed security would require only the security name, deal date and time, settlement date, quantity and price.

Other trades are far more specialised. They may have hundreds of pages of documentation and take months to put together. They will be traded individually and no two trades will be alike. Even these more complicated trades, however, are usually made up of components built from simpler, standard trades.

1.9   WHO WORKS ON THE TRADE AND WHEN?

In Chapter 15 we will discuss the various business functions. Here in Table 1.2 is a summary of the most general activities of each business function and at what point they are performed.

Table 1.2

Business function	Before trade	While live	After maturity
Sales	arrangement		
Legal	checking documentation	dealing with queries, disputes	
Structurer	arranging trade		
Trader	testing trade	execution, active risk management	
Market risk	checking limits	monitoring	
Counterparty risk	checking limits	monitoring	
Trading manager	approval	reviewing performance, monitoring	
Product control		booking, valuation, reporting	
Operations		confirmation, settlement	
Finance		reporting	reporting
Audit		auditing	auditing
IT	systems – development and support	systems – development and support	

1.10   SUMMARY

There are many reasons why people might trade. Financial trading is undertaken by a broad range of companies specialising in various areas and strategies. A trade has both common and specific properties and can be transacted in many different ways. The various business functions within a financial entity will perform their activities at different stages in the trade lifecycle.

2

Risk

Risk is a major part of trading. Not only do most traders need to actively manage risks that arise from their trading (market risk) but the actual processes in the trade lifecycle carry various types of risk. Here we present an introduction to the concept of risk in general.

2.1 INTRODUCTION

The German sociologist, Niklas Luhmann, defined risk as "the threat or probability that an action or event will adversely or beneficially affect an organisation's ability to achieve its objectives".

In the financial services industry, the term *risk* often denotes the market risk of holding trading positions. Risk management is then the action taken by traders to control this risk. This is an important type of risk and one to which we will devote a chapter of this book (Chapter 10), but it is by no means the only source of risk to an organisation engaged in trading. Whenever we use the unqualified term *risk,* we mean the wider connotation of risk as in Luhmann's definition.

2.2 RISK IS INEVITABLE

Imagine you own £ 10 000 in cash and decide to store it in the proverbial shoebox under the bed. You are now certain that you have protected your money – there are no risks attached. Correct? Unfortunately, things are not quite as safe as you think. Firstly, it could get stolen or there could be fire or flood. Secondly, if you leave the cash there long enough, the denomination of the bank notes could cease to be legal tender and banks and shops refuse to accept them. Thirdly, inflation of prices might reduce the real value. In addition to these risks of losing all or part of your money, you are also forgoing the ability to invest your money for profit.

In reality there is no such thing as being free of risk. All activities incur some sort of risk. Trading and its associated processes have many risks; the important thing is to be aware of risks and choose how to deal with them.

2.3 QUANTIFYING RISK

In order to quantify and manage risk, one must define:

- the event upon which the risk is to be measured;
- the probability of the event occurring;
- the loss entailed if it occurs;
- the means by which some or all of the risk can be mitigated;
- the cost of mitigating risk.

Table 2.1

Event	Prob	Amount of loss	Action	Estimated cost
Client does not pay on time	30 %	USD 1500 per late payment	Hire debt collectors	USD 2000 per month
Error in documentation leading to loss of deal	0.1 %	Unknown – depends on deal	No action	Zero
Company exceeding capital adequacy limit	Once a quarter	Regulator could impose fine but hasn't yet	Improve financial reporting	USD 10 000

Both probability and loss calculations are very important in order to have an appreciation of the risk. A catastrophic event that occurs with a remote probability may require greater protective action than an everyday event that causes a small loss.

In practice, it may be difficult to quantify either the probability or the amount of loss entailed or both. With finite resources, an organisation will need to spread the amount it spends on protection against risk according to priorities. However, even an estimation of risk should aid the process of assigning priority. Also, in deciding a future course of action, the organisation should weigh the benefits against the risks in order to arrive at a fair decision as to how to proceed.

In Table 2.1 we give three examples of risk events, a rough estimate of the probability of occurrence, the amount of loss should the event happen, the selected remedial action and the estimated cost of such action.

2.4   METHODS OF DEALING WITH RISK

2.4.1   Ignore

An event carrying risk may be considered of negligible impact and so can be totally ignored. Alternatively, it may be more expensive to protect against the risk than to let the event occur – sometimes an organisation has to just take the hit.

For example, the loss to a hedge fund of being without electricity is negligible compared to the cost of installing its own generator.

2.4.2   Minimise

If it is impossible or too costly to remove the risk altogether, steps can be taken to either lessen its impact or reduce the probability of it occurring.

The skydiver may carry two parachutes in case one malfunctions. (He would rather not think about the probability of both not working!)

2.4.3   Avoid

Again, if it is too difficult to protect against a risky event or the benefits are not sufficient to justify the possible damage entailed, the risk can be totally avoided.

For example, the market risk department might rule that a trade is so risky it cannot be transacted despite the potential profit.

2.4.4 Remove

Removal of risk is certainly desirable, but often difficult to achieve.

An example of risk removal is house insurance. One transfers the risks associated with owning a house to an insurance company. (Obviously there is still a residual risk that the insurance company will default on its obligations, but legislation and regulation generally make this probability negligible.)

2.5 MANAGING RISK

A successful organisation relies on good management. One key feature of management is assessing weaknesses and taking steps to tackle them. In order to do this, a good understanding of risk is essential. Many business functions within a financial entity are partly or fully concerned with the management of risk. All trading activities entail risk. As different parts of the trade lifecycle give rise to different risks, the success of the trade is dependent on the knowledge of its risks and the management of them. Since risk in all its manifestations is part of the business of financial trading, the company that can manage its risk best will be at a distinct advantage.

It should be said that managing risk is distinct from being risk-averse. There are many reasons why a trading desk might take on market risk and manage it successfully. Similarly an institution may decide on a more risky course of action because the likely benefits outweigh the possible losses. As long as the potential risks are understood and estimated, it can be said that risk is being managed.

2.6 PROBLEMS OF UNFORESEEN RISK

No stakeholders in a business – investors, managers, employees and customers – want unforeseen risk. Due to its sudden effect, the organisation is ill-equipped to deal with it and its consequences are unknown. One of the major causes of the recent credit crunch was the failure of many organisations to take into account a particular risk: that so many American subprime mortgage borrowers would be unable to repay their debt. Unforeseen risk points to poor management and supervision and reduces confidence in the financial entity. If risk is present, it should be identified and then sensible decisions can be taken about how to manage it.

2.7 SUMMARY

A financial entity must accept that risks are an unavoidable part of the trading process. When an adverse scenario arises, it will fare better and be able to keep costs down if it is proactive in uncovering them, estimating their probability and effect and deciding how best to deal with them. Controlling risks does not necessarily mean being cautious in business – aggressive trading can reap big rewards. But recognising risk in all its manifestations is a fundamental part of managing the trading process.

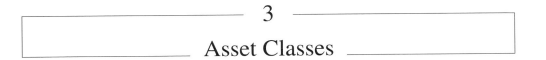

3

Asset Classes

What do we mean by asset classes?

A trade can be executed with a huge variety of underlying assets. It is helpful and usual to group assets into classes. Traders are normally organised into desks, each desk trading the same class of assets. Processes that flow from these trades are also divided by their asset class.

Large parts of the trade lifecycle are generic: trades are executed, booked, confirmed and settled. But the implication of these processes may vary from one class of assets to another. Here we discuss some common asset classes, their particular features and how they affect the trade processes.

3.1   INTEREST RATES

The asset class of interest rates is usually taken to include deposits, swaps and futures in one trading currency.

3.1.1   Deposit

A deposit (or loan) is a simple instrument. One counterparty gives an amount of currency to another counterparty, expecting its return on a future date. At agreed regular intervals, interest will be paid by the receiver to the depositor.

A deposit can be unsecured or secured. When secured, the receiver has to provide some collateral to the depositor and in the event of default, the collateral will be forfeited.

The market for very short-term loans and deposits is known as the money market. Here money can be borrowed overnight, for a few days or for a few months.

A very secure form of short-term lending is known as the repo market (repo is short for repurchase). Here the borrower sells a highly secure bond such a US Treasury bond at an agreed price for repurchase at an agreed future price. The purpose of such a transaction is in order to borrow money more cheaply by using the bond as collateral.

Deposits oil the wheels of financial markets by ensuring participants can acquire cash and proceed with other trading. When short-term lending becomes expensive, as we saw in the credit crunch, raising money for all other trading is negatively impacted.

3.1.2   Future

A future is a longer term deposit. They are standard products traded on exchanges, as opposed to forwards which can be any over-the-counter (OTC) agreement between counterparties. (See Section 4.1 for a fuller explanation of forwards and futures.)

3.1.3   Swap

Technically, a swap is an agreement to exchange one asset for another, however when used without a qualifier it means interest rate swaps (as opposed to equity, foreign exchange

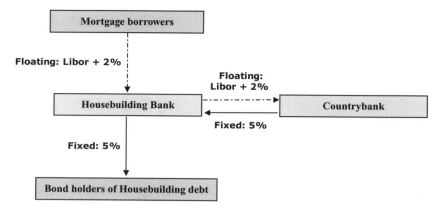

Figure 3.1   Motivation for a swap trade

(FX) or other asset class swaps). Within the same currency, swaps can be customised to the requirements of the counterparties, but the standard trades are float-for-fixed and float-for-float between different indices. Swaps have agreed fixing periods throughout their life when money is transferred.

Float for fixed: one counterparty pays fixed currency. The other pays a floating rate dependent on an agreed index such as LIBOR.

Float for float: one counterparty pays a floating rate based on one index (e.g. Euribor) and the other pays floating based on a different index (e.g. TIBOR).

Although there is an agreed notional for a swap trade, this is only a nominal figure used to calculate the amount owed at each fixing. Swaps are used when a counterparty wants to hedge his exposure across different indices, or when he wants to transfer his payment streams from fixed rate to floating or vice versa.

See, for an example, Figure 3.1:

Housebuilding Bank receives floating rate mortgage repayments (at LIBOR + 2 %) from its customers and needs to service the debt arising by means of a bond it has issued which has fixed coupon payments (5 %).

Housebuilding enters into a swap trade with a counterparty (CountryBank).

Housebuilding receives 5 % from Countrybank and pays its bond holders.

Housebuilding pays LIBOR + 2 % to Countrybank which it receives from mortgage borrowers. Now, Housebuilding has removed his exposure (risk) to interest rate changes.

The combination of deposits, futures and swaps traded in one currency constitutes the market data necessary to produce an interest rate curve. This determines how much that currency will be worth in the future based on information available today. Interest rate curves are used extensively in the financial world. Most trades rely on the interest rate curves to discount future cashflows. The higher the future interest rates in a currency, the less money in that currency will be worth.

Interest rate products are traded in their own right by dedicated trading desks and are also traded as hedges for more complicated trades or cashflow scenarios (as in the swap example above). In most currencies they are very liquid products.

3.1.4   Tradeflow issues

The asset underpinning an interest rate trade is simply the currency. For the purposes of tradeflow, this can be defined very easily – there are a limited number of currencies in the world and each has a very exact meaning and nomenclature. The settlement and delivery mechanism involves having a nostro account in the currency. There are no odd units of transfer, no security documentation and no warehousing issues.

Interest rate products do not have the notion of a buyer and seller, as the same asset is being transacted either by a loan or a swap. Therefore, it is important that trading processes can distinguish the two sides of the loan and the swap and know exactly who is paying and who is receiving during the lifecycle.

When accounting for interest trades in a currency other than the reporting currency, it may be necessary to provide two values – one for the actual amount in the traded currency and one for the reporting currency equivalent.

For instance, a trade might result in USD 600 000 being held in the USD nostro account. The trade report might show:

USD 600 000
EUR 426 994

This allows the reader to see the native USD amount which will stay unchanged day on day, but be able to aggregate all the trades into a single reported figure in EUR.

3.2   FOREIGN EXCHANGE (FX)

Closely linked to interest products are those in foreign exchange. As the name implies foreign exchange is the transfer of one currency for another. The basic trading types are similar to interest rates.

3.2.1   Spot

A spot foreign exchange trade is an immediate transfer of currencies. (Immediate meaning within a few days of execution as dictated by the conventional settlement date for standard trades or by mutual agreement for OTCs.)

3.2.2   Futures and forwards

As for interest rate trades, a future is an exchange-traded standard contract and a forward is any OTC agreement between two counterparties. In essence, for foreign exchange they are delayed spot trades. The exchange rate is agreed upon execution and the future exchange of currencies is mandatory upon the agreed date. The difference between futures and forwards is explained in Section 4.1.

3.2.3   Swaps

As for the interest rate asset class, foreign exchange swaps are a common way of trading fixed and floating cashflows, the only difference being that there is the added ingredient of the exchange across more than the single currency.

Example:

A two-year quarterly payment swap with notional 50 million EUR. A pays fixed 4.5 % GBP, B pays LIBOR + 1 % EUR.

3.2.4 Baskets

A possible variation of FX trades is to exchange a basket of currencies. For example:

sell: JPY 500 million and USD 7 million
receive: EUR 4 million and GBP 50 million

3.2.5 Tradeflow issues

In foreign exchange there is no concept of purchasing an asset with a currency because both sides of the trade involve currencies. Trade lifecycle systems have to maintain at least two entries for the currency and more for baskets. This can present problems when, for example, the system has been designed for other asset classes and is being adapted for FX. Also, the problem of not having purchase and sale leads to errors where staff are not used to dealing with FX.

One of the biggest sources of error arises from the direction of the quoted FX rate. If we write EURGBP 1.154 does that mean you receive 1.154 EUR for every 1 GBP or the other way around? What if the quote is written EUR/GBP? Every time somebody in the trade lifecycle needs to know the exchange rate, he must understand the quote convention in the system he is using. If data flows between different systems during the lifecycle, both systems must understand if they are using the same convention or if it requires inversion. All parties to the settlement process – the two counterparties and their custodians – must have the same interpretation of this exchange rate.

Another problem with FX is the existence of various different nomenclatures for designating the two currencies of the trade (in a standard nonbasket trade), where one is the reporting or home currency. For example, a Canadian bank dealing CAD against USD may use any of these pairs of terms:

CAD	USD
Domestic	Foreign
Riskfree	Risky
Base	Foreign

The underlying asset in a basic foreign exchange is the currency pair. But it is possible that a simple FX spot trade could involve four currencies. The same Canadian bank may exchange EUR for JPY and report in USD.

Then the trading system needs to cope with:

- domestic: CAD
- foreign 1: EUR (sell)
- foreign 2: JPY (buy)
- reporting: USD.

Now the trading and accounting systems will need to know the CADUSD exchange rate and two of CADEUR, CADJPY and EURJPY (the third can be derived from the other two).

The foreign exchange asset class has many of the benefits of interest rate trades, such as a small number of easily defined underlyings (there is a relatively small set of currency pairs available for trading) and easy transfer of assets with very liquid prices.

3.3   EQUITY

Equities are synonymous with shares and stock. They entitle the owner to a part of the company which has sold them. By giving up capital to finance the company, the purchaser of equity hopes to receive a share in the profits. This is a payment known as a dividend. Dividends vary in size and date of payment. There are many different types of shares:

- ordinary – the regular share in the company;
- preference – shares with extra rights sometimes including a guarantee of a fixed dividend and greater chance of reimbursement should the company be wound up;
- cumulative preference – similar to preference, but certain rights can be carried forward into future years should they not be paid in the current year;
- redeemable – the company can buy them back at a future date.

Financial entities buy shares because they expect a return on their investment, both in the form of dividends and a rise in the price of the share. Very often the price of the share is a reflection on the likely dividend to be paid.

Public shares are bought and sold on trading exchanges. There may also be over-the-counter share trades directly between two counterparties.

3.3.1   Synthetic equities (index)

A market has developed for the purchase of a synthetic equity product known as an index. Examples of equity indices are the DAX, Dow Jones Industrial Average and the French CAC 40. The purchaser does not own any real shares in any company; he holds an abstract combination, whose price is determined by the price movements of a defined set of constituent entities. This is a very useful product for someone wanting a representative sample of large French organisations, but not to be overly exposed to the price vagaries of any one of them.

Futures and options also exist on indices as they do for real equities.

3.3.2   Lifecycle issues pertinent to equity trades

Equities are a mature asset class with a straightforward exchange of currency for asset. However, there are some extra issues affecting the processing of equity trades.

With so many different shares in existence, it is very important that the exact identity of the share being traded is recorded. This would include the full name of the company and its mnemonic, the description of issue and, where applicable, the exchange upon which it was traded. For example:

- Full name: Xray Yacht Zebra Trading Co.
- Mnemonic: XYZ
- Type: Ordinary Shares of GBP 0.50
- Exchange: LSE (London Stock Exchange).

Either a custodian would be employed or the operations department would be responsible for registering the shares with the company issuing them in order to qualify for dividends. They would also have to keep the share certificates and prepare to accept and account for dividend payments.

The middle office would have to keep track of ex-dividend dates (see Section 8.7).

Trading of equities could be on any number of shares, but certain equities are traded in multiples of common sizes, known as board lots or round lots. Sizes different to board lots are known as odd lots and might incur higher trading costs.

Index equities should be distinguished from real equities in the trade processes because they bear no dividends and documents, such as share certificates.

3.4   BONDS AND CREDIT

We combine bonds and credit because all bonds except risk-free sovereigns carry credit risk. From a trade process perspective they are often treated separately so we begin the section with a discussion of all types of bonds and then move on to other instruments bearing credit risk. Bonds are related to (short-term) interest rates and the somewhat arbitrary asset class distinction is maturity related with anything under one year being regarded as in the interest rate class. In addition, credit risky bonds and "risk-free" sovereign debt are often regarded as different asset classes.

3.4.1   Bonds

Apart from raising capital by selling shares in the company, there is an alternative by which the company borrows money. This could be a simple bank loan and would be dealt through a retail bank. However, for large capital amounts it is highly unlikely that a single bank would have the funds and the desire to lend by itself. To overcome this problem, companies issue bonds. Purchasers of bonds pay capital to the company, which is repaid to them at the end of the period (term) of the bond. The lenders are rewarded by receiving interest in the form of coupons, in most cases throughout the term of the bond.

Fixed income is another name for the asset class comprising of bonds. The term fixed income is used because, once a bond is issued, the expected income is known. This contrasts with equities, where dividend payments are unknown. Another difference with equities is that bonds have a termination date. A further distinction is that many bonds are issued by governments wishing to raise finance, whereas all equities are corporate.

3.4.1.1   Sovereign debt

Government bonds are known as sovereigns. Rating agencies do not apply credit ratings to sovereigns except where bonds are issued in a currency other than one controlled by the government. In theory, debt issued in the currency of the government itself are risk-free to that currency, because the government can always print more money to repay its debts. (Of course the foreign exchange risk would have to be taken into account. For example, Zimbabwean government bonds are risk-free in Zimbabwean dollars, but as the country's economy declined, the worth of its currency declined, making a sizeable foreign exchange discrepancy.)

3.4.1.2   Types of bond

In order to get a flavour of the difficulties involved in handling bonds, we shall look at some of the common variations. As mentioned, all bonds have a starting date (issue date) when the purchaser pays and a maturity date when the purchaser receives his money back (redemption). The intervening period characterises the type of the bond. In theory, any set of regular or irregular coupon payments can be made at any prearranged date or dates. Here, however, are some common bond types.

3.4.1.3   Fixed

The bond pays the same coupon at regular intervals with the last coupon usually coinciding with the redemption payment. The coupon is quoted as an annual percentage of notional.

Payments are usually quarterly, semi-annually or annually. All coupon amounts can be exactly determined.

3.4.1.4   Floating Rate Note (FRN)

When the coupon is paid at variable rates, the bond is known as a floating rate note or floater. The exact payment is determined only just before the coupon date and is derived from a benchmark index, such as LIBOR. The process of determining the coupon is known as a fixing. The coupon is often an amount over the benchmark (e.g. LIBOR plus 50 basis points). This is known as the margin.

3.4.1.5   Zero coupon bonds

These bonds pay no coupons. The bonds are offered at the issue date for a discounted price (e.g. 63 %) and are redeemed at maturity for par (100 %). The gain to the purchaser arises from this price differential and is an alternative to the coupon payment of standard bonds. This means the issuer does not have to worry about having to find intermediate income to service the coupon payments.

3.4.1.6   Amortising bonds

Sometimes the capital borrowed is repaid to investors in instalments, rather than all at the end. Then the notional of the coupon is reduced over time. Although the fixed coupon rate remains at say 8 %, the notional might have reduced from 200 000 000 to 100 000 000, resulting in a lower coupon pay out.

3.4.1.7   Asset-backed securities

Some bonds are secured using debts owed to the issuer itself. These commonly arise from mortgages (mortgage backed securities or MBS) or credit card repayments. They are amortising bonds, but the amortisation is unknown at time of issue. If the underlying debtors, such as homeowners, repay their mortgages early, then the debt outstanding on the bonds is reduced accordingly.

For simplicity in this example, the payments assume a very crude calculation of dividing the annual rate in half to get the semi-annual payment. In reality, the calculation is more complex taking into account the number of days between coupon payments.

3.4.1.8   Example coupon payments

In Table 3.1 below are several different types of bonds and their coupon dates and payment amounts.

3.4.1.9   Other features

Some bonds combine fixed and floating cashflows; others have clauses specifying when payments are made that depend on market prices. Floating rates can be capped at a minimum level (known as a floor) or restricted to a maximum (known as a cap). Convertible bonds can be converted into equity. Bonds can be denominated in one currency, but pay coupons in another currency, according to predetermined or market exchange rates.

3.4.1.10   Tradeflow issues

One of the key tradeflow issues relating to a bond is capturing its true definition.

Due to the limitless possibilities of coupon types and payments, the safest way of defining a bond is by its set of cashflows. To pass a series of cashflows around the processes of the trade lifecycle is not always practical, however. So, if the bond conforms to a type and standard set of conventions, its definition can be encapsulated by a finite set of fields. It should always be the case that these fields will lead to an exact set of cashflows. A missing or ambiguous set will lead to improper booking and management.

Here are the standard fields required:

- Identifier (ISIN, CUSIP etc.);
- Name of issuer;
- Seniority – bonds are issued at different levels of seniority. This affects the order in which creditors are paid in the event of default;
- Currency;
- Description – a summary of the bond. For instance, Ford SEN 5.5 % 2012;
- Type – whether fixed or float, amortising or fixed notional;
- Day count convention – used to calculate the exact coupon payment;
- Business day convention – when a coupon is due on a weekend day or holiday, this convention indicates when the coupon should actually be paid;
- Holiday calendar – used in conjunction with the business day convention to determine when is a holiday;
- Issue date;
- Maturity;
- Fixed coupon (for fixed bonds);
- Margin (for FRN);
- Reference for fixing (e.g. LIBOR, used only for FRNs);
- Frequency – this is the frequency of coupons;

Table 3.1

	20-Mar-09	20-Sep-09	20-Mar-10	20-Sep-10	20-Mar-11	20-Sep-11	20-Mar-12	20-Sep-12	20-Sep-13	20-Mar-14
Regular fixed										
Fixed	5.5 %	5.5 %	5.5 %	5.5 %	5.5 %	5.5 %	5.5 %	5.5 %	5.5	5.5
Notional	1 bn	1 bn	1 bn	1 bn	1 bn	1 bn	1 bn	1 bn	1 bn	1 bn
Payment	27.5 m	27.5 m	27.5 m	27.5 m	27.5 m	27.5 m	27.5 m	27.5 m	27.5 m	27.5 m
Regular float										
Float	5 %	5.5 %	6 %	6.25 %	6.5 %	6.25 %	6.25 %	6.5 %	7	6.5
Notional	1 bn	1 bn	1 bn	1 bn	1 bn	1 bn	1 bn	1 bn	1 bn	1 bn
Payment	25 m	27.5 m	30 m	31.25 m	32.5 m	31.25 m	31.25 m	32.5 m	35 m	32.5 m
Amortising fixed										
Fixed	5.5 %	5.5 %	5.5 %	5.5 %	5.5 %	5.5 %	5.5 %	5.5 %	5.5	5.5
Notional	1 bn	1 bn	1 bn	1 bn	800 m	750 m	700 m	500 m	500 m	500 m
Payment	27.5 m	27.5 m	27.5 m	27.5 m	22 m	20.625 m	19.25 m	13.75 m	13.75 m	13.75 m
Amortising float										
Float	5 %	5.5 %	6 %	6.25 %	6.5 %	6.25 %	6.25 %	6.5 %	7	6.5
Notional	1 bn	1 bn	1 bn	1 bn	800 m	750 m	700 m	500 m	500	500
Payment	25 m	27.5 m	30 m	31.25 m	26 m	23.4375 m	21.875 m	16.25 m	17.5 m	16.25 m

- First accrual date – sometimes the first coupon is paid at an irregular interval from the issue date;
- Short first coupon – suppose the first accrual date was two months after the issue date for a semi-annual bond. This could mean the first coupon is paid after two months or is deferred and paid after eight months (two plus the regular six);
- Redemption – the amount paid back at maturity: normally set at 100 %.

When nonstandard bonds need to be processed, extra fields may need to be added or the bond marked in such a way that the user of system treats it as nonstandard.

A feature of bond prices is that, for historical reasons, they are sometimes quoted in eighths or sixteenths. Although these can be rounded into fractions, it is helpful if the systems can preserve them in their native price state to make it easier to read and to avoid rounding errors.

3.4.1.11 *Summary*

As we have seen, the booking and processing of bonds can be complicated. It is necessary to keep track of coupon fixings and notional fixings (for amortising bonds) and manage the documentation in the form of bond certificates. Also the coupon payments need to be received and accounted for.

3.4.2 Other credit risk bearing instruments

Credit as an asset class really refers to credit risk. Although all investment institutions have been managing counterparty risk ever since trading with counterparties began, credit risk products are relatively new to the financial industry.

3.4.2.1 *What is credit risk?*

You cannot go and buy a unit of credit risk like you can buy copper or Lloyds TSB shares. It is a synthetic product existing as a structured or derivative trade. Its primary manifestation as a traded product is as an insurance policy against a particular name defaulting. The market has developed in the last 10 years or so, with the underlying trade being the buying and selling of this credit risk and associated structures. Chapter 5 on credit derivatives will explore the nature of the products themselves; here we focus on the asset class and its application to the trade lifecycle.

3.4.2.2 *Why is credit risk different?*

As it is fundamentally an insurance policy, the trading of credit risk confers a different area of emphasis to other products. There is a greater degree of legal risk so documentation becomes more important.

3.4.2.3 *Legal risk*

Insurance is a guarantee that one party (the provider) will pay the other party (the purchaser) if a certain event (trigger) occurs. The purchaser pays a fee (premium) for this insurance. The whole contract relies on the precise definition of the trigger event and on trust that the provider will pay out if required. To bolster confidence in the insurance market, providers of insurance are regulated by independent bodies. These ensure that companies have the means to satisfy claimants and that they will fulfil the insurance obligations they have undertaken.

The purchaser of any insurance must be happy that he will get paid when the event is triggered. Both sides to the insurance must understand the trigger and for that they require full and complete documentation and, sometimes, additional legal assistance.

3.4.2.4 Documentation

As the market for credit risk has developed, some products have become more standard. The International Swaps and Derivatives Association (ISDA) provides industry standard documentation for a variety of products including credit default swaps. In the same way that one more readily trusts a light bulb approved by the British Standards Institution (BSI), so financial organisations are more likely to trust ISDA documentation.

Documentation for nonstandard credit risk trades, such as a cash collateralised default obligation, can run into hundreds of pages. This documentation needs to be maintained throughout the trade lifecycle; individual trade processes may extract relevant parts of it.

3.4.2.5 Example of a credit product

In order to get a feel for credit risk we can look at an example of a credit default swap (CDS).

- France Telecom Senior Subordination has a five-year CDS maturing 20 March 2012.
- Bank A purchases the CDS from Bank B and pays 62 basis points premium per year at quarterly intervals on a notional of EUR 12 million.
- This means that A will pay EUR $62/10\,000 \times 12\,000\,000$ per year which is EUR 18 600 per quarter to B, unless and until France Telecom defaults. This is known as the payment or premium leg.
- Should France Telecom default, B will have to pay EUR 12 million to A, less any recovery. (Recovery is the amount a name will pay to its creditors upon default. This varies according to the seniority of debt and is discussed below.) This is known as the recovery leg.

3.4.2.6 Definition of default

The whole credit risk market depends on a precise definition of default and an ability to see when default has occurred. There are several technical definitions of default, the most obvious being when a company goes into liquidation or when an issuer of debt cannot repay its obligations. This latter definition led to the bizarre situation of the US Government nearly being in technical default when it failed to have its budget approved in the mid 1990s. At the time, companies such as Coca Cola were considered safer than the US Government!

Once the definition of default is apparent from the documentation, the processors of the trade, such as middle office, need to watch for indications of default. In the event of default, they need to prepare back office for reception or payment of the amount insured. Generally, a default does not creep up unexpectedly: steep rises in CDS spreads for a name, or a sharp drop in its equity price are good indications that default may be approaching.

Table 3.2

	1 yr	2 yr	3 yr	4 yr	5 yr	7 yr	10 yr	15 yr
ABN Amro	68.6	75.9	81.4	79.5	78.3	73.3	70.9	70.4

3.4.2.7 Measuring credit worthiness

The credit spread is the premium required by an insurer to provide insurance on a name. It is a measure of the credit quality of the name. Secure names have low spreads; risky names have high spreads. The market indication of credit spread is through credit default swap prices. CDS prices exist at various durations (tenors), the most liquid being five years. It is also common to see quotes for one, two, three, four, six, seven, 10, 12 and 15 years.

3.4.2.8 Example

Table 3.2 shows indicative CDS spreads of one name given in basis points for various tenors.
    The problem with monitoring credit swaps for valuation and risk purposes is that many are illiquid at some or all tenor points. This leads to some of the data engineering techniques, described in Chapter 20 on data.
    Another measure of credit worthiness is the credit rating issued by rating agencies.
    There are three main rating agencies, Moodys, S&P and Fitch. Some of the problems of using credit ratings are:

• Credit rating is only a band, not an exact figure. For example, AAA may cover names with CDS premiums between five and 50 basis points.
• The agencies might disagree as to the rating of any name or they may not supply a rating.
• Agency rating classifications have been called into question since the recent credit crunch and ensuing recession as, in many cases, they did not predict the imminent default of a name.

    Many institutions trading credit risk will use a combination of CDS premiums and rating agency classifications to gauge the credit worthiness of a name.

3.4.2.9 Recovery

A very important feature of the credit risk market is that recovery rate is a key input in the valuation of credit risk products. This piece of market data cannot be measured or known until default actually occurs (and sometimes quite a while after). For calculation and trading purposes this number is estimated or implied. If you know the price of a particular CDS contract and the input CDS premium, then the recovery can be mathematically implied. This will only apply to standard contracts whose price is known; generally the recovery rate is estimated based on historical defaults of similar names and seniority of debt.
    The imprecision caused by this input makes the quantitative approach to credit risk very different from the precise world of interest rates and foreign exchange. Risk managers, used to dealing with these other asset classes, must alter their approach when working with credit risk and its underlying recovery assumptions.

Since there are thousands of bonds currently being traded, identification becomes a major issue. Common identifiers like ISIN, CUSIP and SEDOL have been adopted. Each financial entity may also have its own way of identifying bonds. It is important that the correct static data references are available to link and identify bonds across different identifiers.

Bonds are susceptible to credit risk. If the issuer defaults, future coupon payments and the final redemption are put at risk. For monitoring this risk, the issuer of the bond must be known in addition to its legal parent. A legal database may therefore be required.

Ultimately bonds and equities are linked because they derive from the same underlying company. It may therefore be necessary to provide combined fixed income and equity information in the form of reports to users who have an interest in this connection.

3.5   COMMODITIES

Commodities are the oldest asset class. Since they have been traded over a long period of time before market standardisation took place, many conventions and idiosyncrasies have developed, which can make processing them difficult.

3.5.1   What are commodities?

A commodity is something that is common between different suppliers. It can be defined by its size and quality. The buyer can be certain that he is getting the same object no matter where he purchases it.

Characteristics of commodities:

- odd units of trading
- possibility of physical delivery
- intrinsic utility
- old markets
- diversity.

Due to the range of possible commodities, they tend to be subdivided and traded in smaller groups. Loosely, we can categorise them into agricultural, animal products, energy, precious metals and industrial metals.

3.5.2   Agricultural commodities

Agricultural commodities include:

- Corn and wheat sold in units of 5000 bushels on the Chicago Board of Trade (CBOT)
- Cocoa sold in units of 10 tons on the New York Board of Trade (NYBOT)
- Cotton sold in units of 50 000 lbs also on NYBOT.

3.5.3   Examples of animal products

Examples of animal products are:

- Live cattle, units of 20 tons on Chicago Mercantile Exchange
- Lean hogs, units of 20 tons also on Chicago Mercantile Exchange.

3.5.4   Energy

The two biggest traded energy products are:

- West Texas Intermediate Crude Oil, traded in units of 1000 barrels on New York Mercantile Exchange and the Intercontinental Exchange (ICE)
- Brent Crude also in 1000 barrels units on ICE.

Other energy products include heating oil, propane and natural gas.

3.5.5   Precious metals

There are four main precious metals all in units of troy ounce. Gold and silver are traded on CBOT; platinum and palladium on NYMEX.

3.5.6   Industrial metals

Industrial metals are traded in metric tonnes on the London Metals Exchange (LME). They include aluminium, aluminium alloy, copper, lead, nickel, tin and zinc.

3.5.7   OTC commodities

Above we have listed exchange-traded commodities but in fact the over-the-counter (OTC) market in commodities is bigger. OTC trades may be on any exchange-listed or non exchange-listed commodity and can be on amounts different from the standard exchange lot sizes. In the case of energy for instance, there are hundreds of grades of oil and related products which the refiners will produce and consumers will buy. Particular grades of oil have become the standard traded product in their field for financial markets, due to their liquidity and volume of trade. The exchanges can only offer the main products, but specialist oil brokers will obtain prices for many of the smaller derivative oil products.

3.5.8   Localised nature of production

Most commodities are grown, smelted or produced in particular localities. They are subject to local forces, such as natural events and changes in political circumstances. Bad weather, forest fires, earthquakes and political turmoil can drastically affect supply in one region and become a major factor in the market price.

Traders and salesmen are dependent upon good knowledge of all the factors affecting supply and production. Commodities demand very specific research.

3.5.9   Time lag

If there is a sudden demand for a commodity it may take considerable time for the supply to catch up. Many commodities are stockpiled to meet short-term requirements, but they will not be able to cater for more sustained demand.

3.5.10   Utility of commodities

When dealing with commodities, it is important to bear in mind that the underlying is not a synthetic financial instrument but a real product. Although commodities are traded as financial products with the expectation of profit, they hold residual utilitarian value. This means they cannot default and be worthless, unlike, for example, a corporate bond. There is some minimum price which reflects this intrinsic usefulness of the product. (The exception is with perishable goods and livestock which can obviously wither or die.)

3.5.11   Precious metals as a currency

A currency is an accepted medium of exchange. It is relied upon to retain its value either because it contains intrinsic worth, such as gold or silver, or it has token value, but is guaranteed by government. Precious metals can therefore be treated as currencies or as commodities with intrinsic value.

This dual nature of gold and silver makes it possible for trade processes to consider them as an extra currency alongside euros and dollars, or as commodities alongside tin and aluminium. A decision has to be made as to which will be a better fit, depending on the organisation trading them.

3.5.12   Physical settlement

Since commodities are traded between producers and consumers who require physical delivery, any financial entity involved in trading must either be able to cope with physical delivery or convert it into cash before delivery is made. Many contracts offer a choice of physical or cash settlement. Middle and back office procedures must be aware of the type of settlement. Some metals are held in warehouses and oil on barges, so physical settlement could simply mean transfer of ownership documents while the commodity remains in situ. But other commodities do present problems – not many financial entities want to own inventories of cattle and wheat and would not have storage facilities for crude oil and pork bellies!

3.5.13   Other tradeflow issues

Trading in and settlement of commodities can be complex.

Settlement can be defined by using an average of prices rather than the price on the date of settlement.

As an illustration of the complexity involved in settlement prices, here is a quote from the trading at settlement (TAS) rules on NYMEX for Brent crude oil:[1]

> Trading at settlement is available for the front two months except on the last trading day and is subject to the existing TAS rules. Trading in all TAS products will cease daily at 2:30 PM Eastern Time. The TAS products will trade off of a "Base Price" of 100 to create a differential (plus or minus) in points off settlement in the underlying cleared product on a 1 to 1 basis. A trade done at the Base Price of 100 will correspond to a "traditional" TAS trade which will clear exactly at the final settlement price of the day.

---

[1] Quoted from New York Mercantile Exchange website.

As in the examples above, commodities are traded in lots of specific amounts and units. Processes must be able to cope with this range of units and rules.

As we have seen, commodities are not homogenous and are not like other asset classes. Therefore great care must be taken when designing processes and systems for commodity trades, so that currently traded and potential trading products are catered for.

3.6   TRADING ACROSS ASSET CLASSES

Sometimes traders want to take advantage of price discrepancies between closely related asset classes. There may be a hedge strategy, whereby there is perceived limited market risk, the multiple trades involved cancelling out exposure to the underlying asset or assets – this is known as basis trading.

Examples of basis trading:

- spot and futures on the same underlying instrument;
- credit default swaps and bonds on the same underlying bond.

There may also be no arbitrage, but the trading strategy is such that one is only interested in the relative positions of two different instruments or asset classes. Examples:

- In the next six months aluminium will be more in demand than copper and its price will be relatively higher.
- Eastern economies will fare better than European economies and hence their currencies will be stronger.
- Long-term interest rates will rise and commodity prices will fall.

For trading across asset classes, it is important that the trader can book and view all parts of his portfolio for price and risk. This can be particularly challenging when different systems are used for different asset classes. Other business functions have similar aims, especially when they are monitoring risk at a trader level.

Trading across asset classes may involve more than one of the support functions such as use of the interest rates' back office and commodities' back office and hence increase risks of miscommunication.

3.7   SUMMARY

Each of the major asset classes was discussed in this chapter. We also illustrated the differences between them and what to look out for when designing elements of the trade lifecycle to cope with a particular asset class.

4

Derivatives, Structures and Hybrids

4.1 WHAT IS A DERIVATIVE?

Any trade that derives from an underlying asset, but does not involve the direct purchase or sale of that asset, is known as a derivative. Common classes of derivatives are forwards and futures, swaps and options. Derivatives are often divided into linear and nonlinear.

4.2 LINEAR

The simpler set of derivatives are linear products. This means that the payoff is related linearly to the spot price of the underlying asset. (We disregard unexpected or unknown extra payments, such as share dividends from this consideration.)

For example, suppose on 3 January 2009 you purchase a six-month forward silver contract at USD 17.05 per troy ounce. The profit or loss six months later is as shown:

Spot price on 3-Jul-09	Profit per unit
15.05	−2
16.05	−1
17.05	0
18.05	1 etc.

Clearly the profit is linearly related to spot price. The same is true for swaps.

Differences between futures and forwards: in the financial industry, there are some technical differences between trades called forwards and futures, although the overall purpose is the same, namely to lock in a price now for some exchange of assets in the future (see Table 4.1).

4.3 NONLINEAR

When the payoff versus spot price is nonlinear for some or all spot prices then we say the trade is a nonlinear derivative. The most common nonlinear product is an option.

An option can be on any underlying financial or nonfinancial instrument. The option trade references the underlying instrument in order to determine the exercise procedure but the option trade is separate to the underlying unless and until exercise occurs.

A call option is the right but not the obligation to buy an instrument or commodity at a specific price at or before a particular time in the future.

A put option is the same as a call option except that it refers to the sale rather than purchase of the underlying.

We can illustrate the call option by the following example from outside finance. Groucho wishes to sell his piano – he wants 1000 euros for an immediate sale. Harpo thinks this is a good price, but he wants to check the market so he gives Groucho 50 euros as a nonrefundable means to hold the sale for one week at the same price. If Harpo finds similar pianos on sale

Table 4.1

Futures	Forwards
Exchange traded directly by the counterparties or through intermediaries who deal on their behalf	Direct agreement between the two counterparties with no other involvement
The exchange is the ultimate counterparty for each side of the trade so there is no counterparty risk (except for the credit worthiness of the exchange itself)	Counterparties bear full risk themselves. If the other side defaults they lose all expected money that cannot be reclaimed during insolvency and legal proceedings
Trading is in specific quality and quantity of the underlying	Any mutually agreeable trade is transacted
Daily margin must be posted by the counterparties which will fluctuate as spot prices change	Unless there is a specific collateral agreement between the two parties, no money will change hands until the forward date

for 1200 euros he will return to buy it for 1000 euros from Groucho (known as exercising his option) and then sell it, making a 150 euros profit (200 – 50). If he finds pianos are cheaper he will simply buy elsewhere (and accept the loss of 50 euros).

As the profit and loss (dark line) in Figure 4.1 shows, Groucho has limited his loss to 50 euros but his profit rises linearly with the market price of pianos. Note that the value of the option is a curve (light line) and hence the option has nonlinear value.

A put option is like an insurance policy. Groucho may insure his piano for 1000 euros and pay 50 euros per year to the insurance company. This is essentially a put option. If the piano is stolen or damaged, it is worth nothing but Groucho receives 1000 euros. If nothing happens to the piano, Groucho could sell it at its market value (and will only have lost his 50 euros premium).

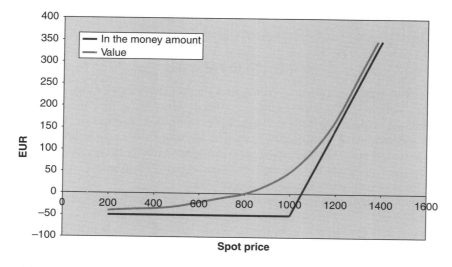

Figure 4.1   Call option

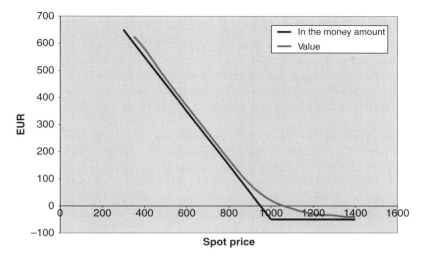

Figure 4.2 Put option

As Figure 4.2 shows, profit rises as market price falls, but the maximum loss is still limited (in this case to the 50 euros premium).

4.3.1   Trade process issues relating to options

Options can be applied to any underlying instrument. The processes involved in dealing with options are somewhat different from those of linear trades.

4.3.2   Exercise

Exercise is the taking up of the option to buy or sell the underlying in the option contract. The traders, middle office and back office have to be prepared for the possibility of exercise, as described in Section 8.9.

4.3.3   Optionality

The cashflows on an option cannot be completely determined from the time of execution, because of the uncertainty of exercise. This means that all processes must be able to cope with a possible but not certain flow of assets.

4.3.4   Leverage

The purchaser of an option has a maximum loss, which is simply the premium paid. The writer (or seller) of the option potentially has an unlimited loss. In the case of a call option on Coca Cola struck at $ 10, if the price at exercise is $ 1000, the writer of the option would have to purchase the underlying shares for $ 1000 in the market place and receive only $ 10 from the option buyer, making a huge loss. It could get even worse if the underlying price climbs even further, as can be seen from the put graph above.

A put option has a limit because the underlying price cannot fall below zero, but even so, there could be a huge loss to the writer as for call options.

The potential to gain or lose more than the original amount invested is known as a type of leverage. People and systems trading leveraged products need careful supervision. Most of the spectacular downfalls of finance houses have arisen on leveraged trades.

Even though the purchaser of options is not putting the assets of the financial entity at undue risk, he is subject to leveraged counterparty risk which the credit control department will need to be aware of.

One way of containing leveraged risk is to trade out of the position when the amount becomes too large. For example, in our call option case the writer of the option might put a limit at spot price of $ 30 and enter a trade to reverse his exposure or sell the trade he holds in the market. Obviously he will still make a big loss by doing so, but at least the loss is contained. A common problem is that people hang on to bad trades because the cost of trading out of them is high, even though it will be much higher if nothing is done.

The above strategy for dealing with leveraged positions only holds good for liquid products. If no buyer could be found for the trade it wishes to sell, an organisation could be left holding onto a rapidly deteriorating situation with no way of stopping it.

Another, better way of managing leveraged risk is to use hedging. Hedging is a process of transacting one or many additional trades in order to offset the risk of a currently held position. For example, if I sell a call option on an equity, I could buy the underlying equity as a hedge. If the price rises, I will lose money on the option, but that loss will be exactly offset by the gain in holding the underlying (the hedge). Although there may be a transaction cost in putting on the hedge, the exposure to the equity price will be covered and the risk is controlled. Hedging will be discussed in greater detail in Chapter 10 on risk management.

Other examples of leveraged positions:

4.3.4.1   Selling short

This means entering a trade with a commitment to selling an underlying in the future that the trader does not hold at time of execution. The trader expects the market price to fall so that he can purchase it cheaper than the agreed sell price. This is a linear trade as the profit is linearly related to the spot price. But it is leveraged because, if the price starts rising, the trader will have to commit an unknown size of funds to buying the underlying in order to fulfil his trading obligations.

4.3.4.2   Credit default swaps

As credit default swaps (see Chapter 5) are an insurance product, they are leveraged trades. This can be illustrated as follows.

Suppose a five year credit default swap trades at 200 basis points per annum. If spreads stay fairly constant, the buyer of protection will have paid about 1000 basis points over the life of the trade (equivalent to 10 % of the notional). On the other hand, the seller of protection will pay 100 % of the notional (less recovery) in the event of default.

4.3.4.3   Dealing with leveraged positions

Risk managers and control departments have various ways of dealing with leveraged risk. They may insist that the trading desk posts a reserve into an account to be held for losses

Table 4.2

Product/Term	0–1 month	1–3 months	3–12 months	1 year–5 years
Short call options	2×	4×	8×	15×
Short put options	1/2×	1/4×	1/8×	Maximum loss
Short sell	1×	3×	5×	10×
Writing credit	1/50	1/25	1/10	1/5

Explanatory notes
For options and selling short we assume spot prices will change more over a greater period of time.
2× indicates the loss incurred when the spot price doubles, 8× when it is multiplied by eight etc.
For products involving the writing of credit insurance, loss is a fraction of the total payout in the event of default.
(For example, if the maximum credit loss were USD 50 million, the 3–12 months tariff would be USD 5 million.)

on leveraged trades; they may allow some degree of leverage, but under limits; or they may enforce a hedging strategy.

When leveraged trades are naked (i.e. they are not covered by hedges for whatever reason), the problem of marking infinite or very high maximum exposures arises. To do this they may use a tariff for estimating assumed maximum loss (see Table 4.2).

4.4   SOME OPTION TERMINOLOGY

European: these options can only be exercised on the maturity date.

American: these options can be exercised at any time up to and including the maturity date.

Bermudan: somewhere between a European and American. There is more than one exercise opportunity, but not a continuous set as for American options. It could be that the exercise is allowed periodically (e.g. one day every three months) or there is a period of no exercise (e.g. first five years) and then exercise is allowed every day thereafter (e.g. for the final six months).

At-the-money: this describes the current position of the option. At-the-money means that the strike is the same as the current spot price.

Out-of-the-money: means the current spot price is below the strike price for call options or above for put options and so would not be exercised if exercise were today.

In-the-money: means the current spot price is above the strike price for call options or below for put options and so the option could be exercised if exercise were today.

Swaption: a swaption is an option with the underlying being a swap. Swaptions generally refer to options on interest rate swaps. A payer swap gives the purchaser the right to enter into a swap paying fixed and receiving floating. A receiver swap gives the purchaser the right to enter into a swap paying floating and receiving fixed.

4.5   OPTION VALUATION

There are certain attributes which characterise an option and enable it to be valued.

Spot price: the current market price of the underlying (market data, changes every day).

Strike price: the price at which the option was struck (trade data, fixed).

Interest rate: for one-currency trades, this is derived from the interest rate (or discount) curve for that currency. For foreign exchange and other options involving multiple currencies, there will be several interest rate curves (market data, changes every day).

Table 4.3

Date	Spot price for date	Resettable strike value
Start date	Irrelevant	124
After 3 months	130	143 (the bigger of 124 and 110 % of 130)
After 6 months	108	124 (the bigger of 124 and 110 % of 108)

Time to maturity: the amount of time left until the option matures (based on trade data, changes every day).

Call or put: whether the option is a call or a put (trade data, fixed).

Volatility: this is a well-defined measure of price variation over a given time period. See Chapter 20 on data for more information.

These six pieces of information are inputs to the valuation model for options, which is normally based on the classical Black–Scholes options pricing formula.

4.6   EXOTIC OPTIONS

Having defined the basic option, which is known as a "plain vanilla" or "vanilla", we go on to discuss exotic options. Any trade based around a vanilla option but modified in some way is known as an exotic option. Here we shall give a sample.

Resettable strike: there may be a clause in the option contract that allows for the strike to be changed during the life of the option. Suppose a USDJPY option is struck at 124 (see Table 4.3). After every three months, the contract allows the strike to be adjusted to be the maximum of 124 and 10 % over the spot price on the resettable fixing date.

Barrier options: there are three standard barrier options: an upper barrier, a lower barrier and a double barrier. Each one can be knock in or knock out.

> Knock in. This means that the option cannot be exercised unless the barrier has been hit at some point in the lifetime of the option.
> Knock out. This means the option can never be exercised if the barrier is reached.

Average trades: in vanilla options, the payout is determined by the spot price on the maturity date (for European style) or on the date of exercise (for American style). In average option trades, the average spot price over several time periods is used to determine the payout.

Basket options: as mentioned in Section 3.2 on foreign exchange as an asset class, baskets of currencies or other underlyings can be traded. An option on the basket would set a strike at the total equivalent worth of one currency of all the currencies in the basket. The valuation of baskets requires several interest rates and cross volatilities between each of the currency pairs in the basket.

Ratchet options (Cliquet): this is a series of forward start options, each one beginning when the previous one terminates. The strike is set at the beginning of each period, such that the option is at-the-money.

Digital or binary option: instead of the payoff being the difference between the strike and spot upon exercise, a digital option has a predetermined payoff amount. It is similar to a bet: if the spot finishes above the strike (for a call option), the purchaser receives a set amount, if not he gets nothing.

4.6.1 Issues with exotics

- Exotic derivatives generally require more ongoing attention than other trades. Ve.
the spot price must be carefully tracked at all times during the life of the option. Al
middle office is used to marking spot prices once a day for valuation, this is more complex,
because the spot price may be required continuously to see, for example, if a barrier has
been breached.
- A strict legal interpretation must be given as to what constitutes the current spot price,
otherwise the counterparties might be in conflict over whether and when a trade is knocked
out or exercised.
- Traders who execute the trade and decide on exercise, must work closely with middle office
which books and processes the trade, including the administration of exercise procedures.
- All the control functions must fully understand the risks associated with exotic trades.
- All of the contract details of these trades must be entered into a system that is capable of
holding them.

4.7   STRUCTURES AND HYBRIDS

A structure is one very specialist bespoke trade or a set of different trades bound together to
produce a required set of exposures. The structure may encompass many types of derivative
and spot trades. A hybrid is similar to a structure, but straddling different asset classes.

For instance, an Australian processing company wants advice from the structuring desk of
an investment bank.

- They produce bronze from copper and tin.
- They sometimes require aluminium and silicon.
- They buy raw materials in USD and sell to all parts of the world particularly in Europe and
Japan.
- They have a floating rate loan on their plant payable in AUD.
- It takes six months from acquisition of raw materials to sale of product.

Staff on the structuring desk will ascertain which risks the processing company wants to
reduce or eliminate and which risks it is happy to live with. They will then put together a
combination of derivative and simple products, to try to handle the risks according to the
client specification. When they think they have come up with a solution, they will test it using
indicative and historical market data. They will then write a report or prospectus for the client,
illustrating in nontechnical language the proposal and explaining all the costs and assumptions
involved. The client will pay a fee for the consultancy and if he likes the proposal, he may
engage the bank to trade on his behalf.

In addition to investigating client requests, structured trades may arise from gaps or mis-
matches in the market. For example, if credit spreads are high reflecting poor credit worthiness,
but bond prices are high reflecting the opposite, a structure might be put together to take advantage of the difference, with little or no inherent risk.

The lowest common denominators of any structured or hybrid trade are the cashflows. The
structurer is, in essence, trying to massage the cashflows to produce the maximum likely
returns, while containing the risk to acceptable areas and sizes. This is by no means an easy
task: cashflows may be occurring on different dates, the amounts may be unknown and there
are the complications arising from the optional component of many derivatives.

Structures are, by their very nature, individual trades or groups of trades. They are therefore hard to process in a systematic way. This often means they are treated as exceptions outside the normal trade processes. Every time an exception is allowed, all the trade lifecycle processes have to cope with the exception. This means the exception cannot be so easily aggregated with trades in the normal process and all business functions have to know how to manage and control the exception. This can be expensive in terms of time devoted to the exception and in terms of the extra operational risk incurred.

Where the structure consists of a group of smaller, simpler trades, it is important that the constituent trades are marked with their links to the overall structure. That way the risk assessment can be done on the structure as a whole.

Structured trading can, however, be a very profitable part of the business. With the control and support functions understanding and managing the trade processes, structurers can look beyond one asset class or one type of trading. They can evolve safe and profitable strategies for taking advantage of market conditions and enriching the services the financial entity can provide to its customers. Additionally, they can be a research arm, testing and pioneering new products and business areas.

Structured trades generally take longer to come to fruition and require a greater degree of scrutiny from business functions, such as the legal department.

4.8   IMPORTANCE OF SIMPLER PRODUCTS

Whenever a trading desk is involved in derivatives it needs to make use of simpler products to manage its risk. Thus a future may require a spot trade; an option may require a future and a spot trade; all trades may require deposits and foreign exchange futures and spots. A network is established where the more complicated trades require the simpler trades.

One of the most important desks is the treasury desk, which holds the money that traders can borrow in order to finance their trading. The treasury will pool all the requirements of the traders and attempt to borrow money at the lowest rate available. It will then lend out from the pool it has acquired to the other trading desks, charging them for this service. Internal charging is usually seen as good business practice, as it leads to efficiency and costs are shown where they are incurred.

For instance, without charging for finance, the efficiency of the treasury desk in achieving cheap funding may be obscured by inefficiencies in the swap desk, and nobody would know where the fault lay.

To promote interaction between trading desks, the seating arrangement once played an important part: spot traders and treasury needed to be accessible to everybody. More derivative products were closer to quants, and structurers close to traders of all products with which they were involved. With modern electronic communications, the physical seating has become less important, but face-to-face communication is still optimal, especially for important decisions or for complicated discussions.

The evolution of trade processes and systems is such that the simpler products had a mature and active market before derivatives arrived on the scene. The legacy systems were designed to work with the products available when they were being developed and so, when derivatives processing was required, either new systems had to be built from scratch or the existing ones modified.

Table 4.4

Asset class:	Interest rates	Foreign exchange	Equities	Fixed income	Commodities	Credit
Product type:						
Spot trades						
Forwards and Futures						
Swaps						
Vanilla options, swaptions						
Exotic options						
Structures and Hybrids						

Although most organisations arrange trading desks according to asset class, the support and control functions are very often grouped by product type. For instance, there might be separate IT systems for spot, nonlinear and option trades – each one crossing many asset classes.

4.9   TRADE MATRIX

Differences in processes arise from:

• different underlying asset classes
• different type and complexity of trades.

This can be represented as a two-dimensional table with the various asset classes in one dimension and the range of trade types in the other as shown in Table 4.4.

Control and support must be provided for every product type in every asset class. This can be done vertically (e.g. equities for every product type), horizontally (e.g. options for every asset class) or with a mixture of both. The decision should take into account availability of systems, distribution of knowledge, trade volumes and complexity and a range of related issues.

4.10   SUMMARY

In this chapter we have explained some of the types of derivative products. Options are a major category of derivatives and we discussed the mechanics of an option. We showed how more complicated products are built from simpler products. Finally we showed the range of product types across all the major asset classes.

5
Credit Derivatives

This chapter was written in collaboration with Dr Geoff Chaplin, Reoch Credit Partners LLP.

We shall now examine one asset class in detail. We have chosen credit derivatives because they are topical, complicated and combine many of the features of other asset classes and derivatives described in the previous two chapters.

5.1   INTRODUCTION

You cannot buy a quantity of credit in the way you can buy a barrel of oil or shares in a company. However, credit risk in the form of counterparty risk (see Chapter 12) has been known and managed since financial trading began. In addition, certain products such as bonds and loans carry intrinsic credit risk: that the underlying issuer or borrower will default and fail to fulfil their obligations.

Since many companies were left with unwanted credit risk on their books, a market was started to trade credit risk with other companies that were prepared to carry the risk in return for some financial incentive.

As ever, the market started with simple products and has advanced to the more complicated and structured products, such as collateralised debt obligations (CDOs).

We begin our discussion of credit derivatives by examining all of the main products, and then show how credit products differ from other asset classes.

5.2   CDS

A credit default swap (CDS) is a contract between two parties referencing an entity or asset: a buyer of protection, also known as the seller of risk; and a seller of protection, also called the buyer of risk.

A simple example would be: JPMorgan buys protection from Banco Santander referencing Ford Motor Credit (Ford Motor Credit is the reference entity). The contract would have a specific term, say five years; an agreed notional amount, say USD 10m; a pre agreed premium, typically called the "CDS spread" say 800bp = 800 basis points = 8% per annum – so the annual premium is approximately 10m × 800/10 000 = USD 800 000 per annum; an agreed list of "credit events"; and other details including payment method on a credit event.

A credit event triggers the termination of the contract and a capital payment. Typical credit events include bankruptcy, failure to pay, or restructuring of outstanding debt. In the context of credit derivatives, the term "default" is often used to mean "credit event" (in contrast, "default" for bond assets typically only means failure to pay).

When a credit event occurs, the seller of protection pays either:

- physical settlement: USD 10m in return for USD 10m notional of Ford Motor Credit debt; or
- cash settlement: a net sum representing USD 10m less the value of Ford Motor Credit debt in the marketplace.

Table 5.1

Credit default swap	Insurance
Financial contract	Insurance contract
No requirement for insurable interest	Requirement for insurable interest
Central bank as regulator	Insurance regulator
Insured is loss of value on the debt of a reference entity	Insured is a physical asset

In the above example, Ford Motor Credit debt in the marketplace may be trading at 20 % of notional value (USD 2m in this case). The figure of 20 % is referred to as the recovery value and the balance is the "loss given default".

A useful analogy is an insurance contract between the insured and the insurer on a particular asset, for example, a car, ship or camera. If a defined event occurs (say, accidental damage), the insurer may pay the repair costs to restore the asset to its former value.

Table 5.1 lists the differences between a credit default swap and an insurance contract.

Recently in the Credit Derivatives "big bang" and "little bang" several changes have occurred to the trading of CDS. Now, many CDS contracts are quoted with a fixed ongoing premium of 500 basis points (sometimes 100 basis points) and a variable initial (known as "upfront") premium. There has been a move away from physically settled CDS contracts (where default results in the protection buyer delivering the defaulted asset to the seller and receiving the amount under protection) to cash settlement (without any asset delivery upon default) and a variety of other changes. Also, there now exists an auction on many CDS contracts that facilitates more open participation and the standardisation of prices.

In addition to "single name" CDS contracts, it is possible to purchase a CDS on an index which is a contract offering protection on a basket of entities.

5.3 CLN

A simple "credit linked note" (CLN) repackages a single name credit default swap in the form of a bond. The buyer of protection (generally a bank) creates the note under a "Limited Recourse Note Program".

This means the bank can issue defaultable notes if a third-party credit event leads to non payment on the note, but does not affect the credit worthiness of the issuing bank.

In the example above, Banco Santander could issue a five-year note referencing Ford Motor Credit which JPMorgan would buy for, say, USD 10m. It would receive in turn coupons of LIBOR plus 800bp. On the occurrence of a credit event, the note would terminate and JPMorgan would receive a cash sum representing the value of Ford Motor Credit debt in the marketplace. Note that a CLN purchaser has credit exposure to both Banco Santander and Ford Motor Credit.

Credit linked notes can be used to repackage more sophisticated and complex credit default swaps.

The term "credit default swap" is also used to describe any credit derivative, where premiums are paid regularly, but exchange of a capital sum only takes place on a credit event. Such products are also referred to as "unfunded". In contrast, if the credit default swap is packaged into a credit linked note, then the product is referred to as "funded".

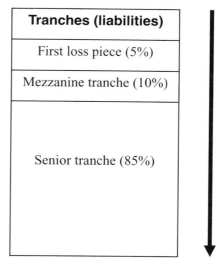

Arrow on right shows direction in which defaults eat into the tranches

Figure 5.1 Anatomy of a CDO

Single name credit default swaps have been widely used by banks and other entities to manage and exchange risk to corporate, bank and sovereign entities. Compared to CDOs, they are relatively simple, high volume, and liquid instruments.

5.4 CDO

A CDO structure is a credit derivative which references not just a single name, but a portfolio of risks (see Figure 5.1). There is one further key difference: tranching of risk. This relates primarily to the capital flows when credit events occur in the reference pool.

A CDO is linked to a "reference pool". This is a portfolio of reference risks – often bonds or default swap contracts (the "asset side"). This portfolio may exist only as a list of reference instruments. It need not exist as an actual portfolio of assets. The purpose of the reference pool is to define cashflows on the CDO tranches. The reference pool typically includes 30 to 200 (but sometimes thousands) of risks. For example, Ford Motor Credit (USD 5m), Unilever (USD 7m), Toyota (USD 10m) ... Let us say, the total of the individual notional amounts is USD 100m.

The "liability side" of a CDO is made up of tranches of risk which are, in effect, passed on to the buyer of risk. For example, these might be the first 5 % of risk (USD 5m) – often called the "First Loss Piece (FLP)"; then the next 10 % (USD 10m); then the remaining 85 % (USD 85m). If reference assets default, the loss (notional exposure less recovery on the reference entity debt) hits the first 5 % tranche, but the other tranches are unaffected. As losses mount up, the 5 % tranche may get eliminated and then losses start to eat into the 10 % tranche. However, the 85 % tranche is unaffected until losses exceed 15 % of the original exposure.

For example, suppose Ford Motor Credit defaults with a 20 % recovery – a loss of USD 4m. The first tranche is reduced to USD 1m. The buyer of risk on the FLP pays USD 4m on the occurrence of the Ford credit event.

If Unilever then defaults with zero recovery (USD 7m loss), then the buyer of risk on the FLP pays USD 1m and that tranche terminates. The buyer of risk on the 10 % tranche pays the balance (USD 6m). The tranche continues with USD 4m notional. If Toyota defaults with a 50 % recovery (USD 5m loss) then the buyer of risk on the 10 % tranche pays USD 4m and that tranche terminates. The buyer of risk on the 85 % tranche now pays USD 1m and the tranche continues with USD 84m notional.

The premiums paid to the risk takers on the various tranches differ. The FLP is the highest risk tranche and carries the highest premium – possibly thousands of basis points. The most senior tranche is the lowest risk and may carry a very low premium – just a few basis points in some cases.

Credit triggers are typically the same as for single name credit default swaps. CDO tranches are often issued in funded (credit linked note) form. This means the notional of the note declines as credit events are called. The notional will reduce to zero if that tranche of risk is eaten up by credit event losses.

The reference pool may or may not exist as a portfolio of assets. In cases where all tranches of risk are sold, a simple "hedge" would actually be to buy all of the risky assets. It is also common to sell individual tranches of CDOs done. The hedge assets would then be different from the reference pool.

CDOs are an example of "structured credit". It is the structuring of risk, rather than having an untranched portfolio, which brings a new element to the product and which makes pricing difficult. The term "CDO contract" typically relates to a specific tranche, rather than all tranches, and may be in unfunded (CDS) form or in funded (CLN) form.

5.4.1   CDO reference pool

Reference pools of CDOs can vary widely. A pool of corporate reference entities (Ford, Unilever, etc.) and banks (RBS, Wells Fargo, etc.) has been common. The reference pool may be investment grade risks, or "high yield" (sub-investment grade/junk risks). Sovereign risks are often included in such pools ("emerging market risks"). Generally, the reference entity risks mentioned in this paragraph are relatively easy to price, although some reference entities do not trade regularly.

Other types of reference pools are also found. Pools of mortgages (residential or commercial) are common, but other assets are also found: lease/rental contracts, credit card debt, and others. Underlying assets here are difficult to price because they do not trade in the open market.

A tranche of another CDO may be included in the reference pool. If there are many such tranches in the reference pool, then the term "CDO squared" is often used to describe the CDO. If one of the tranches is a tranche of a CDO squared, then the term "CDO cubed" is sometimes used. CDO tranches are usually less transparent than sovereign or corporate debt, which makes it harder to obtain price quotations on and easier for issuers to manipulate. That is because investors cannot easily assess either the initial or the ongoing default risk of the reference assets. Price and yield information is not readily available on major public sources of information, such as Reuters.

A "cash CDO" has a reference pool of bonds and/or loans (or other assets) and the reference pool actually exists as a portfolio of assets. Typically, all tranches of the liability side of cash CDOs are sold in order to fund and protect the default risk on the assets. A "synthetic

CDO" has a reference pool typically of CDS contracts or simply a list of reference entities or reference assets. There may be no actual portfolio of assets and often only a single tranche of a synthetic CDO is sold.

5.4.2   Static and managed CDOs

The CDO is referred to as "static" if the reference pool is defined at the outset and not changed, except through defaults or mergers. A "managed CDO" is one where the reference pool may be changed subject to constraints ("compliance rules"), described in more detail later.

It may be useful to give some background to the development and application of managed CDOs.

The ability to substitute assets in a CDO predates the credit derivatives market. Generally, the right to substitute is granted to the originator of the deal, to a third-party asset manager or, more recently, to the investor.

Originator-managed CDOs: the Collateralised Loan Obligation or "CLO" was one of the CDO market's predecessors. It was used throughout the 1990s as a mechanism for banks to manage their loan portfolio. The so-called "Balance Sheet CLO" involved a bank (the "originator") selling, say, 100 loans with notional of USD 10 million each from its own balance sheet into a special purpose company ("SPC"). This financed the purchase by issuing tranches of debt with differing tranches on the pool of loans (junior, mezzanine, senior etc.). In an "Arbitrage CLO" the same structure is used, but the loans are sourced from other bank balance sheets via the secondary market.

In order to facilitate the sale of the mezzanine debt, it was common for the originator of a Balance Sheet CDO to buy some or all of the equity tranche. The theory was that since the first few percent of losses within the portfolio of loans would be sustained by the originator, he would rigorously monitor the credit quality of the borrowers.

Third-party managed CDOs: the concept of third-party managed CDOs is not new – fund managers have been managing debt funds for a long time. Most of the management pre 2001 had taken place in cash deals; synthetic deals were a new product and the management of them came a little later. Investing in cash assets and synthetic assets is not the same thing and the skill sets are not completely interchangeable. For this reason, the number of debt asset managers, who also understood credit derivatives, was limited. As with other structures and asset classes in a third-party managed deal, there will be a portfolio management agreement. This details the roles and responsibilities of the portfolio manager and puts the necessary controls in place to ensure independence.

The role of a manager in a CDO is confused by the fact that a substitution is not necessarily good for every investor. Depending on whether an investor holds the first loss (equity), mezzanine or senior debt of a CDO, a substitution may have a positive, neutral or negative effect. An example is where one credit is replaced with something of identical credit quality, but a credit that increases the chance of defaults bunching together. This is likely to result in an increase in equity value, a decrease in senior value and possibly have no effect on the mezzanine debt. However, if a manager is acting on behalf of multiple tranche investors, his priority is likely to be to minimise realised losses. Where there is just one tranche, it would be possible to fine-tune the manager's mandate.

Compliance rules: managed structures are governed by constraints over what can be taken out and what can be substituted in. Such constraints vary widely. They may be very restrictive:

for example, allowing only capital from maturities to be reinvested. Or they may be very lax: allowing assets to be sold and new ones bought in. The following rules are examples of the sorts of constraints that are often found in managed CDOs.

(a) Concentration Limits. These might state a maximum notional amount in any one of:
    (i) name
    (ii) industry
    (iii) asset class (e.g. loans, structured assets or mortgage debt)
    (iv) rating band, or other.
    In addition, other numerical measures of **diversity** might be used such as Moodys diversity score – a means of assigning a measure to the mix of industries and countries represented in the reference pool.
(b) Rating Limits
    (i) Substituted names may have to satisfy a rating requirement (e.g. at least BB or better rated than the name taken out).
    (ii) There may be requirements to maintain a certain average rating. Numerical measures such as WARF (weighted average rating factor – which converts rating to a number and weights by the notional amount in that name) might be used.
    (iii) Spread constraints may be present and WAS (weighted average spread) might be used.
(c) Other constraints may apply, such as turnover limits. They may become tighter or laxer according to the performance of the structure.

The purpose of compliance rules is to constrain the portfolio in a certain "shape" and to limit the manager's ability to make substitutions which are not in the investor's interests.

5.4.3 CDO pricing methodology

Valuation and understanding of the risks in a CDO requires a mathematical model of the underlying financial product and data in order to use that model. There are two approaches to valuation data in common use.

The "natural measure" or "fundamental/actuarial pricing" is often used by investors – what is this *really* worth? What income do I anticipate I will receive? In the context of CDOs, this means using estimates of default rates often derived from historical default studies by the rating agencies.

The "risk-neutral measure" or "pricing off one's hedge" is typically used by banks – what is the cost to me of hedging this transaction, so that I can lock-in a known profit with minimal risk? In the context of CDO pricing, this means using CDS premium data to "imply" (mathematically) default rates.

The mathematical models are often the same under either measure – the difference being the data put into the model, rather than the sums being done.

The standard mathematical model for CDO products in use by banks since the late 1990s is the "Normal Copula" model, which correlates default times of the various reference entities. Default and recovery rates for each reference entity are then used together with a correlation assumption to value a CDO tranche of risk. Recovery rates used to be assumed as 40 % for senior and 20 % for subordinated debt. Nowadays, particularly on United States reference entities, each reference entity has a (unique to that entity) quoted recovery rate alongside its CDS premium.

The two data approaches will give different answers. How different these answers are – and indeed which is higher – will depend on the make up of the CDO and the assumptions being made.

The former data choice is intended to answer the question "What do I anticipate will actually happen?"

The latter is intended to answer the question "How much will it cost to hedge this risk and how much profit do I expect to make from the deal?"

First, consider a simple example of a single corporate bond. We generally talk in terms of "spreads" – the excess yield of the bond compared to good quality banks' yields ("swap rates"). An investment grade (say, "A" rated) bond may stand at a spread of 100bp (0.01 %) in the market place (equivalent to the risk-neutral measure). However, if we look at historical default and recovery rates as a guide, we may find that the bond only needs to stand at a spread of 20bp to compensate for the default risk. This corresponds to the natural measure price. The difference of 80bp is the "reward for risk".

Instead of an "A" rated bond, if we took a "B" rated bond we may find the bond stands at a spread of 500bp in the market. But historical data suggest that a fair compensation for the actual risk is 400bp, with 100bp being the reward for risk.

The pricing of CDO squared products is difficult and even now there is no agreed "accurate" method of "risk-neutral" valuation.

5.4.4   Other terminology

Rating: ratings are provided by independent rating agencies – S&P and Moodys being the most widely used and best known. These ratings are a guide to default risk and the methodology for rating corporate (and banking) entities has a long history and is well-established. Ratings are not a perfect indication of risk. Indeed, no perfect indicator of risk exists. However, spreads are believed to be a better indication of default risk than rating because they react more quickly to changing situations and represent the sum total of market knowledge, rather than the opinion of a few analysts. The market's perception of the risk of an entity is quickly reflected in its spread, whereas the rating agencies are often slow to re-rate names.

Structured assets are also rated by the agencies. This is relatively new and the methodologies used have changed over time. Structured asset ratings are viewed cautiously. Generally structures carry a spread which is significantly higher than the average spread for corporate entities of the same rating. In addition, structured assets may not be regularly re-rated. A structured asset may suffer several defaults which, if the asset were to be re-rated, would mean a serious deterioration in value and rating. The "latest" rating may be quite old and not indicative of current risk. Even where re-ratings take place, these are lagging indicators of what has happened. This, among other reasons, makes the presence of structured assets in a reference pool undesirable from an investor's perspective.

Investment grade means bonds or loans which are rated from AAA to BBB by one of the main rating agencies. Bonds rated below BBB (BB, B, CCC, etc.) are sub-investment grade and often referred to as "Junk".

Gearing: the term "gearing" refers to a higher risk than would be obtained by a holding of a portfolio of risks. For example, consider the following two exposures:

(a) EUR 20m exposure to 40 reference entities (each of 0.5m).
(b) EUR 20m exposure to the losses on the same 40 reference entities but now each exposure
     is 2m (with a total notional of EUR 80m): a "25 % First Loss Piece".

If 16 reference entities default with an average loss of 0.3m (0.5m × 60 % loss given default) then exposure (a) loses $16 \times 0.3 = 4.8$m. So 15.2m is left of the original 20m. Exposure (b) loses $16 \times 2 \times 0.6 = 19.2$m and there is only 0.8m of the original 20m left. Exposure (b) is said to be "four times geared" relative to the underlying portfolio.

Additionally, a geared structure is relatively insensitive to the better quality names. If we take a reference pool with spreads ranging from 150bp to 1000bp and construct a first loss piece (say 0 to 25 %), we can calculate the expected loss on the entire pool and also on the FLP. Improving a handful of the best (lowest spread) names in the reference pool to a 10bp spread (from an average of around 175bp), reduces the expected loss (EL) on the FLP by only 5 % of the EL, but reduces it by over 16 % in the case of the unstructured pool.

The impact of gearing is also felt on more senior tranches. As spreads increase, the value of a geared structure is impacted far more harshly than an ungeared structure.

5.5   DATA RELATING TO CDOs

As described above, CDOs are different from most financial products in that they often require active management, as well as valuation and risk assessment. Here we discuss some data specific to CDOs and go on to look at practical aspects of management and valuation.

5.5.1   Reference pool data

The reference pool of assets may change over time. There are two principal causes of change:

(i) Default of a name in the reference pool will automatically cause it to be removed from the CDO.
(ii) The CDO manager may substitute a name in the pool. This substitution will involve some or all of that name's notional being removed and a new name replacing it. In the following illustration, it is worth bearing in mind two examples – the iTraxx series 9 CDO and a managed bespoke CDO. The first is a static structure – a data source – and may exist as an actual transaction; the latter is a transaction.

Each reference entity in the pool contains static, semi-static and market data. Note that reference entities may disappear from the pool or new ones appear. In particular, mergers may lead to one or more names disappearing and consequent changes to the tranching structure.

Static data (rarely changes)
- Reference Entity (its legal name) and other identifiers such as RED code
- Parent name
- Sector
- Country
- Region
- Notional holding of this name in the reference pool
- Currency
- Seniority
- Contract clauses – such as restructuring clause.

Semi-static data (changes, but not on a frequent basis)
- Rating assigned by one or more rating agencies
- User's own rating ("internal rating" – sometimes defined as a function of rating agency data)

- Recovery rate – prior to 2008, this would have been semi-static for investment grade names; post 2008 US names moved to dynamic recovery rates ("market data" below).

Market data (changing on a daily or frequent basis)
- CDS spreads at various tenor points
- Recovery rates (for some names – see above).

5.5.2 Tranche data

Static data
- Attachment point – except for managed CDOs where it is semi-static
- Detachment point – as above
- Maturity
- Currency
- Reference curve (fixed coupon, floating: LIBOR plus a fixed spread)
- Payment details – Day Count, Day Roll, Frequency, Holiday Centre.

Semi-static data
- Rating – initial rating is fixed; bespoke deals may be re-rated.

Market data
- Tranche price (spread)
- Correlation.

5.5.3 CDO deal details

- Start Date
- End Date
- Size
- Security ID
- Rating.

5.6 PRACTICAL ASPECTS OF CDO MANAGEMENT

A CDO management system would be expected to provide the following information in addition to audit trails.

5.6.1 What is happening?

CDOs are complex instruments comprising several underlying structures across different asset classes. The user will want to know the current state of the CDO, both from an absolute viewpoint and relative to a previous point in time, usually yesterday, last week or last month.

The system must provide an assessment of the overall current position of the CDO or CDOs which it is managing. Common techniques for monitoring the CDO are: composition measures, weighted average scores, individual winners and losers.

Composition measures: this analyses the entire reference pool and provides measures such as mean, maximum and minimum for:

- Industry sectors
- Rating buckets – these could be the actual ratings or user defined groupings such as investment grade, sub-investment grade
- Geographies – usually country or rating agency defined region
- Notionals
- Diversity – the rating agencies have devised methods for assessing the diversity of assets within the reference pool usually by analysing the composition of industries. Diversity Score is one such measure.

Weighted average scores: this is a group of calculations, each one finding the mean across the reference pool of the individual score of the asset multiplied by the asset's notional holding in the CDO. Typical scores are:

- WAR (Weighted Average Ratings). Generally each rating is given a score. 1 for AAA, 2 for AA+ etc.
- WARF (Weighted Average Weighting Factor). The rating agencies ascribe a factor to each rating to reflect the relative safety of higher ratings and the more risky nature of lower ratings.
- WARR (Weighted Average Recovery Rate).
- WAS (Weighted Average Spread). Five year credit default spreads are the most liquid credit instruments in the CDO.
- WAM (Weighted Average Maturity).

Individual winners and losers: a list of individual names in the reference pool for which one of the following data items has changed significantly; or else a list of the best and worst performing assets for that data item.

- Rating change including a watch being imposed or removed.
- CDS spread – generally at the most liquid five year instrument and a move of more than x % or y basis points overnight/week/month.
- Credit event.
- Change in recovery rate of more than z overnight/week/month.

5.6.2   What has happened?

Trustees, CDO managers and investors in CDOs need to be able to track the historical progress of a CDO. They will need to receive periodic reports on a variety of data connected to the CDO from its inception to the present. Usually these reports are generated monthly. They contain narrative together with statistical breakdowns in tabular and graphical formats. Typical reports comprise:

Composition changes: how the composition measures outlined above have changed over time.

Weighted average score changes: how the various weighted average scores have changed over time.

Substitutions: an historical record of all substitutions noting the substitution made, the reason, the immediate effect of the substitution on the portfolio and the cost of substitution in terms of fees paid or received.

5.6.3 What is likely to happen and what is the worst that can happen?

If a CDO system is functioning correctly and data is being input regularly and accurately, it should be possible to alert users to imminent events and reduce the element of surprise.

Easy predictions: the system can keep a diary of future expected events, such as cashflow payments. This would give the user a view on future coupon payments, tranche fees, interest payments etc. If the user is required to take action or make a decision on a certain day, the diary is an easy means to give early and final warnings to ensure good management of the CDO.

Harder predictions: a future credit event is obviously hard to predict, but will have significant consequences for the CDO. A sophisticated CDO system could stress test the portfolio for a range of scenarios and report the effects of, say, a given number of downgrades or defaults. These tests may take time to run, so could be batched up and processed at quiet times, such as overnight or at the weekend. The user should also be able to see the effect of a scenario of his choosing, such as a particular name suffering a credit event. Remember that in scenario testing, the user will be keen to see the net effects of change across all the portfolios he is holding, so there will need to be aggregation of results for all CDOs.

It is important that a system should have the flexibility to accommodate user specified stress tests and changing requirements over time.

5.6.4 What opportunities do I have?

A CDO manager sees the world of assets as being divided into those he owns in one or more CDOs, and those he does not. The user should be able to view information about assets in these two groups. In practice, this means keeping lists of:

- the universe of all assets;
- all those assets held in one or more CDOs (held universe);
- all those assets not currently held (nonheld universe).

Obviously, the first set is the union of the other two.

Like for like identification: if a currently held name becomes undesirable or a nonheld name becomes desirable, the user may require a means to identify similar names across the held and nonheld universes. The similarity might be defined by rating, CDS spread, industry, country or some other means.

Trading one feature for another: alternatively, he may want to be offered the cost of changing risk profile. For example, he may want to improve the credit quality by switching an asset rated BBB+ for one rated A−. He will want to know how much such a change will cost and which is the cheapest asset matching his new criteria.

System suggested substitutions: a sophisticated system might be able to suggest substitutions on a regular basis by comparing the current portfolio with alternatives in the currently nonheld universe. This requires an algorithmic method of scoring a given group of names and then systematically choosing different names and re-scoring.

What would have been? Knowing the full substitution history allows the system to inform the user of what his CDO would look like, had he not performed the substitutions he did. It is informative to track the progress of the original portfolio against the evolving one over time, assuming the original is still in existence. This allows the user to see if his substitutions were beneficial and provides information as to which factors have affected performance.

5.6.5   Reporting

As mentioned above, a key piece of functionality in any CDO management system is reporting. Likely reporting requirements will be:

- daily reports for managers;
- ad hoc progress reports for business managers, potential clients etc.;
- trading reports for middle office, operations, finance departments;
- end of month formal reports for investors, trustees etc.;
- end of year financial reports;
- regulatory reports.

Some of these will have fixed formats and be generated at known times. Others will be individual, ad hoc queries. A flexible system will need to provide:

- capture of all market, static and trading data at the atomic level;
- a user interface allowing the user to specify the query on the data;
- the ability to slice, dice and aggregate the atomic data to satisfy the query;
- a sufficiently comprehensive formatting of output to satisfy all of the reporting requirements.

5.6.6   Limits

Many CDOs constrain their managers by imposing portfolio limits on the reference pool. These limits are often based on the composition measures and weighted average calculations described above. Examples are:

- weighted average spread to be no higher than 350 basis points;
- not more than one region to have greater than 15 % of notional holding;
- the sum of the two most concentrated industrial sectors – no more than 40 % of portfolio.

To cope with limits and tests, the CDO management system will need to provide the following functionality:

Ability to specify a new limit or amend an existing limit: this is not trivial because there is a vast array of possible limit tests. Generally, however, there are two aspects to each test:
- defining the unit of the test – e.g. WARF, Average spread, Region concentration;
- defining some combination of unit scores, e.g. top two, average, minimum etc.

Calculation of tests and limits: the system must be capable of applying the full set of portfolio tests to a particular CDO and discovering how close each test score is to its limit. The calculation may need to be run:
- on a periodic basis, such as every morning;
- on demand, when the user is particularly concerned about the state of the portfolio; or

- after a given action on the portfolio such as a substitution. The user may also want to know the effect of a substitution on the portfolio tests, before it is performed.

5.6.7 Alerts

The user will want to know when a limit is approaching and when it has actually been breached. He will then need to take action to bring the portfolio back within the limit or, for internal limits, take steps to get the limit changed temporarily or permanently. Alerts could be transmitted by various means, such as on-screen messages, reports or machine-generated emails to interested parties.

5.7 PRACTICAL ASPECTS OF CDO VALUATION

The purpose of this section is to highlight some issues relating to CDO valuation and risk management.

Missing data: it is common for some input market data, such as CDS spreads, to be missing on an occasional or regular basis. Here are some suggested solutions to the problem:

- prompt the user to enter a value;
- use the previous day's value;
- engineer a value based on data from similar inputs. For example, in the case of a missing automobile spread, one could calculate the average movement of all automobile spreads from the previous day and apply that change to the previous day's spread of the missing name. Another simple example is to use a "proxy" name – e.g. RTW Engineering is assumed to have the same spread as BMW.

Generally the user will want a report when any piece of market data has changed considerably or when it has been stale for a period of time. A dramatic change could indicate something important happening which will affect the entire CDO or it could be an error. Stale data could be caused by a reference identity changing or an error on the part of the supplier. Missing data may arise because the name has defaulted or been taken over.

Pre valuation: CDO valuations can take a long time to process. The optimum time for this is overnight. If, however, data is missing or wrong, the user will want to be told beforehand so that he does not arrive the following morning to find nothing has been valued. One way to check that market data is complete and within an acceptable tolerance, is to perform a quick valuation on the portfolio. A simple, price only valuation or reference entity calibration is generally quick enough to be run at the end of day before the users leave the office and will reveal most errors that will prevent a full valuation.

Calibration: CDO valuation models have a dependency on all assets they are using to be calibrated to produce a survival curve (or hazard rate). The production of these survival curves is called the calibration process and uses the asset's CDS spreads at various maturities to derive its curve.

An individual reference entity only needs to be calibrated once, no matter in how many CDO reference pools it sits. Furthermore, unless CDS spreads (and other data such as discount factors) change, the calibration process need not be re-run for different scenarios or simulations. For these reasons, it is more efficient to divide the valuation process into two – the first for calibration and the second for CDO valuation using the survival curves. This division requires the calibrated survival curves to be held in memory and each one has a unique identifier.

Registration: due to the compartmentalised nature of CDOs, it is often useful to be able to build individual components in memory and refer to them in later stages of the valuation process. This is particularly useful in a spreadsheet. One might have:

- individual sets of discount factors for each currency;
- a full universe of calibrated reference entity survival curves;
- a full universe of stressed reference entity survival curves (for sensitivity analysis);
- individual CDOs holding reference pool and tranche data;
- standard deals (such as ITRAXX and CDX.IG) with their market data spreads or correlations.

A common approach is to register each component in memory and return an identifier. The valuation process can then use these references as parameters which means that:

- less data needs to be passed as input in one go;
- it is easier to track which part of the process is currently being run;
- revaluation makes use of already registered units making it quicker;
- if data is changed, fewer components need rebuilding.

Bespoke and standard reference deals: a distinction must be made between reference deals such as iTraxx and CDX.IG (which may not exist as actual transactions) and the user's own CDO transactions. Reference deals provide market data inputs to the valuation by either quoting price or correlation. The quote will be for a given series, maturity and tranche (e.g. iTraxx series 8, 7 year, 6–9 %).

A bespoke deal may be a transaction on one or more reference deals or may have different reference entities and tranching structure. When the bespoke deal contains reference entities which differ from those in the iTraxx and CDX pools, the user will have to provide a mapping between the reference entity and the standard deal whose correlation structure is considered most appropriate. The default would be European names linked to iTraxx, US investment grade names to CDX.IG and US high yield names to CDX.HY.

Common valuation requests: defined and implied data: we think of the valuation of a CDO as deriving the tranche price from its correlation, but very often the user may wish to reverse this process: input a tranche price and view the derived correlations:

- Valuation plus sensitivity analysis.
- Change in subordination: before a user makes a substitution he may want to see how the subordination will change in order to keep the value of the CDO the same.
- Aggregation: the user may want to aggregate a CDO with several individual CDS trades. In addition, he may have bought standard tranches of reference deals for hedging and may want to see the combined aggregation of risk between his bespoke CDO and the bought tranches.

5.8   WHY ARE CREDIT DERIVATIVES DIFFERENT?

Mix of market data sources: credit derivatives combine data from interest rates, foreign exchange, standard quoted credit instruments, such as credit default swaps and the more specialist index quoted CDO series such as Markit iTraxx and CDX, and volatility data. In addition, most credit derivative systems require inputs of rating agency data such as ratings (current, outlook and warnings) plus historical recovery rates and transition matrices. The diversity of market data means dealing with many different suppliers; presenting both business acquisition issues, such as purchasing contracts; and technical concerns, such as a variety of input media.

Dependency upon accurate static data: as with most credit products, accurate static data is required. Many models use static data from individual assets to derive correlation assumptions – industry sector, country, legal name and relationship to any other child or parent entities. The IT solution will need to source the original static data and keep it up to date.

Complex valuation: the pricing and risk management of credit derivatives is far from easy and there are a variety of analytic solutions available. Many organisations require CDOs to be valued using multiple models and many variations of input parameters. Valuation is time consuming. A sophisticated solution may require the use of parallel processing or grid technology to make optimal use of available hardware. This involves identifying atomic units of valuation which can be distributed, ensuring that each unit has all input data required, and then amalgamating all the unit results to produce the correct overall valuation.

Scenarios: after generating a basic valuation result, it is often required to test the CDO valuation in various scenarios. Here are some examples:

- Choose particular historical market data combinations (Black Wednesday, 9/11 etc.).
- Make some virtual substitutions to the reference pool.
- Take user defined correlation or recovery rate assumptions and override those from data suppliers.

High sensitivity to assumed data inputs: perhaps what makes credit derivatives especially different from most financial products is their sensitivity to two inputs which are difficult to measure or derive from the market – asset recovery rates and correlation.

The problem of dealing with these two unreliable inputs to valuation means that the software solution must allow the user:

- to experiment with different combinations and see the effect of input parameter changes upon the final output;
- to ascribe to every output (including stored and reported results) the input assumptions which were made. Valuation results are meaningless if the underlying assumptions are unknown or unclear.

Cashflow waterfalls: cash CDOs require a "waterfall" definition. The waterfall describes how cash generated from the reference pool is applied – including payment of coupon and/or capital to the tranche holders – and may incorporate a range of tests determining whether a distribution is to be made or whether income is to be held in reserve. These definitions are unique to each CDO. This presents a challenge to the IT solution:

- to allow the user to specify the waterfall to the computer;
- for the machine to implement the algorithm when there is no generic set of inputs or processes.

Problems caused by CDOs: some of the problems caused by CDOs are explained in Chapter 5.

5.9 SUMMARY

Credit derivatives are a complicated but often useful set of financial instruments. We have defined various types of credit derivatives, how they are used and where they differ from other asset classes.

6

Liquidity, Price and Leverage

Before moving on to the trade lifecycle, this chapter considers three important aspects connected to trades themselves.

6.1 LIQUIDITY

6.1.1 Two types of trading

An apple grower wanting a fixed price for his crop come harvest time enters into a forward trade with an apple wholesaler and receives a guaranteed price from which he can budget for the future. The trade he has agreed will not be re-traded with another counterparty; the apple grower is happy to see the trade through to maturity and collect profit for supplying apples.

A metals trader in an investment bank can see that the future price of lead is lower than should be the case, based on industry fundamentals, and so buys lead futures. He has no intention of waiting for the futures to expire into a delivery of lead – he will sell his futures when he believes the time is right.

6.1.2 What is liquidity?

Whenever a financial entity wants to sell a trade executed with one counterparty on to a new counterparty, there must be a market for that resale to occur. Many trades are conducted with the expectation of being able to re-trade at any time and therefore require markets to be available continuously (or at least during normal trading hours). Others may have fewer potential buyers and sellers.

When a market has an abundance of buyers and sellers, we call it liquid. When there are few, we call it illiquid. Liquid markets have the advantages of:

- competitive prices
- small bid/offer spreads
- plenty of information about the products
- availability to buy and sell as required.

6.1.3 Asset liquidity

In addition to specific markets and products having variable levels of liquidity, so individual assets have liquidity. One asset may have greater utility than its peers and hence be more liquid. For instance, certain bonds are more popular than others, because they can be used as collateral in the repo market.

6.1.4 Measuring liquidity

It is hard to give a precise measure for liquidity and it is misleading to compare liquidity across different markets as each will have its own idiosyncrasies, but the best indicators of liquidity are difference between bid and offer prices and total volumes of trades being conducted in a given time period.

6.1.5   Risks associated with liquidity

The two areas where liquidity needs to be considered are:

- trading products
- using market prices for valuations.

There is nothing wrong with trading products that are illiquid, provided that the trader himself and the control functions around trading are aware and take into account the illiquid feature of the trade.

Similarly, illiquid market prices can be used for valuation, provided that it is made clear to all readers of valuation reports that they are using illiquid data.

There is a risk if a product or price changes from being liquid to illiquid. This can happen in certain markets and requires the trading support teams, such as middle office, to be aware and mark the trade or price accordingly.

If a product is traded with a false assumption of liquidity, it can lead to an unrealistic reliance on its market value.

A valuation based on market prices that are not as liquid as assumed, can also cause decisions to be made based on false assumptions.

It is therefore important to take into account liquidity whenever a piece of market data is being used or trade is executed and watch for changes in liquidity over time.

6.2   PRICE

6.2.1   Over-the-counter price

The price of an over-the-counter (OTC) trade is the amount the buyer will pay and the seller will accept to transact the trade. It is only applicable to the instant the trade was executed: one second later the price may be different. Another pair of counterparties transacting a different trade with the same terms and conditions at exactly the same time as the first trade may reach a different price. The price of an OTC may be derived from a similar process to that of a house for sale:

1. look at prices of similar houses recently traded;
2. assess the advantages and disadvantages of this particular house compared to its peers and estimate the price difference these features will make;
3. take into account the vendor's desire to sell and the purchaser's desire to buy.

6.2.2   Exchange price

An exchange or market place often insists that participants publish prices, which they are committed to honouring, for standard trades conforming to known terms and conditions. The prices are normally quoted as bid/offer. The price is therefore common to anyone wishing to transact, but prices will still vary over time.

6.2.3 Broker price

Brokers bring together buyers and sellers and often publish prices. From the price perspective, they are very similar to exchanges.

6.2.4 What can we infer from price?

Exchange trades are generally more liquid because of the guaranteed supply of participants. The price is therefore a better indication of market sentiment. Since many products are valued using prices of other products, it is important to find a realistic market price. If trading is liquid, the price is likely to be more useful. Many product and risk control functions in financial entities will accept liquid trade prices, but will be wary of illiquid prices.

For example:

The risk based on a quoted price is calculated as 16 000 euros.
If the quoted price were liquid, the risk allocation remains as 16 000 euros.
However, if the price were illiquid, the allocation is set more conservatively at 20 000 euros.
Generally a price for a trade will only be considered liquid if a few (say, three to five) brokers or any one exchange is quoting prices for that trade.

6.2.5 Cost of unwind

Unwinding a trade means reversing all the asset flows and commitments of the trade in order to arrive at a situation where it is as if the trade had not been executed. The cost associated with this process is very dependent on the liquidity of the trade. To give an example: someone thinking of buying a new car may be swayed by how easily he could resell the car if he found it was not to his liking. If there were a great demand for that model, resale might not involve much reduction in price. But if the model were illiquid, the owner might have to come down considerably to persuade someone to take it off his hands. Since most traders are very concerned with the cost of unwind, the price of a trade is affected by its liquidity.

It may not be possible to unwind very bespoke or structured products, because there is nobody in the market place who wants the exact product. In such cases, the trade will be broken into its constituents to be unwound separately. But this will probably involve additional costs.

6.2.6 Volumes

In the local supermarket, the more one buys of an item, the lower the price. In financial trades, it is likely to be the reverse. Since, within reason, it is harder to resell large quantities of an asset, people are less willing to take on the trade and this means the price will rise. Usually exchange and other quotes are for standard quantities or they state the maximum quantity applying to the quoted price. The volume of a trade is the quantity of the underlying asset transacted.

For example, a European investment banking holding a large quantity of Japanese yen and wanting euros might ask several foreign exchange spot traders to sell the yen rather than putting it all through one trade.

Table 6.1

Trade type	Buyer	Seller
Spot	No leverage	No leverage
Future	Leverage partially offset by margin call	Leverage partially offset by margin call
Forward	Leveraged	Leveraged
Option	No leverage on trade but leveraged counterparty risk	Leveraged
Insurance such as credit derivative	No leverage on trade but leveraged counterparty risk	Leveraged

6.3 LEVERAGE

When a spot trader buys aluminium he pays in full on the settlement day. Whatever happens to the price of aluminium, there is no additional payment required to meet his obligations arising from the trade. We say that spot trades are not leveraged.

When a bank sells a put option, it receives the premium and pays nothing. If the trade is exercised, it will have to pay the difference between the strike and spot price at exercise. The bank has paid nothing upfront but has created a possible future pay out. Hence we say that options are highly leveraged.[1]

Futures and forwards are leveraged in a different way (see Table 6.1). The parties to a forward agreement pay nothing until the transaction is settled and then they pay the difference between spot and the forward price. The future trade is similar, but the degree of leverage is partially offset by margin payments to reflect the spot price fluctuations between when the deal is executed and when it is settled.

We define leverage as the use of borrowed capital or debt to increase possible return on investment.

From the point of view of the purchaser of the put option, he has paid the premium and may receive many times the premium as a payout, should the option be exercised. His bank will, however, be concerned for the leveraged counterparty risk – see Chapter 12 on counterparty risk.

6.3.1 Advantages of leverage

The investor can use leverage to buy more investment potential per dollar he invests. For example, a share trades at 10 dollars, an option on 100 shares costs a premium of 10 dollars. An investor with 1000 dollars could buy:

- 100 shares outright or
- 100 options giving him control of 10 000 shares.

This process is sometimes known as gearing – a small investment leading to a much bigger reward potential. With finite capital available, it is very tempting for investment organisations to use leverage to "create" more investment opportunity.

---

[1] Leverage and "gearing" are both terms applied to the "more than one for one" change in the value of the asset compared to an identical sum invested in the underlying asset.

Table 6.2

Spot price on expiry (cents)	Buyer receives (dollars)	Seller receives (dollars)
0	−100 000	100 000
10	0	0
20	100 000	−100 000
100	900 000	−900 000

6.3.2   Disadvantages of leverage

Leverage creates risk: it has the potential to overstretch the investor by making him liable to pay more than he has available in the form of capital. Even if one is owed money, this can be a problem because of counterparty risk. Both market and counterparty risk control departments try to measure and control leverage. As well as internal limits, regulators place external limits on the permitted degree of leverage.

6.3.3   Measurement of leverage

Leverage arises when there is a definite or possible debt. Forward settling and insurance-based products create leverage. Options can be considered as insurance products. Sometimes leverage can be quantified, other times it is limitless. Here we look at the degree of leverage in some common products.

A six month cash settled forward trade of notional one million units is set at forward price 10 cents.

Table 6.2 shows that there is a maximum loss to the buyer of 100 000 in the event that spot drops to zero. The seller, on the other hand, has an unbounded loss if the spot price should rise.

Call option trades have similar behaviour: if the price rises the profit to the buyer (and loss to the seller) is unlimited. If prices fall there will be no payout.

Put options always have limited downside, because the price of the underlying cannot fall below zero. When prices rise beyond strike there is no payout.

Derivatives on asset classes such as shares and commodities can exhibit huge spot price variations and so estimation of leveraged positions is an issue. For interest rate products and bonds the price fluctuations are generally tighter and hence leverage is more manageable.

Products such as credit derivatives have enormous leverage. The premium received on providing protection on a company defaulting is a lot less than the amount of payout should the company default. The problem is compounded by the payout being very unpredictable, because it is dependent on the recovery rate which is not known at all before default and sometimes not until well after default has occurred. (See Chapter 5 on credit derivatives.)

In cases where leverage cannot be determined, an estimate will be made. This will take into account:

6.3.4   Current market position

This includes market predicted forward prices, which will give some indication of the likely payment obligations.

6.3.5 Time

The longer the debt exists, the greater the likely change in price. So leverage can be divided into time intervals – the shorter intervals having less estimated leverage than the longer ones.

6.3.6 Asset class

As mentioned, some products have greater volatility of prices than others. Sometimes there are known factors that affect the longer term prices, such as the mean reversion property exhibited by oil prices.

6.3.7 Monitoring of leverage

Even though estimation of leverage is often required, it can be tempered by the fact that it is rare for asset prices to suddenly jump up or down by more than a few standard deviations of their current level. Provided there is continual monitoring, upward or downward trends can be detected and acted upon. This means that the degree of leverage can be controlled, even in trades that have potentially unlimited loss or gain, assuming that the trade has enough liquidity to allow it to be reversed when required.

6.3.8 Summary

Leverage increases risk. A trading organisation and everybody involved in risk monitoring and control should be aware of how much leverage exists and in which trades and books.

Part II
The Trade Lifecycle

7

Anatomy of a Trade

A trade ticket is the combination of all details relating to a trade. In order to discuss the lifecycle of a trade, we begin by looking closely at the components of a trade ticket. These will vary according to the type and asset class of the trade being transacted.

7.1 THE UNDERLYING

This is the basis for the trade. It is the fundamental unit upon which the trade is constructed. The actual underlying will depend upon the asset class. The underlying could be:

- a particular share traded on an exchange (equity);
- a bond (fixed income);
- two different currencies for exchange (foreign exchange);
- one currency for future exchange or swap (interest rate);
- a particular measure (size, weight, volume) of a real substance (commodity);
- some other financial instrument.

We will divide the ticket into the major subcategories that apply to most trades and give a specific example to illustrate the concepts. As an illustration, details of the example deal are set out at the end of each section below.

Suppose My Trading Bank bought 20 000 Cadogan Petroleum ordinary shares quoted on the London Stock Exchange from The Bank Next Door on 3 June 2009.

7.2 GENERAL

Some features are required by all parts of the trade process and hence do not fall into any one subcategory. Among these are the identification details. These ensure that all processes know which trade they are acting upon and the status of the trade, so that it is clear where the trade currently sits.

Identifier: E091003
Asset class: Equity
Type: Spot
Status: Awaiting confirmation
Trade date: 3 June 2009
Transaction time: 11:09 London (GMT+1)
Transaction location: London

7.3   ECONOMIC

These are all features of the trade relating to the value of the trade such as the date, size, asset identifier and price.

Buy or Sell: Buy
Notional: 20 000
Ticker: CAD
Exchange: LSE
Currency: GBP
Price: 10.38p

7.4   SALES

Certain trade details are recorded purely to reward the salesperson arranging the trade. These have no bearing on the economic value of the trade or on any future trade process. Salesmen are generally rewarded according to the size of the trade and the possibility of profit it affords using a formula to determine the number of *sales credits* the trade has generated. When sales commissions are allocated, the number of sales credits is used as a measure of each sales person's performance.

Salesperson: Tanya Carter
Sales credits: 150

7.5   LEGAL

As mentioned above, many trades are transacted at high volume and with standard agreements. However, more specialised or complicated trades may have legal addenda which form part of the terms and conditions of the agreement. This is commonly a document which will be attached to the trade ticket in soft or hard copy. It comprises a master agreement, a schedule relating to the master agreement, both of which are standard for all trades of the same type with the same counterparty, and a confirmation that is specific to the trade itself.

Legal: No special instructions
Jurisdiction: England

7.6   BOOKING

After execution, the trade will be accounted for at several layers within an organisation. Internal processes require a description of where to place the trade. The details are very much driven by the way the organisation arranges its books and records.

Desk: Equity trading
Folder: European stock
Trader: Giles Milner
Assistant: Mark Best
Trading book: GBP Equity trading

7.7 COUNTERPARTY

It is essential to know all the details of the counterparty in order to confirm and settle the trade successfully, to investigate queries and process any post execution requirements.

Counterparty: The Bank Next Door
Department: London interbank
Branch: London City
Address: The Old Grange, Wickmore Street, London
Payment Type: SWIFT
Payment Code: UIT TRY XXX XXX
Counterparty reference: LCE393_93B
Settlement Date: 5 June 2009
Special Settlement Instructions: None
Delivery Type: Delivery versus Payment

7.8 TIMELINE

7.8.1 Dates relating to a trade

Trade date: the date upon which the trade is agreed and executed. From this point the trade is live and has exposure to market forces.

Maturity date: the date the trade closes or expires. All of its cashflows are known; the trade no longer has exposure to market forces.

Final delivery date: the date upon which all cashflows are settled; there is no longer any counterparty risk.

7.8.2 Fixed cash or asset exchange dates

These dates apply to trades that have at least one exchange of cash or assets prior to the final delivery date such as swaps or loans:

Value date: the date upon which the exchange of cash or assets is supposed to occur. In some sets of terminology, this is known as the settlement date.

Settlement date: the date upon which the exchange of cash or assets actually did occur.

7.8.3 Unknown cash or asset exchange dates

When certain future cash or asset exchanges have uncertain amounts they have the value date and settlement date as for fixed flows but in addition:

Fixing or reset date: the date a flow is fixed according to some piece of market data or other agreed criteria. From this date, the size of the cash or asset flow is completely determined.

7.8.4 Example

The hedge fund Fencing LLP requires a one year loan from Capital Bank for EUR 50 000 (see Table 7.1). The agreed interest is 10 %.

Table 7.1

Date	Action
15 Sep 2008	Trade date – no money changes hands yet
17 Sep 2008	Value date – EUR 50 000 is due to go from Capital to Fencing
17 Sep 2008	Settlement date – the money is transferred
15 Sep 2009	Maturity date – the trade expires but no money changes hands
17 Sep 2009	Final delivery date – Fencing pays EUR 55 000 (principal + interest)

Note: in this example there are no fixing or reset dates because the cashflows are fixed and known from the trade date.

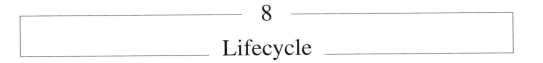

8

Lifecycle

This chapter examines the full lifecycle of a trade.

8.1 PRE EXECUTION

Systems and processes need to handle two common pre trade situations. Both cases outlined here give rise to a virtual trade ticket necessary for keeping all of the requisite trade details. The virtual trade can then be converted into an actual trade if and when it is executed.

8.1.1 Provisional trades

For a complicated or structured deal comprising many parts, the trading parties might design a provisional trade. They will agree on a period of time for due consideration and amendments before a final execution date. There may also be conditions and penalties if one side pulls out of the agreement to trade.

Such provisional trades will need to be circulated to interested parties such as:

- the legal department for scrutiny;
- market risk control to stress test;
- credit risk control to determine whether sufficient credit facility (or line) is available with the particular counterparty;
- trading desks to prepare other trades required to hedge the risk of the provisional trade.

Many investment banks and hedge funds have special non trading portfolios for such provisional deals. These maintain the division between real and virtual trades, but allow for the provisional trades to filter through required checks and processes and make it easier to convert the provisional trade into reality when the execution is enacted.

Risks associated with provisional trades: the extent to which a provisional trade carries a legal responsibility must be clear and transparent to anyone acting upon or using that trade. Falsely assuming a provisional trade to be completely abstract could cause loss and is therefore a risk.

Additionally, there may be clauses attached which make one or other party liable if they do not follow certain causes of action by given deadlines. Examples are:

- supplying information to the counterparty;
- guaranteeing that the organisation can meet its responsibilities;
- completing due diligence;
- signing a contract.

Operational processes would need to be put in place to ensure such obligations are acted upon well before the deadline.

A clear risk exists if the provisional trade automatically becomes live when a counterparty does not withdraw by a given date.

There may be a tendency to apply less stringency with the writing and checking of a provisional trade ticket because it is not real. This bears risk because, in the event the trade is executed, it might be simply transferred to a live trading book with the falsely applied assumption of accuracy. Review of provisional trades before execution is essential.

A system designed to capture and process real trades must bypass all provisional trades, so that they do not contribute to any official books and records. This requires proper design to ignore provisional trades, carry out thorough testing and ensure the correct implementation by people involved in entering them into the system.

8.1.2 Orders

When a trader is instructed to carry out a trade, the instruction is called an order. Orders can arise from:

- a salesman communicating between clients and traders;
- electronic requests by clients or other financial entities;
- automatic generation. Examples are stop orders where an instrument must be sold when its price falls to a specified level and limit orders where an instrument is bought once its price reaches a specified level.

The order may be unconditional and hence definitely result in a trade or be conditional upon price, time or some other factor. Orders may be aggregated to make trading more efficient.

For example, metals trader Mandy has the following orders on her books (see Table 8.1).

She will execute one trade to buy the balance, which is to buy 100 000 pounds thus satisfying the five individual orders and reducing her transaction costs.

Risks associated with orders: an order is an instruction to trade and therefore it is important that orders are correctly input and processed. As orders and trades may not match one to one, it is useful to have a means by which trades can be reconciled against their composite orders for audit or tracking purposes and to prevent mistakes. Any trading process must have the capability to deal with orders where they exist.

There may be a tendency to assume that once an order has been instructed, the deal is done. Since execution of a trade is distinct from order capture, there is a possibility that due to human error, machine malfunction or process delay, the trade may not yet have been created.

Since pending orders will give rise to trades and rebalance the organisation's exposures, it is essential that known orders are visible to traders and market and credit risk functions.

Table 8.1

Order type	Size (pounds of aluminium)
Buy	70 000
Sell	60 000
Buy	95 000
Buy	85 000
Sell	90 000
Net	Buy 100 000

8.2   EXECUTION AND BOOKING

8.2.1   Execution

When both parties have agreed to a trade, the trade is said to have been executed. This could occur in a number of ways:

Telephone: the spoken word has no lasting record. Even when telephone calls are recorded, which is now the norm in the financial sector, there is the possibility of one or other party mishearing or misunderstanding the details, information being omitted or language communication problems, any of which could lead to a claim that the trade was incorrectly executed. Most trades dealt on the telephone will be backed up with some form of written communication. Although outlawed by many organisations, some trades are transacted on mobile phones. This carries real problems: the trader may be away from his desk and hence away from proper systems to implement the trade.

Email: although details are in writing and subject to less ambiguity than trades transacted over the telephone, emails have dubious legal validity and carry a risk of impersonation. It is difficult to prove who the person sending the email actually was. Another problem with emails is that if one side sends an email with full trade details and the other replies "yes" or "confirmed", are they actually agreeing to the same trade? Timing delays between emails being exchanged could lead to doubts as to whether and when execution actually occurred.

Electronic chat: this is very similar to email but has the advantage of almost immediate reply, reducing some of the timing problems.

Electronic systems: electronic systems can be unique to a financial entity or used by the whole market as for broking systems. Electronic systems can be fast, accurate and eliminate human error. Details can be checked, confirmed and seen by all relevant parties and automatically fed to processing systems removing the need for secondary booking.

They will only work, however, for standard trades conforming to the templates with which the system was designed. Also, they rely on all parties having constant access to the system. When lines go down due to power cuts or natural disasters, for instance, there must be alternative means to gain access to trade details and, if necessary, continue trading.

The risk of sabotage or industrial espionage must also be considered. The electronic system only works if all its users have full confidence in its integrity and accuracy.

In person: the old-fashioned, open outcry exchanges involved two traders talking or signalling their agreement to a trade. These are almost obsolete, but nowadays salesmen often meet their clients in person and will transact deals using portable computers or written notes with a signature. It is essential that these trades enter the proper booking systems quickly and accurately.

Post: in an age where communication happens instantaneously, it may seem curious that some trades are still executed by post. Cashflow collateralised debt obligations, for example, might have contracts running to hundreds of pages, comprising legal ISDA agreements and precisely defining complicated cash waterfalls for the movement of money over time. These trades are sent out, reviewed and only come into effect when signed and returned by post.

8.2.2   Booking

When a trade is executed, a record must be created. In the London Stock Exchange of old, this used to be the stock jobber (market maker) making a note on his dealing pad. Nowadays, nearly all trades are recorded electronically. The principles of booking remain the same, however:

all trade details need to be recorded together with the time and place of transaction. Usually both counterparties make separate records, unless one is responding to an offer by another on an electronic exchange. In this case, although the trade ticket is written once, the system will send out full details to both sides, so effectively there are always two records. Once a trade is booked it confers full legal responsibilities on both sides to deliver the obligations associated with it.

As explained above, there are many parts to a trade ticket. Traders are busy and keen to assess the impact of their trades immediately. Hence, when two traders agree a trade, they may only record the sections relevant to them, which will be economic, and some basic internal booking and counterparty details. It will be left to their trading assistants or other business functions, such as middle and back office, to complete the ticket. Also, traders have a penchant for jotting down trades on a pad, known as a trade blotter, and it will be left to others to input the trade into the correct booking system. (This is not an eccentric quirk of the trading profession – if a manager tries to insist the trader books a trade in full, he may be impairing the trader's ability to carry out his primary responsibilities of trading and risk management. The loss entailed by this should be weighed against the losses caused by partial or inaccurate booking.)

Straight Through Processing: in essence, execution and booking should be simultaneous processes. So the quicker a trade reaches the booking system from the time it was executed and the fewer people involved in booking it, the lower the risk of errors.

The paradigm to which many organisations aspire is known as Straight Through Processing (STP). This means all actors in the trade lifecycle are working with the same data. The trade is entered once at time of execution, with all its details and the system carries the trade through all its checks and actions throughout the organisation. Every amendment is noted alongside the trade and a full audit of who did what and when is available, reducing many risks associated with booking.

There are risks associated with STP. A fully automated system means that mistakes are fully automated. The machine cannot respond to potential or actual errors unless it has been programmed to do so. Due to the varied nature of trade booking errors, the design of the system cannot be relied upon to catch them all and, even when they are caught, the process requires human beings to take appropriate action. Also, some business functions are required to *merely* check trades in the STP. Since checking is a passive activity, it is easy for mistakes to slip by.

STP systems are often expensive to produce and, once fully implemented and tested, there is a resistance to adapt or modify them. This means that when the business evolves and new trade types are transacted, there is a tendency to shoehorn them into the existing system. The desire to make the system do something for which it was not designed can lead to many errors, often occurring at unexpected times or in exceptional, but nonetheless damaging, circumstances.

We believe that STP systems require the utmost planning and wide consultation with all users before being implemented. The future growth of existing business and expansion into new business must be taken into account; everybody concerned must be aware of what the system can and cannot do.

8.3   CONFIRMATION

The process of confirmation involves representatives of both counterparties to a trade agreeing to all the particulars of the trade (except internal details). This role is usually carried out by the back office. The actual method of confirmation will vary according to the nature of the deal. In reality, there are two activities: matching and confirmation.

8.3.1 Matching

Before confirmation of a trade can begin, both counterparties must match their records to ensure they both have a record of the trade and that they are referring to exactly the same trade. In a high volume trading environment, this may not be quite so easy. Ideally, each party to the trade execution (the traders) will have recorded the other party's trade identifier at the time of booking. If not, the trade can be matched by its time, trader and some headline details.

For example:

Yvonne at Ordinary Bank records a sale USD 5.05 million of US Treasury bonds at 15:05 on 13 January.

Zena at Special Bank has a record of 5.055 million of the same asset being bought from Yvonne at the same time.

The records are not identical, but the two interpretations are close enough to assume they refer to the same trade and hence start the confirmation.

Where a trade cannot be matched at all, it is likely that either it was never received and executed by the counterparty or it was dealt with a different counterparty and the counterparty details were misbooked. In the latter case, the real counterparty will be trying to match and will contact the counterparty who made the error, so the mistake will be identified and corrected.

For example:

A trades with B, but A has recorded that it traded with C.

A attempts to match with C, but C has no record.

B attempts to match with A, and the mistake is identified.

8.3.2 Confirmation

Once the trade is matched, all the details must be confirmed. There are three circumstances upon which a trade may need to be amended during confirmation.

8.3.2.1 Omission

If details are omitted, they will need to be agreed and added. Unless they affect the value of the trade these details can generally be decided by the back office itself without recourse to the traders who executed the trade. If an important economic clause, for example the currency of the trade, was omitted, then the traders would need to agree to its inclusion. If the omission has only occurred in the ticket of one counterparty, it is likely the other counterparty can supply the missing data.

8.3.2.2 Error

An error may have occurred on one side. The confirmation process should identify it and then either it will be accepted and corrected or there will be a dispute as to which interpretation is correct. This dispute may be settled between the counterparties themselves or, in serious cases, by an independent arbiter or court of law. It is rare that anyone will deliberately try to misrepresent a trade he transacted, as it may endanger his reputation in future trading. With a limited number of counterparties, there will be internal pressure to settle disputes so that trading possibilities remain open for both sides.

The one exception is where a conflict arises either after a period of time or after significant movements in the market place. Here the difference in value of the trade between the two interpretations could be significant and make resolution more difficult.

8.3.2.3   Ambiguity

Where a particular trade detail is incompletely filled out, it could lead to ambiguity. Generally, consulting the traders as to their intention behind the ambiguity will resolve the issue.

8.3.2.4   Confirmation risk

If an organisation has a speedy and thorough confirmation process it will deal with errors efficiently and gain a reputation for being a good partner in business. Since confirmation is a two way process, other organisations will quickly see how effectively the process is being conducted and inferior individuals and organisations will be exposed.

The longer mistakes remain in the trade lifecycle, the more costly they are to correct. The confirmation process is essential to ensure a smooth trading practice.

8.3.2.5   Feedback from confirmation

It is inevitable that mistakes will sometimes be made on trade booking and the confirmation process will correct them. The people carrying out confirmations are, however, in a very good position to assess the booking procedure and systems and advise on improvements. Common or costly errors and omissions can be reported back to those responsible for booking and better systems and processes for checking and catching mistakes can be designed.

Internal confirmation (reconciliation) between different input systems is another aspect of confirmations. Once a match has been found, it is useful if the corresponding trade identifier is attached, so that a trade can be fully audited through all the systems.

For example, a copper spot trade with identifier CST0014 is entered into the front office system *Jeopardy* and later is entered into the middle office system *Resolute* with automatically generated identifier 342002. If the trade in Jeopardy can hold the ID 342002 and the trade in Resolute can hold CST0014, the tracking process is enhanced by this double incidence of cross-reference.

8.4   POST BOOKING

8.4.1   Trade scrutiny

Once trades are booked in the trading system, they require scrutiny to ensure they are correct and fit in with the other processes comprising the trade lifecycle. Middle office has the responsibility for this scrutiny (see Section 15.6).

8.4.2   Enrichment

The person booking the trade may not have all the trade details to hand at time of booking. Therefore, these missing details must be completed later. They are unlikely to comprise economic details but could include counterparty, settlement or custodian information. This process may involve liaison with the original trader and with the counterparty or custodian.

8.4.3   Cashflows

At this point a calculation of the expected cashflows relating to the trade may be performed. This is useful to check that everything relating to the valuation of the trade is complete. Cashflows also define the responsibilities that the trade has devolved on the organisation trading it and are an alternative and meaningful representation of the trade for many subsequent processes.

8.4.4   Fees and duties

Once a trade has been executed it may incur certain duties. Examples are:

- broker fees (for buying or selling);
- stamp duty when an equity is purchased (but not when it is sold);
- exchange charges on a per trade basis;
- commissions to external parties for arranging the trade;
- legal fees (if the firm does not use its own lawyers).

These fees must be recorded, checked and payment arranged by the due date.

8.4.5   Error reporting

If anything is amiss it should be reported at this stage to allow maximum time for correction. This also prevents errors spreading through later processes which, in the case of settlement for example, could be costly.

8.5   SETTLEMENT

A trade might have been executed, booked and confirmed and is legally binding on both parties, but until settlement, nothing physical has changed hands. Settlement is the process by which the counterparties to a trade fulfil their obligations to exchange. We often think of a trade as A buying something from B, and then A would exchange cash in return for a financial instrument, document or commodity. However, many trades involve both parties transferring cash. Examples would be:

- foreign exchange where one currency is exchanged for a different one;
- interest rate swaps where one party pays a fixed amount every six months, the other side paying a floating amount dependent upon the current rate of an agreed index, such as LIBOR;
- credit default swaps where one side pays a fixed premium per year and the other side will only ever pay if the underlying asset defaults.

8.5.1   The importance of settlement

Few activities in the trade lifecycle carry as much importance as settlement. Settlement is a physical exchange, materially affecting the assets held by the trading party. As in any business or personal situation, whenever money leaves the door, it must be carefully checked. The person authorising payments for settlement bears great responsibility. Most organisations will insist on two different individuals being involved in the settlement – requiring either two signatures or, in the case of an electronic settlement, two authorised operators. Senior staff are generally employed directly or in a supervisory role in this task because they will have greater experience to spot mistakes or suspicious transactions.

8.5.2   Settlement instructions

A key part of the trading ticket are the details for settlement. These are known as settlement instructions. The two main types of settlement instructions are delivery versus payment (DvP) and Free of Payment (FoP). The former requires both parts of the exchange to happen simultaneously and will generally involve the generation of one settlement instruction between the client and the custodian. The latter allows for there to be two distinct settlements at different times and hence there will normally be two settlement instructions between client and custodian – one to expect a receipt of cash or security and one to make a payment.

8.5.3   Custodian

The custodian holds cash, securities or both on behalf of a trading entity and can effect a transfer with the custodian of the counterparty. The custodian also has knowledge of local trading practices, providing valuable advice to his client. He can supply transfers at a customised level of security to meet the requirements of the trading party – a large transaction requiring a greater level of encryption and participant identification than a smaller one.

8.5.4   Cash or physical

As mentioned above, any of three different entities could be involved in settlement – cash, documentation or physical commodity.

8.5.5   Cash

This will involve an account being credited or debited by the settlement amount. As bank accounts are generally only held in their domicile currency, institutions trading in foreign currencies will either need to hold domestic or offshore accounts in those currencies or employ the services of bank in the country of the currency being traded.

8.5.6   Documentation

Share certificates, bonds, loans, warrants and insurance guarantees are all examples of documents that may be traded. These may be held by the counterparty themselves or stored by the custodians. They are vulnerable to being lost, stolen or damaged and are costly to replace.

8.5.7   Physical commodity

When commodities are traded, they often involve the exchange of physical goods ranging from grown produce, such as coffee beans, through precious metals to barrels of crude oil. The recipient of such a commodity transfer will need to provide shipping from the warehouse, factory, depot or port where the goods are to be collected and safe storage, once transportation is complete.

8.5.8   Cash settlement of commodities

Many banks and hedge funds have no interest in using bought commodities: they buy in order to resell them at some point in the future. Therefore, they do not require physical delivery and in fact would not know what to do if a lorry load of aluminium arrived on their doorstep!

Such traded commodities remain in the same warehouse or place of storage after settlement, only the document of ownership being exchanged.

Many forward and future trades stipulate cash settlement for commodities. This involves one counterparty paying in cash the difference between the agreed future price and the prevailing market price on settlement day.

For example:

In May, Helen buys 45 tonnes of coffee beans for November delivery at an agreed price of USD 140 per tonne.

On the day of settlement in November, the price is USD 150 per tonne. Instead of receiving coffee, she will receive USD 10 per tonne in cash. (Had the price fallen, she would have to pay the price difference.)

8.5.9   Nostro accounts

Deriving from the Latin word *noster* meaning ours, the term "nostro account" is used to describe a cash account held in our name by you. Nostro accounts must be held with a local clearing bank, so Bank A may have a:

- EUR nostro account in France with Bank F,
- JPY nostro account in Tokyo with Bank J, and a
- HKD nostro account in Hong Kong with Bank H.

Part of the process of settlement is to update the various nostro accounts. Additionally, transfers between nostros may need to be enacted to ensure they stay within overdraft limits or to prepare for imminent withdrawals.

In order for the finance department to understand the true position of the institution, it needs to gather together all the current nostro account details supplied by the back office. For examining past settlements in the event of a problem, the nostro will be the indicator of exactly how much was paid or received and when.

8.5.10   Risks

1. Theft: a big risk in the settlement process is theft. This could occur where the settlement process is intercepted by criminals or where staff involved in the process (including those writing or operating a computerised settlement system) divert part or all of the money to their own bank accounts.

2. Cost of recovery: the settlement process may fail if money is transferred to the wrong account, too much is transferred to the correct account or the transfer is on the wrong day or at the wrong time. Even if there was no deliberate attempt to steal money, it may cost a significant amount to recover it and cause severe embarrassment.

3. Legal: settlement is a legal obligation arising from execution of a trade. If a counterparty fails to settle the right amount at the right time and according to the given settlement instructions, he risks being sued by the wronged party. The legal process, even if settled out of court, will be expensive and time consuming.

4. Reputation: any missed or erroneous settlement will cause damage to the reputation of the counterparty at fault. Trading works to a large extent on trust and poor settlement will quickly lead to trading lines being reduced or withdrawn. A failure to settle will arouse doubts as to the competence of the organisation concerned because trading is one of the main activities of investment banks and hedge funds, and because settlement is the most visible face of the institution to its peers.

5. Unexpected charges: a party to a trade may be expecting a large receipt of money upon settlement. If that settlement is delayed for any reason, it will lose the use of that money, which could involve not being able to pay off a debt charged at a daily interest rate.

6. Other trades: a counterparty may have a trade with settlement expected on a given day. It may then have executed a subsequent trade, anticipating using the first trade settlement to pay the second trade in cash, financial instrument or commodity. A delay on the first settlement will have knock-on effects for other settlements dependent upon it.

As discussed later, in order to limit the losses involved in the event that a counterparty defaults, most investment banks and hedge funds impose limits (known as trading lines) on the maximum amount that a given counterparty can owe at any one time. (These lines will vary between different counterparties – the more secure having greater line.) While a trade remains unsettled it is using up some of this line and may prevent opportunities for more trading with the same counterparty.

8.5.11   Advantage of quick settlement

Possession is nine tenths of the law. However binding a trade upon its participants and however strong the regulation and law enforcement authorities might be, there is no substitute for a quick settlement. This means both sides have confidence that whatever they have traded will quickly come to fruition and risks will be reduced. Many exchange-traded instruments have stipulated settlement periods. These are often one or two days after execution to allow each side to arrange and carry out the settlement details, although it is increasingly common to see same-day settlement now that many processes are automated.

8.5.12   Multiple settlement dates

Some trades require more than one settlement. A good example is a bond which might pay 5 % coupon every three months through the life of the bond plus a redemption and final coupon upon maturity. Each settlement is regarded as a separate process and all of the above explanation applies to it. The trading agreement will specify the full settlement schedule and what to do if a settlement falls on a non trading day such as at the weekend or on a public holiday. (Typically the next business day will be used, but there may be exceptions when the next day is in another month or is the final payment.)

8.5.13 Breaks

A major part of back office time is spent tracing "breaks", where a settlement has not been enacted. These breaks are very expensive in time and human resources. Sometimes huge numbers of unpaid settlements are built up, because operations do not have time to chase them. It may seem obvious that breaks will either cause loss of profit where the firm is not paid, or cause reduction in future profit, where mis-settlements are realised later and claimed back by counterparties, yet there is very often reluctance to invest time cleaning up breaks – they are often swallowed up in the general, huge costs involved in investment banking.

8.6   OVERNIGHT

8.6.1   Individual trade and aggregation with other trades

The trade is an agreement imposing responsibilities upon the trading parties. It has many processes performed upon it and remains as an individual unit throughout its lifecycle.

To the internal financial entity that traded it, the trade is often considered in aggregation with other trades. The aggregation may be done in many ways. Here are some examples – by:

- asset class
- trading book
- maturity
- currency
- counterparty
- exposure to different market data.

At some point the trade must be joined into the various aggregation and reporting processes. This generally occurs at the end of day roll in the first night after it is booked.

Some business functions examine individual trades, some look at groups and some do both. For example, the legal department will generally scrutinise an individual trade whereas finance will look at the overall effect of a group of trades in a book or department. Market risk will examine both how individual trades and the whole portfolio stand up to market price changes.

Thus, the trade has a duality of existence as an individual and as part of a compound or many compounds.

8.6.2   Date and time

Trade tickets have certain dates when events happen. For example, the actual trade date, one or many settlement dates, maturity date and final delivery date. Processes and calculations work on whole calendar days and not on part days. (The only exception is booking, where time might also be recorded to help with matching and confirmation.) Since time of day is not relevant but actual date is, we need to have clearly defined dates.

8.6.3   Internal and external trade dates

Trades are transacted in a given jurisdiction that may be different from the location of either or both counterparties. For legal purposes, the trade will follow a stipulated time zone (usually that of the jurisdiction) and all dates on the trade are relevant to that time zone – this is the external date. However, internally it must be grouped with other trades. An internal process, say the end of day calculation, must run on all trades taken together. Therefore, the trade needs the concept of an internal date; the end of day for an organisation determines which date that should be.

8.6.4   Deciding time for end of day

In most organisations, people arrive at work in the morning and leave in the evening, so it is an easy decision to set the end of the previous day and start of the next day at some point in the night. In a multi time-zone trading environment where trades are being executed and booked around the clock and staff are always on the premises, deciding the end of day may be harder. Usually the organisation will fix the end of day on the basis of its principal trading time zone.

For example, if Bank TwentyFourSeven trades on both the Chicago Mercantile exchange and has extensive Australian commodity dealings, but is based in Germany, the bank may take the middle of the German night as its end of day. This may lead to problems where a trader is dealing with Australian trades just before or just after German midnight – the timestamp on the booking could be used for determining the internal trade date.

Note that it is irrelevant that the counterparty has a different time for its end of day. The internal date does not affect processes between counterparties which will use the external date. (This mutual external date will be agreed at execution and checked at confirmation.)

8.6.5   End of day roll

Every time the end of day is reached, the trades will be rolled into the next day and for internal purposes, a new day will begin. For accounting and monitoring, the trades are often split into the following subdivisions:

1. **New:** those that have been dealt in the previous day and are appearing on the books for the first time.
2. **Amended:** those that were amended the previous day. Some systems treat an amended trade as a new trade, but they will have a link to the original trade for prior reconciliation.
3. **Deleted:** a trade may be deleted because it was mistakenly booked or because both counterparties have agreed to rescind it. Generally auditors will require deleted trades to remain in the system (suitably marked) and have processes for dealing with them, because it is dangerous to allow business functions to simply remove them.
4. **Expired:** when the trade rolls past its maturity, it is said to have expired. It may still require processes to be performed on it, such as delivery, but it no longer makes a contribution to profit and loss.
5. **Open or current:** all other trades are open or current. The end of day roll marks the process by which previously new or amended trades become current.

8.6.6   Overnight processes

The night is a good opportunity for time consuming and resource-hungry processes to run. It is also the first chance a new trade has to be aggregated with other trades.

Many valuation, risk generation and reporting processes run overnight. These include:

- P&L
- market risk
- counterparty risk
- balance sheet
- trading activity
- calculation of collateral requirements.

8.6.7   Pre overnight checks

Overnight processes rely on complete and accurate input data. It is very annoying for any business function staff to arrive at work in the morning and find the overnight processes have failed due to a lack of good data. Much time has been lost and it may be difficult to run processes during the daytime when people are working. One solution would be to have staff available at night to check systems have run and correct any errors that arise. This is usually expensive and does not do much for morale. An alternative is to have the system perform a mini calculation earlier in the evening before people leave. This must be sufficient to detect most errors, but it is not too time consuming.

Getting the balance between human and machine activity on overnight processes will depend on cost, intricacy of processes required and quality of staff. It is possible to automate virtually all the activities or to have all but the heavy calculations performed manually. Here is an example of a mixed human and machine end of day process:

16:30–17:30 End of day market data is ready for overnight processes
17:30 Middle office checks quality of data
18:00 Pre overnight process is run
18:30 Middle office checks process has run and corrects any errors
22:00 Overnight process begins:
    Trades are rolled
    Calculations are performed
    Reports are generated
08:00 Middle office checks reports and, if satisfactory, distributes to relevant parties.

8.6.8   Amalgamation between systems

Where a finance house trades different asset classes, it may have different systems performing valuations. These systems must be coordinated so that output results can be combined for aggregated reporting. It is of course necessary that amalgamation occurs after all contributing systems have completed their end of day processes successfully. Dependencies across different systems mean that the designer of an overnight process must allow time to cope with overrun.

8.6.9   Stale data

If a process fails to run, it may have left stale data in a position where new data is expected. Subsequent processes may inadvertently assume the stale data to be new and use it.

If data is missing completely or too big or too small, it will either cause the system not to run or to produce obviously incorrect results. Stale data, on the other hand, is potentially more dangerous, because it can easily go undetected and is a common source of calculation and reporting errors. Some systems provide comprehensive diagnostics to allow the user to examine exactly which data was used in all calculations; others are rigorous in their checking of input data to ensure it is not stale. The old adage of garbage in, garbage out particularly applies here.

8.7   CHANGES DURING LIFETIME

The trade has experienced its first night, has made a contribution to P&L and risk control reports and is now extant in the system. This section discusses changes that might occur to the trade during its lifetime. We also consider payments or receipts due on assets arising from the trade. Changes to assets will require processes whether or not they are booked separately from trades. For convenience, we group them with other trade changes.

The trade should have all its details and components fully confirmed and readily available to all processes that require trade data. If the system is operating correctly, each time any trading report is run, the trade should appear on it. Each day until its maturity, the trade is assumed to be identical to the previous day unless one of the events listed below occurs:

- changes as a result of corporate actions to assets holdings;
- changes as a result of market data;
- counterparty changes;
- changes to the trade;
- changes in underlying;
- changes as a result of asset holdings.

We begin this section by discussing a group of events known as corporate actions. These involve an issuer of a security (bond or equity) distributing benefits or when the structure of the issuer changes.

8.7.1   Dividends

At certain times, companies may pay dividends to their shareholders. These are discretionary and depend on the financial health of the company. (Even preference shares usually have delay clauses, so are not guaranteed.) When a dividend is due, the financial entity holding the stock must accept the dividend and account for the money received in its books and records. Processes must be in place to perform these activities and a business function must be made responsible for performing them.

Although dividends do not affect the trade itself, they should have reference to the trade from which they arise, so that P&L can be properly accounted.

When making a dividend announcement the issuing company will state the payment date, the date of record and the ex-dividend date – all of which should be recorded on the trade details.

Table 8.2

Accrual date	Payment date	Amount	Type
30 Jan 2007	1 Feb 2007	LIBOR + 40bp	(float)
30 Jul 2007	1 Aug 2007	LIBOR + 40bp	(float)
30 Jan 2008	1 Feb 2008	4.85 %	(fixed)
30 Jul 2008	1 Aug 2008	4.85 %	(fixed)
(and so on)			

For example: Segro PLC announces a payment of 1.4p per share to be distributed on Friday 20 June 2008 to all recorded shareholders on Friday 6 June 2008, ex-dividend date Wednesday 4 June 2008.

Therefore if an institution held Segro shares on or before 4 June, it will expect dividend payment on 20 June even if it has subsequently sold those shares. These dates and the dividend amount need to be recorded against the trade so that the correct dividend will be processed on the correct date.

8.7.2   Coupons

A sovereign or corporate body wishing to raise capital may issue bonds. Bonds pay coupons at regular intervals. These coupons may be fixed or floating or both. A fixed coupon is a known amount, such as 5 % of the notional. A float amount is based on an index such as LIBOR, plus a given number of basis points. Some bonds pay floating coupons for a period and then fixed for the remainder.

An example coupon schedule is shown in Table 8.2.

Accrual date is the date used for coupon calculation; payment date is a fixed number of days after the accrual date when the coupon is actually paid.

Although the dates of coupon payments are usually known when the bond is issued, floating coupon amounts can only be known on the accrual date. In this case, a process will need to be performed to consult the relevant index on the relevant day and "fix" the coupon. The fix is made on the accrual date, so that the receiver knows the exact amount to expect on the payment date.

8.7.3   Other corporate actions

Mergers, demergers, rights issues and other changes to issuers of equities and bonds will alter the size and value of the assets held.

8.7.4   Changes as a result of market data

8.7.4.1   Fixings

Apart from floating bond fixings described above, many trades require fixings against market data during their life. Each counterparty to the trade must find and record the relevant fixing to ensure:

1. All processes and calculations can work with the anticipated flow: until the fixing is made, calculations must use an estimated value from the best available market data. For example, a CHF floating swap rate of LIBOR + 30bp due to be fixed in one month, might use the CHF one month LIBOR. This will change daily causing the input to the calculation to change. After fixing, this rate will be known and so the cashflow can be fully defined in the system.

2. Correct settlement of cash (or asset) flow on payment date: just as in trade confirmation, both sides must agree on fixings affecting all asset settlements. A fixing made from a published reference indicator such as LIBOR will not be subject to misinterpretation or dispute, but some fixings are from more bespoke criteria and therefore each party to the fixing will want to ensure they have recorded it correctly. An example fixing might be the average of five broker prices quoted between 14:00 and 15:00 on the fixing day.

8.7.4.2 *Products using fixings*

Swaps: any swap agreement which has a floating leg will require a fixing for every accrual date in a similar way to a bond.

Trades using average market rates: many trades use an average of market data across many dates to arrive at a figure used for settlement. An example might be an oil future trade that uses the quoted oil price over the last 30 days of the contract, rather than just the price on the last day. In any trade using average market rates, the fixings for every date in the average must be recorded.

Trades changing in behaviour according to market data: some more exotic trades actually change their behaviour according to changes in market data (see Chapter 4). Such changes will materially affect the asset flows in the trade and therefore market data fixings must be recorded on all relevant days, so that the trade can be properly managed. For example a nickel barrier option has:

- spot USD 13 800
- strike USD 15 000
- lower knock out barrier of USD 12 000.

This means that if the price of nickel falls below USD 12 000 at any time, the option expires and the buyer receives nothing.

Another example is a convertible bond trade which, depending on certain conditions, converts from a bond into an equity. Since systems may treat equities and bonds as completely different trades or there may be a separate system to handle each, a convertible may require considerable work to process it properly.

8.7.5 Counterparty changes

If the counterparty changes its settlement details (such as its custodian or bank account) then the settlement process will need to be alerted and act on the change. This involves changes to the trade separate from the settlement of asset flows.

8.7.6 Collateral

If a collateral agreement is in place, margin must be calculated on a daily basis and then a cash transfer executed between the parties. This has to be performed all the time the trade is in existence. See Section 12.7 for a fuller discussion of collateral.

8.7.7   Changes to the trade

8.7.7.1   Settlement

One or many settlement dates may exist in the trade. Settlement is discussed in a separate section.

8.7.7.2   Amendment

Both sides might agree an amendment to the trade at any point in its life. The amended trade will have an effect on all processes and calculations. Conceptually, it is the equivalent of deleting the old trade and creating a new one with the amended details. Many systems treat it thus, but record the original trade on the amended trade to ensure a proper audit trail.

8.7.7.3   Cancellation

Both sides might agree to cancel the trade. Auditors will generally insist that records of the trade are kept in the system. Some processes such as P&L Attribution (see Chapter 14) will measure the effect of cancellation on the day it was done. Simply removing a trade without trace is not sensible, so cancelled trades do flow through trade systems.

8.7.7.4   Exercise and maturity

These are covered in separate sections below.

8.7.7.5   Exotics

Some exotic derivatives such as knock-in and knock-out options (see Chapter 4) require careful monitoring of market data to see when they are approaching limit conditions. Sometimes a combination of machine and human process is used, whereby the machine is allowed to conduct a preliminary check. If the limit is a long way off, no further action is required. If it is close, the machine sends a warning and the human takes over, monitoring the market to determine if and when it was exceeded.

8.7.7.6   Changes in underlying affecting the trade itself

Trades are executed on a wide variety of underlying assets. Many of them will not change their details during the lifetime of the trade, such as gold, Japanese yen and US Treasury bonds.

Those that do change, however, may result in a different asset holding or a monetary payment as described above (dividends, equity holdings). A different type of underlying does materially affect the trade, rather than the assets resulting from the trade. The prime example is credit. If protection is bought or sold involving a corporate or sovereign name, a credit event on that name will cause certain payments or receipts, as defined in the trade contract. Moreover, for single name protection the trade will expire upon a credit event. Trades which are susceptible to changes in their underlyings need careful monitoring to ensure that any changes are noted.

Table 8.3

Trade(s)	Event	Underlying	Action
T110	Coupon payment date	Bond: BRD2020	Expect receipt
T304, T30	Averaging date	Nymex WTexas Oil	Fix
T737,T373	Swap fixing	LIBOR CHF	Fix
T167	Settlement date	Fix/Float GBP	Settle
T35, T36, T37	Ex-dividend date	Segro PLC	Record
T22	Maturity date		Process Expiry
T772	Close to knock-out	EUR/JPY	Check market

8.7.8 Management of changes

It is difficult for any one process to detect and record changes, because they can occur over diverse areas – the trade itself, a wide variety of market data, a counterparty, an asset (dividends, bonds), changes to an underlying (credit events). A common technique in handling many of the possible changes is to use a diary. The diary may consist of events, the trades and underlyings they relate to and the action to be taken.

Each day the diary is opened and all events for that day are processed.

In Table 8.3 we show example actions common to both middle office and back office but in reality there would be separate reports for each business function.

When events occur every day (such as margin calls or the possibility of a credit event) they can be given their own process.

When there is no predicted date such as for a trade amendment, a process will need to be undertaken on demand and cannot be diarised.

8.7.9 Risks

Changes to a trade or its assets cause risks to the institution holding the trade. One of the biggest risks is that changes are missed. Then:

- counterparties may demand unexpected payments;
- opportunities for receiving money may be passed up;
- undesired increase in exposure may occur.

Another risk is that the change is detected and reported but no action is taken. This has a similar effect to missing the change. It is important that the institution understands exactly what trade changes are likely or unlikely to happen when a trade is executed. Procedures should be put in place for every possible change.

The institution must organise itself such that changes are communicated to all relevant parties within it. For example, a credit risk department might detect credit events promptly in order to manage counterparty exposure, but neglect to inform a trading desk that has just traded its first credit derivative.

8.8 REPORTING DURING LIFETIME

Even when a trade has not changed it will need to be tracked and reported upon every day of its existence. The reporting has been briefly mentioned above and is discussed in greater depth in Chapter 21.

8.9   EXERCISE

At some point during the life of an option trade, the buyer has the right to exercise the option. In a call option, this means the right to buy the underlying asset at the strike price. For a put option, it is the right to sell the underlying. Exercise is a very important component of an option trade and processes must be in place to deal with it.

8.9.1   Exercise date

This is the final date by which notice of exercise must have been given. The trade details will stipulate the hour of the day and the means by which exercise is performed.

The style of the option is very important in defining whether there is one single or a range of exercise dates.

- American options can be exercised on any day from the start of the trade until the exercise date.
- European options can only be exercised on the exercise date.
- Bermudan options are a mixture – there is a period during which they cannot be exercised and then a period when they can be exercised on many or all dates (the name Bermuda deriving from the island which lies between Europe and America).

8.9.2   When to exercise

Exercise is an economic decision. If the option purchaser stands to gain more by exercise than letting the trade expire unexercised, he will exercise. Generally if the spot price of the underlying asset is greater than the strike, a call option will be exercised and the reverse for a put option.

It is usually clear ahead of the exercise date whether the option is "in the money" and therefore worth exercising or "out of the money" and not. However there are borderline cases where the exact market data close to exercise must be known and conveyed to the person making the exercise decision. Generally the trader who dealt the trade or someone on his desk will make the decision and the middle or back office will give the counterparty notice of exercise.

8.9.3   Cash or physical

The trade will stipulate whether exercise is performed into cash or into a physical asset. When the exercise is physical, the seller sometimes has a choice of exactly which asset to deliver. For example, the trade may stipulate one of a set of bonds all being the equivalent to a defined benchmark bond. The seller can then choose the bond that is cheapest for him to buy in the market for delivery to the purchaser, or one that he currently owns.

For cash exercise, the difference between spot and strike is used to calculate the optional component of the trade and that is delivered as a cash payment to the purchaser in the currency of the trade.

8.9.4   Exercise as a process

The exercise date is another (possible) settlement date in the trade lifecycle. The size of the settlement is unknown and could be zero, involving no processing. The institution buying options must be able to manage the additional tasks of deciding whether to exercise and informing the counterparty of exercise. One selling options must expect exercise and be ready to deliver the amount and type of asset required. For American and Bermudan options, there is the added complication of several possible exercise dates.

Both counterparties to an option will need processes for monitoring the relevant market data to determine exercise. This monitoring may begin from straight after trade date because it affects the value of the option. When options get close to their exercise date, alerts need to be triggered to warn decision makers and implementers to take action.

8.9.5   Fugit

Some option traders like to attach a date known as a fugit to the trade. (This can be added as a diary item – see section on trade changes.) Fugit comes from the Latin *tempus fugit*, time flies. In this context, it means the first date at which an American style option is likely to be exercised.

8.9.6   Risks associated with exercise

There are obvious risks, such as poor communication between traders and middle office, leading to exercise being missed when it should have occurred or being performed when it should not have occurred.

There is also a problem when market rates are very volatile and an option is at-the-money. A sudden swing could take the option into the money and make it worth exercising. Systems showing market data must be accurate and up to date – the timing of market data may be as crucial as its actual value.

Another issue arises from at-the-money options with volatile market data. When a trader expects an inflow of assets, he takes steps to hedge his position and reduce his risks. The problem of last minute decisions about option exercise is that the asset changes cannot be managed so effectively, and this can result in greater hedging costs or greater exposure.

8.10   MATURITY

The trade's maturity date is agreed and set out in the trade details during execution and booking. The following are features of a trade that reaches maturity:

- The trade is no longer subject to market risk.
- All of its cashflows are known and fixed even though they may not have been settled.
- The trade no longer makes a contribution to P&L.
- The trade changes from being live to being expired.

Reporting processes that deal with live trades will no longer report on a matured trade. Other processes used for audit and historical purposes may report on matured trades.

8.10.1   Final settlement date

This is the date on or after the maturity date when the final settlement has been made and no more exchanges of cash and assets need to occur. This is the point when the trade ceases to have counterparty risk. Unless there is a subsequent dispute, the final settlement date represents the date when the counterparty becomes irrelevant to the trade.

8.11   EXAMPLE TRADE

In trading language:
(a) 2Y Swap
(b) Fixed: GBP 3 %
(c) Float GBP LIBOR + 30bp
(d) Nominal GBP 10m
(e) Freq: semi
(f) MF
(g) Act / 365
(h) Payment: 2bd
(i) Holiday Centre: London.
(j) TD: 9th June 2009

Translation:
(a) This is a two-year swap with
(b) one side pays a fixed 3 % of notional in GBP.
(c) The other side is floating rate set at LIBOR fixing plus 30 basis points (which is plus 0.3 %).
(d) The nominal for calculation is GBP 10 million.
(e) Payment is made semi annually using a
(f) modified following business day convention and
(g) an actual divided by 365 day count convention.
(h) Settlement date for each fixing is two business days after the accrual date.
(i) Business days are defined as working days in London.
(j) Trade is transacted on 9 June 2009.

8.11.1   The trade lifecycle

9 June 2009
10:28 Trader checks he has sufficient counterparty line to deal
10:29 Trader checks this trade will not breach his personal and desk trading limits
10:30 Deal executed by trader
11:05 Trading assistant books basic deal details into booking system
11:25 Middle office book rest of trade into system, asking trader to confirm missing details
11:30 Trading system generates accrual and payment dates for this trade
14:00 Back office begins deal matching
14:40 Back office faxes confirmation to counterparty
14:45 Counterparty phones with queries on settlement details
15:50 Confirmation agreed with counterparty
17:30 Official market data download enters valuation system
18:30 Pre overnight process completes satisfactorily

20:30 Overnight process begins

20:30 This swap trade enters valuation and reporting system

20:30–03:00 Trade is valued and reported in a slew of overnight reports on a single and aggregated basis.

10 June 2009

07:30 Trader checks his P&L and the new trade have valued correctly. Also checks a variety of trading reports including P&L explained (see Chapter 14)

08:00 Product control check P&L and other overnight reports

08:00 Market risk start using the new trade to view current market exposures, VaR etc.

08:00 Credit risk monitor effect of trade on counterparty exposure.

11 June 2009

Trade appears on weekly balance sheet report.

30 June 2009

Trade appears in its first month end report.

11 June 2009 to 9 December 2009 (first accrual date)

Trade appears every day on all relevant reports and is monitored.

Trader will hedge expected cashflows.

Management will monitor profitability of trade and exposure it has caused.

Control functions will ensure that market, credit and other risks are known and contained within appropriate limits.

9 December 2009 (first accrual date)

11:00 LIBOR fixing is taken and entered into trading system

11:02 Trading system calculates a net receipt of GBP 34 000 is due on payment date

11:30 Back office confirms payment amount with counterparty and rechecks settlement instructions.

11 December 2009 (two business days after accrual date)

07:00 Settlement instruction is generated

08:30 Settlement is enacted

08:45 Back office check payment has arrived of the correct amount.

(and so on for all accrual and payments)

9 June 2011 (expiry date)

11:00 LIBOR fixing is taken and entered into trading system

11:02 Trading system calculates a net receipt of GBP 37 500 is due on payment date

11:30 Back office confirms payment amount with counterparty and rechecks settlement instructions

20:30 Trade rolls off system and is booked into matured trades system. It no longer appears on trading and P&L reports.

13 June 2011 (final settlement date, two business days after expiry date)
   07:00 Settlement instruction is generated
   08:30 Settlement is enacted
   08:45 Back office check payment has arrived of the correct amount.

8.12   SUMMARY

Many people and processes act on the trade throughout its lifecycle. Here we explained typical processes that may occur, and at what time, and some of their features. We also looked at how trades changed over the course of their life and what happens at maturity.

9

Cashflows and Asset Holdings

9.1 INTRODUCTION

The trade is an instruction to carry out various asset and cash exchanges at one or many points after execution. The trade lifecycle is a means by which executed trades are turned into cash and assets.

We define cash to be an amount of money denominated in any recognised world currency. An asset is a holding of something other than cash. It is convenient, however, to have one term to describe the flow of cash or assets. So in this book, we use the generic term "cashflow" to mean the flow of either currency or commodity.

An asset holding is a position in currency or commodity. A cashflow will add to or subtract from the holding. The effect of a trade is to change the holdings by means of cashflows. A holding differs from a trade because it does not expire.

Holdings are defined by type and amount. Table 9.1 shows some sample holdings for a bank.

Let us work through an example trade and see how holdings and cashflows come together (see Tables 9.2 and 9.3). (We are going to use the more unusual case of physical settlement to show the movement of commodity as well as currency.)

Bank de Nord based in France buys a European call option on gold
Today: 22 July 2009
Strike: USD 1000 per troy ounce
Delivery: physical
Notional: 1m troy ounces
Maturity: 1 year
Premium: USD 0.2 per troy ounce
FX: 1 EUR = 1.15 USD on 22 July 2009.

We can summarise the generic effects on holdings and cashflows of different times in the trade's life in tabular format (Table 9.4) and in a diagram (Figure 9.1).

Table 9.1

Asset type	Unit	Amount
GBP		3 400 000 000
USD		77 254 590
CHF		19 584 020
EUR		500 000
Palladium	Troy ounce	31 230
Cocoa	Tonnes	732 400
WTI Crude oil	Barrels	2 341 892
Shares in France Telecom		74 504
Shares in BP		1 703 200

Table 9.2   Holdings

	USD	Gold (oz)	EUR	Notes
Before trade	0	0	500 000	1
FX for funding	200 000	0	326 807	2
Trade settlement	0	0	326 807	3
Bank loan	1 000 000 000	0	326 807	4
Exercise	0	1 000 000	326 807	5

Table 9.3   Cashflows

Date	Asset	Amount	Notes
22 July 2009	EUR	−173 913	2
22 July 2009	USD	200 000	2
24 July 2009	USD	−200 000	3
22 July 2010	USD	1 000 000 000	4
26 July 2010	USD	−1 000 000 000	5
26 July 2010	Gold	1 000 000	5

Notes
1, Before the trade is entered into, Bank de Nord holds EUR 500 000, no USD or gold.
2. Bank de Nord is about to execute the trade and so converts enough of its EUR holding into USD to be able to settle the trade; this involves two cashflows: one out of EUR and the other into USD.
3. Two days after execution the trade settles and Bank de Nord must pay its premium in USD to the counterparty. This involves one cashflow out of USD.
4. Exercise day is 22 July 2010. On that day, the spot price of gold is USD 1010 per troy ounce, making exercise worthwhile. Bank de Nord contacts its counterparty to indicate it wants to exercise its option. On the same day it needs to arrange funding to purchase such a large quantity of gold. There is one cashflow which is the loan of USD 1bn coming into its account.
5. The exercise of the option actually occurs on the exercise settlement date which is 26 July 2010. This involves the purchase of gold at the struck price of USD 1000. There are two cashflows, payment of USD and reception of gold.

Table 9.4

Before trade	Original set of holdings	No cashflows
On execution	Original set of holdings	Anticipated cashflows
During life	Some holdings are altered as cashflows occur	Actual cashflows may have occurred and anticipated cashflows remain
After maturity	New set of holdings	No more cashflows

Note that the cashflows can be of three distinct types:

- known date and known amount;
- known date with unknown amount (e.g. floating rate notes or swaps);
- unknown data and amount (e.g. options or insurance products).

9.2   HOLDINGS

Holdings are not static. Interest payments and other charges may add to or detract from their size.

How to treat asset holdings is often a very tricky question in considering lifecycle trade processes. Much emphasis is placed on the trade, because it is the focus of the institution's

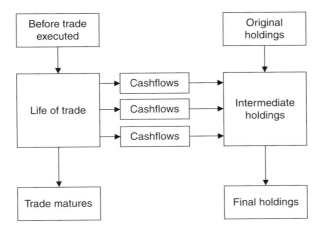

Figure 9.1 Cashflows and holdings

activities and it has a clear start and finish point. Holdings fall into a somewhat ill-defined region of the lifecycle because:

- they have no defined start and finish points;
- they arise both because of trades and independently of trades – an institution might have a holding for historical reasons or through non trading activities;
- they are not of direct relevance to traders, being the by-product of trades and other activities.

There are many reasons why the holdings are just as important as the trades. They require accurate and comprehensive processes to manage them. Holdings:

- determine the composition of the balance sheet;
- can be used to check if trade processes have worked;
- reflect the value of the financial entity;
- are subject to risk;
- enable trading to occur by funding trades and acting as collateral for trades.

We saw above that holdings can be consolidated into type and amount. This allows us to treat a holding generically in the processes no matter whether it is lead, cattle or currency.

9.3   VALUE OF HOLDING

The holding has two aspects of value. Its amount is the expression of its value in its native unit of holding. In order to get an aggregated view across all holdings, it is, however, necessary to convert each holding into a common unit. This is done via the reporting currency.

Here is an example list of holdings with reporting currency EUR (Table 9.5).

By looking at current market prices for each holding, it can be converted into an equivalent amount in the reporting currency. These amounts can be summed for an expression of the overall value.

Another reason for representing the value in the reporting currency is to get an idea of risk. Each holding is a risk to the company holding it, because market prices may change. A feel

Table 9.5

Asset	Native currency	Value in native currency (m)	Value in reporting currency (m)
GBP	GBP	6.4	7.070
USD	USD	77.25	52.751
CHF	CHF	19.58	12.898
EUR	EUR	270	270.000
Palladium	USD	5.85	3.995
Cocoa	USD	0.1725	0.118
WTI Crude oil	USD	1.23	0.840
France Telecom shares	EUR	0.256	0.256
BP shares	GBP	0.004	0.004

for the exposure to each underlying holding can be determined by varying the market price of each one individually and seeing the overall effect on the total reporting currency value (see Chapter 10 on risk management).

Due to these two aspects of value, most financial entities will keep track of the amount they hold in the native unit and value it daily in the reporting currency. To convert everything into reporting currency and lose the native amounts would be unwise, because it would be hard to see whether a change in value was caused by an underlying change to the amount held or by a change in market prices.

To value a holding we need to mark it against the medium for reporting, which is usually known as the reporting currency. This only holds for current prices and so the value is only a snapshot in time. By converting to the reporting currency, we can aggregate all holdings into one amount. We can perform generic risk analysis by varying market prices and looking at their effect on this total value.

There are two main approaches to handling both trades and holdings. Either they can be processed in different systems or consolidated into one. Since trades and holdings are fundamentally different objects, it is sometimes very hard to integrate them because each one has to be treated differently. One possible solution to this problem is to treat a holding as a perpetual trade. In this way:

- value of the holdings and the trades can be consolidated;
- risk can be monitored and managed across both simultaneously;
- consolidated reporting of asset holdings and trades is facilitated;
- actions on holdings such as interest payments can be handled the same way as actions on trades.

9.4   RECONCILIATION

Whether or not holdings and trades are integrated, there needs to be a means by which trades can make cashflows and these cashflows cause a change in the holdings. The nostro accounts, described in Section 8.5, are a means of holding foreign currency. Nostros only apply to cash holdings. Alternative means must be found for handling security holdings (such as equities) and commodities.

At various points in the trade lifecycle, a reconciliation needs to be made between actions the trade should have caused and what has actually occurred. Among these reconciliations is a check between the historic cashflows of the trade and the actual change in holdings. If the cash, commodity and security holdings are in one system, each with the same way of reporting, the job of reconciliation becomes much easier and less error prone.

Much middle and back office time is spent chasing issues arising from non reconciliation. Sometimes it turns out to be unnecessary as there really was no problem but the systems were inadequate to perform a true reconciliation. At other times, there is no mismatch reported, but in reality there are differences. Either fault is expensive and puts the company at risk.

9.5   CONSOLIDATED REPORTING

The aim of consolidated reporting is to be able to report answers to questions, such as:

- What is our total holding?
- What will be our total holding in six months' time with the current trades on the books?
- Are we making money?
- Where are we making money?

All business functions benefit from having information reported in a consolidated format. Having to interrogate different systems for different pieces of information makes reporting much harder. Also, different systems will store results in different ways and at different levels of detail. It may thus be impossible to aggregate across systems to the required level of detail. Even when data is stored in different systems, the aim should be to maintain it at its lowest possible level – that way aggregation can be done later and information is not being lost.

9.6   REALISED AND UNREALISED P&L

A trade with expected cashflows can be valued and compared to the value at execution and thus a profit or loss recorded. This is unrealised P&L, because it is not certain. Market forces might alter the amount of the cashflows (for trades such as options). Even when the future cashflows are known, their value is still dependent upon interest rates and foreign exchange.

Realised P&L is when a trade is bought at one price and sold for a different price – the change in value is certain.

A change in asset holdings is a realised profit or loss in the unit of the holding. The P&L in the reporting currency is however unrealised until the asset is sold, because it is still exposed to the market price of the asset. For example, if as a result of a day of trading my CHF holding has gone from 2.5 million to 3.3 million, I have a realised P&L of CHF 0.8 million. But if I report in euros my P&L can only be estimated from the CHF/EUR rate and is therefore unrealised.

9.7   DIVERSIFICATION

Most financial entities will try to maintain a balance in the range and size of the assets they hold. On the one hand, they want to diversify their risk, not putting all their eggs in one basket. On the other hand, they want to be able to manage the risk on assets they know and understand and not be caught holding an asset for which they have little expertise.

As traders tend to deal in specialist areas, it is left to business managers to define a diversification strategy and market risk to monitor the breadth and depth of exposure to different assets across the organisation.

9.8   BANK WITHIN A BANK

Traders must raise funds to make their trades. They can do this from the treasury desk at their own institution or go into the market to borrow money. Additionally, they must post collateral on exchange-traded deals and on OTCs, where the counterparty insists on a collateral arrangement. In risky areas, traders or trading desks may have to keep reserves of cash ring fenced and separate from their trading activities, in order to make up for market reverses. That way it is the individual rather than the institution that carries the market exposure.

For all of these reasons, many firms set up internal bank accounts for individual trading desks or for traders within the desks. These might be over a range of currencies and receive interest when in credit or pay interest when overdrawn. This is a tighter way of binding the traders to the cash holdings of the firm and ensuring that the cost of funding, collateral and risk is attributed to those using it. The responsibility of managing one's own account is thought to be more motivational than managing an account shared across an entire division or the entire company.

Of course any money held in these individual accounts belongs to the firm and shows in the balance sheet. The disadvantage of their use is the extra processing and reporting required to keep accurate records – for small hedge funds or asset managers this may outweigh the advantages.

9.9   CUSTODY OF SECURITIES

Trades on certain assets such as equities and bonds involve the transfer of documentation relating to the asset holding. In the case of equities, the purchaser or holder of shares must prove their ownership in order to receive a dividend. The same is true for bond holders in respect to coupons and the final redemption. Securities can be either registered or bearer.

9.9.1   Registered securities

The issuer will maintain a list of the holders of the security typically by employing a registrar or transfer agent. The essential details such as the name and address of the holder and the quantity and date of holdings will be recorded. When a dividend or coupon payment is due, the issuer will easily be able to arrange payment to the registered list of beneficiaries.

The owner of the registered security must still anticipate payment and check that they have received the correct amount and that there was no mistake in the registration process. When changes occur, such as selling some or all of the holding or purchasing additional holdings, the registry must be updated accordingly.

9.9.2   Bearer securities

These securities are not registered and are more commonly associated with bonds. The issuer will print certificates which provide proof of ownership. When a sale is processed, the seller will transfer the relevant number of certificates to the purchaser. Bearer securities are very similar to ordinary bank notes in the sense that anyone holding them can claim full rights of ownership. Although it is the responsibility of the issuer of a security to make payments in accordance with the schedule of coupons, these payments cannot be automated because the issuer is unaware of the holders. Therefore the bearer will initiate the payment process by presenting the coupon (which is a detachable part of the certificate) to the issuer.

Clearly bearer securities present the risk of loss or theft. In addition, they place the burden on the holder to claim his payment. If he is late he will be missing the interest he could have earned on the payment had he claimed it on time.

9.9.3   Use of custodians

Where a custodian is employed to handle and hold securities such as shares, the custodian will normally receive the dividends. The custodian will be expected to check the details, collect the payment and pass it on to the true owner.

9.10   RISKS

When trades, cashflows and asset holdings do not match up there are problems. Either the systems are not reporting what is going on, or the processes are not being properly executed – both sources of major operational risk. Since these activities and measures are so intrinsic to the whole trading process, it is important that proper systems and controls are in place for managing them.

9.11   SUMMARY

Trades cause cash and assets to change hands. In this chapter we have discussed how such transfers occur and some of the financial and operational methods of dealing with them.

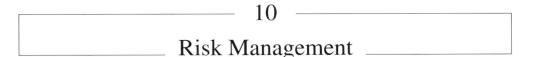

10

Risk Management

In this chapter, we consider the management of a very specific type of risk which is ongoing through the life of a trade or group of trades. Even though it is commonly known as risk management, the term is used in the context of market risk actively managed by traders and not in relation to counterparty, operational, reputational, legal and other risks. As explained earlier, trading involves actual and potential flows of assets. The price of assets varies according to market conditions and so trading carries with it market risk. We define risk management as the process of managing this market risk.

We now look at how risk management impinges on different people in the trade lifecycle.

10.1 TRADERS

Risk management forms a major part of the daily life of the trader. By trading, a trader is taking on positions that expose him to the risk of market prices changing.

10.1.1 Desirable exposure

This exposure might be desirable, as in the case where he expects the market to move in a certain direction and wants to take advantage of this move and convert it into profit. For instance, expecting the price of sugar to fall, the commodities trader sells a future in sugar. When the future is due for delivery he can go into the market and purchase the sugar to satisfy the obligations of the future at, hopefully, a lower price than he received for it.

10.1.2 Undesirable exposure

When the trader is uncertain of the direction of a particular market price, he will not want to be exposed to it. He may be uncertain either because he has no clear view or because he has no expertise or interest in that particular market – any exposure he has acquired is as a by-product of another trade. For example, our sugar trader knows all about sugar, but has no expertise in foreign exchange. His sugar trade is in dollars but his domestic currency is yen and so he will automatically be exposed to the USD/JPY exchange risk by dealing in sugar.

10.2 RISK CONTROL

The control department's interest in risk management is to ensure that it is being carried out, that limits are being adhered to and that management and other relevant people are cognisant of all the market risk in the organisation. Chapter 11 describes the market risk control function in detail.

10.3   TRADING MANAGEMENT

The trading managers will also monitor risk. They need to ensure that traders are keeping to the approved trading strategies. Part of these strategies will involve staying within limits set by the management and the market risk control department. If these limits are breached, the management will have to offer explanations and may be involved in tactical fire-fighting to reduce exposure.

10.4   SENIOR MANAGEMENT

Senior managers have to balance legitimate risk taken in order to make profit, with unnecessary risk – putting the assets of the financial entity in potential danger. They need to ensure proper risk management is being conducted at all levels of the organisation. They also need to monitor the size and composition of the market risk to ensure it is manageable and balanced. In effect, they are acting as referee between traders and risk control.

10.5   HOW DO RISKS ARISE?

In order to get a feel for the various market risks that can arise, let us look at a selection of common trades, their risks and how they can be offset (see Table 10.1). The risks described here relate to those which are actively managed by traders. (Other market risks, such as prospective dividend yields, lending fees and taxation also affect the price of a trade but may not be actively risk managed.)

10.5.1   Spot trades

Entering into a spot trade will increase or decrease the exposure to the underlying asset (currency, equity, bond, commodity etc.). If funding was needed to put on the trade, there will also be an exposure to interest rates. Additionally, there may be some foreign exchange risk. This applies even with a non foreign exchange asset where, for instance, the reporting currency of the institution is different from that of the trade.

10.5.2   Futures and forwards

The promise to buy or sell at a fixed price in the future obviously brings exposure to the underlying spot price and interest rates with again the possibility of foreign exchange risk.

Table 10.1

Trade	Exposures	Offset by buying or selling
Spot	Spot price, interest rate, FX	Spot, interest rates, FX
Futures/Forwards	Spot price, interest rate, FX	Spot, shorter dated future/forward, interest rate, FX
Options	Spots, futures, interest rate, FX	Spot, futures, interest rates, FX
Bonds	Credit of issuer, float or fixed income interest rates	Credit default swap, interest rate swaps
Group of equities	Many equity prices	Trade on index or individual equities

10.5.3   Options

Unlike forwards, the option delta risk is nonlinear. Unique to options is volatility risk, known as vega (see Section 10.9 below).

10.5.4   Exposures to fixed or float income streams

These can be offset by swaps going the other way. For instance, someone expecting income from a fixed coupon bond can offset his exposure by selling fixed for float swaps.

10.5.5   Exposure to debt

Debt products, such as bonds, create exposure to the default of the issuer. This can be offset by purchasing credit protection in the form of products, such as credit default swaps.

10.5.6   Exposure to group of products

A group of different underlying exposures might have their risk offset by trading a basket or index product.

10.6   DIFFERENT REASONS FOR TRADES

Many trades crop up frequently as a means of offsetting risk. When used in this context, they are known as hedging trades. Some trades have been created expressly for the purpose of offsetting risk and act like insurance products in everyday life – a good example is the credit default swap. Other trades started life as a means of offsetting risk and then became traded in their own right, such as interest rate swaps.

One of the most common hedging trades is spot foreign exchange, which is also actively traded for non hedging purposes. Generally speaking, more complicated trades use less complicated trades for hedging.

10.7   HEDGING

Whether the risk is desirable or undesirable it still requires careful handling. It must be monitored and action taken when it reaches what the trader considers an unacceptable level. The process of managing risk on current exposures by buying and selling other trades is known as hedging.

Whatever policy is adopted for hedging, the trader has to watch and act upon a wide variety of circumstances. He needs to:

• know his current exposure to all underlying market risks;
• know the acceptable limit of these risks;
• decide the best method of hedging, assess its benefit in reducing his exposure and calculate the cost of putting on hedging trades.

All the time he is monitoring his positions and his risks, which will be changing as the market data changes. Whenever he puts on a trade or investigates a potential trade, he must be aware of how this will affect all his market exposures. The process of trading has been compared to keeping hundreds of saucers spinning on top of poles. It calls for the ability to process vast amounts of information and make very quick decisions.

10.8   WHAT HAPPENS WHEN THE TRADER IS NOT AROUND?

The requirement to hedge applies to all traders, but the degree of connection to the ever-changing market data landscape varies. Some trading strategies require constant adjustments to market conditions, others need less attention. The question then arises as to how positions and risks are managed when the trader is away from the desk.

10.8.1   Availability of other traders

Most trading desks consist of more than one trader. If a trader is temporarily away intra-day, sick or on holiday, other traders trading the same or similar products can step in to maintain the risk management on his behalf. In fact it has become a regulation that all staff connected to the front office activities of investment banks take a period of two weeks away from their positions each year. This is to allow any irregular or illegal activities to be noticed without the perpetrator being around to cover his tracks.

Many markets are open around the clock, especially in interest rates and foreign exchange. When traders in one place go home for the evening they may hand over their risk management to those in another location. On at least one occasion, London traders in exotic foreign exchange trades stayed at their desks throughout the European night, dealing on the Australian and Asian markets.

This has occurred on other trading desks too when important news affecting the economy is due at night. One example is a bank providing food and sleeping facilities for traders on the night of a tight American presidential election.

10.8.2   Stop and limit orders

When no other traders are around to deal on their behalf, the traders can set up automatic orders to be executed when certain market conditions arise. These orders may be placed with brokers or via an electronic exchange.

10.8.2.1   Stop orders

To limit the loss incurred in holding on to a position or to prevent erosion into a profit, a stop order can be placed. This means the order is activated when the price falls below or reaches above a certain value, depending on the direction of the holding.

For example, aluminium is trading at USD 1.972 per metric tonne and Brenda holds aluminium. She places a stop order to sell at USD 1.962 to prevent her being exposed to unlimited losses should the price of aluminium start falling.

Conversely, Colin is short GBP which is trading at 1 GBP for 1.65 USD. He places a stop order to buy at 1.68 to prevent exposure to high rises in the price of GBP.

10.8.2.2   Limit orders

If a trader does not want to buy at current prices but wants to take advantage of a drop in prices overnight or while he is away, he can place a limit order. This guarantees the upper limit for a purchase, or conversely the lower limit for a sale.

10.9   TYPES OF RISK

We shall now discuss the types of market exposures which require risk management. An overview of the techniques for calculating these exposures can be found in Chapter 22. (The risk measures are designated by Greek letters of the alphabet, except for Vega which is the brightest star in the Lyra constellation. It was also known as Kappa which is a Greek letter, but this is less common nowadays.)

10.9.1   Delta

This is a measure of how the price of a trade moves when the underlying asset price moves. The value of delta may change as the underlying asset price changes. For example, an option in IBM shares might have a delta of close to one when well in-the-money – that is, every dollar change in IBM share price leads to a one dollar gain in option value. Conversely, when well out-of-the-money, a change in IBM share price of one dollar results in a negligible change in option value, so the delta is close to zero.

10.9.2   Gamma

Gamma is a measure of how delta changes. In the example above, when the option is well in- or out-of-the-money, the delta stays very similar as spot changes and so gamma will be very small. Near to the strike price, the delta changes quickly indicating a high gamma. Gamma is a second order measure and is equivalent to the second differential of trade value, with respect to underlying spot price.

10.9.3   Vega (sometimes known as Kappa)

Vega measures the change in trade value caused by a change in the volatility of the underlying asset. Volatility is an input to many trade calculations such as options. Because of the way options are priced, an increase in volatility makes both put and call options worth more.

10.9.4   Rho

Rho is a measure of the exposure to interest rates. Interest rates have a bearing on the price of many trades, even when they are on other underlying asset classes. Rho is calculated in a very similar manner to delta, except that the interest rate curve is bumped and the change in trade value caused by the bump is measured.

10.9.5   Theta

Theta is a measure of how the trade value changes as time passes. Usually the trade is revalued as if the current date were one or seven days hence, keeping all market data constant and the difference in value is the theta or time decay. Although time decay is unavoidable, it is useful to have a measure so that planning for the future can be undertaken.

10.9.6   Additional risks for credit products

Since credit derivatives have a different set of input market data, they have some additional risks beyond those described above. These are discussed at more length in Chapter 5.

10.9.7   Default risk (or jump to default)

A default is a binary, irreversible event – a name has either defaulted or it has not. Default risk is a measure of the change in trade value when one name in isolation is assumed to have defaulted, with the payout determined by the recovery rate.

10.9.8   Recovery rate

This is calculated on every name in the credit derivative by increasing the recovery rate for that name, leaving all the others unchanged, revaluing the trade and finding the difference in value caused by the recovery rate change.

10.9.9   Correlation risk

This is a measure of how a change in correlation affects the trade value. The precise mechanism for perturbing the correlation will depend on which type of correlation assumption is being used in pricing the trade. A common type of correlation used for pricing a single tranche of a CDO is **tranche correlation** which is the single correlation assumption for all assets in the reference pool. Suppose it is 4 %. Then the correlation risk is calculated by revaluing the CDO with a tranche correlation of 4.01 %, the difference between this value and the original being the correlation risk.

Since recovery rate and correlation are major factors on the credit derivative and are notoriously difficult to estimate, their sensitivity measures are very important to give a feel for how much they affect the value of the trade.

10.9.10   Risks in general

The advantage of the sensitivity calculations we have described is that they are all expressed in the same terms as the valuation of the trade itself. For example, if the trade has an NPV expressed in euros then the theta risk will also be in euros. This means that aggregating risk for many trades is easy, so that an entire portfolio or trading book can be managed effectively.

10.9.11   Dreaming ahead

Predicting how the future might look is an important part of risk management. With a complicated trading book, many anticipated future trade events and cashflows and a plethora of future market data, it is sometimes very difficult to work out what the trades will look like at some point in the future, let alone their future values.

Dreaming ahead began as a trading exercise and developed into an additional risk management tool in a front office trading system. Imagine that we are standing six months from now and assume no new trades have been traded. What will our portfolio look like? Which trades will have expired, which will have received coupons and dividends? Which will be near to exercise?

Now take the predicted future values of market data. The six month forward FX rate of today will be the dreaming ahead spot rate, the 12 month forward will be the new six month rate and so on.

Taking the dreaming ahead trading and market data landscape, we can revalue our portfolio and attempt a glimpse into the future. Of course this method assumes that today's future prices are an accurate prediction of what will actually happen, but provided we are aware of the assumptions being made, the exercise may be useful.

10.10   TRADING STRATEGIES

Before examining hedging strategies, it is worth mentioning that the kind of hedging employed will be determined by the overall trading strategy. It is beyond the scope of this book to discuss trading strategies in detail, but we point out two types of trading.

10.10.1   Front book

The aim of this type of trading is for a trader to take advantage of his position as a market maker. He takes no view on the future direction of the underlying market nor does he seek a profit from directional trading. In fact he seeks to eliminate his exposure to market changes by a complete hedging of market risk. His profit comes from buying low and selling high on the same products, often by means of the bid/offer spread and typically within a short period of time (generally less than a day and often as short as a matter of seconds).

10.10.2   Back book

The trader has a view on the future direction of the underlying market and wants to profit from his view. The view might be:

- prices will go up – he will then be long the underlying (buy now, sell later);
- prices will go down – he will be short the underlying (sell now, buy later);
- he does not know whether prices will go up or down, but thinks they will move sharply in either direction (this is called being long volatility).

The back book trader will construct his portfolio by buying and selling trades to capture the direction he expects. He will also use hedging to eliminate extra risks and limit existing risks if his predictions are wrong.

10.11   HEDGING STRATEGIES

The aim of hedging is to offset potential future loss. Hedging costs money because every new trade has to pay at least the bid/offer spread plus an operational cost. There may be additional costs, such as transaction or handling fees and stamp duties. Every trader will evolve his own strategy to offset his risk in the cheapest and safest manner. Here we discuss two general examples of hedging strategies.

10.11.1   Delta hedging

Remember that delta is a measure of how much the trade gains (or loses) in value for every unit change in spot price. Delta hedging seeks to reverse the delta risk by entering into a trade, creating an equal and opposite change in value to the original trade for a movement in the spot.

Suppose we bought a call option with notional 10 000 on the French CAC share index which is now trading at 3402 (see Table 10.2). At this time, our delta is 0.5 which means we gain 5000 if CAC rises to 3403, but lose 5000 if it falls to 3401. Now, if we sell a future on CAC with notional 5000 at 3402, we should reverse our position.

Now let us suppose that when spot reaches 3422, the delta is 0.7 and at 3382 it is 0.4.

It can be seen that as delta changes, the hedge fails to eliminate all of the risk. A delta hedging strategy requires constant hedging in order to achieve its purpose. After a while, many hedges will have been put on. The idea then is that the overall book of original trades plus hedges can cover most or all of the potential deltas arising from changes in spot. The hedging strategy is applied to the book, not the individual trade.

10.11.2   Stop-loss hedging

The purpose of this strategy is to limit the losses caused by the market going against the direction it was expected. There are several ways of achieving stop-loss. As we mentioned, there are stop-loss trades that are activated at certain market prices. In addition, a call or put option can serve a similar purpose.

Suppose that a trader expected nickel prices to rise. If he bought a put option on nickel, when prices fell below the strike he would gain and offset the other losses in his portfolio. Before the price falls to strike, the option is not making an impact on either profit or loss (apart from the fixed premium he has paid). Thus his downside has been capped, leaving him the ability to take advantage of potentially unlimited upside.

Table 10.2

Price	Delta	Gain from option of increase of 1	Gain from future of increase of 1	Total gain
3401	0.5	−5000	5000	0
3403	0.5	5000	−5000	0
3421	0.7	−7000	−5000	−2000
3423	0.7	7000	5000	2000
3381	0.4	−4000	−5000	1000
3382	0.4	4000	5000	−1000

10.12   SUMMARY

Good risk management is intrinsic to the success of a financial trading organisation. It involves the formation of a sound strategy and skilful implementation by means of hedging techniques. Risk must be identified, quantified and controlled. Management, risk control and trading functions must cooperate to use risk to further profit in a controlled and transparent manner.

11

Market Risk Control

The purpose of the market risk control department in a financial entity is to monitor and control the exposure to market risk. Market risk is the risk to changes in market conditions.

We can illustrate market risk with a simple example. Suppose one buys an oil painting as an investment. The price paid for the painting was GBP 150 000. The value of the painting on any given day is the amount someone in the market will pay for it – this could be more or less than the purchase price. We say the oil painting is subject to market risk. The risk is the amount that is lost by a change in price. If the painting could only be sold for GBP 100 000, the risk would be GBP 50 000. In this case, it is only subject to one type of market fluctuation, but in general an asset can be subject to many different market forces. In addition to looking at day-to-day price fluctuations we can look at market risk in other ways, for example VaR – what is the maximum loss I could reasonably expect to make in a day (week, month, etc.) and some of these approaches are addressed below.

Of course for a painting market risk is one of the less important risks – fire, damage and theft are other more relevant risks. For financial assets too there are other risks – legal (can we be sure we own it?), counterparty (credit) risk, documentation risk and others. This chapter assesses market risk in isolation.

Before examining the process of market risk management, let us look at various ways to consider market risk.

11.1 VARIOUS METHODOLOGIES

Measurement of market risk is not an exact science. A market risk control department might employ one or many of the common methodologies we describe below. In addition they may develop their own means to monitor market risk tailored to the products their company trades.

11.1.1 Scenario analysis

One technique for assessing market risk is to use scenario analysis. This means creating a set of market conditions and assessing how much the firm would have gained or lost under those conditions. The difference between that and the current position is the risk. The scenarios might be run as relative to current prices or as absolute values. Examples of relative scenarios would be:

- all share prices down 3 standard deviations
- all bond prices down 30 %
- all market data inputs down 25 %.

Absolute scenarios could be:

- foreign exchange rate between GBP and USD set at 1.00
- recovery rates for credit products at 1 %
- all shares set to their lowest point in the last two years.

Alternatively, scenario analysis might try to replicate the effect on the market of a particular event in history such as:

- Black Wednesday (16 September 1992)
- 9/11 (11 September 2001)
- the Lehman crisis (15 September 2008).

The process here would be to move each piece of market data by the same proportional amount and direction it moved on the day of the event in question.

The purpose of scenario analysis is to measure the risk caused by something unusual, but not impossible, occurring and to factor in some correlation between different types of market risk (as opposed to sensitivity analysis which perturbs each set of market data independently).

11.1.2   Value at Risk (VaR)

VaR is another risk measure. It attempts to state the maximum loss that will occur within a period of time. Since the maximum loss is in effect unlimited, the VaR puts a probability on the maximum loss occurring. For example, there is a 95 % probability that the maximum one-day loss will be 12 million euros. In other words, 19 times out of 20 the loss will not exceed 12 million euros. The converse is that once every 20 times (about once a month) the loss will be more. It may not be very comforting to the board of a firm to know that VaR is likely to be exceeded once a month, but it is an industry standard measure and helps to make comparisons with other organisations to compare their risk exposures.

Usually VaR is computed over an aggregation of trades in one division or from the whole organisation. It is given target limits and breaches of these limits require action in the same way as other market risk limit breaches.

11.1.2.1   The VaR calculation

1. Decide the time horizon: VaR is quoted over a time interval known as the time horizon. Since market data changes every business day, the most common time horizon is daily. Some less liquid trades may receive market data updates less frequently, in which case VaR may be quoted over a week or month. Due to the time effect of risk, the longer the time horizon, the greater the risk. Comparisons between different VaR figures must take into account the time horizon on which they are being quoted.

2. Assemble the market data: this is far from simple. The market risk calculation is in theory attempting to replicate every possible combination of market data. Some simplifications have to be made because each piece of market data is technically a random variable and its connection (or correlation) to other market data is very hard, if not impossible to determine.

3. Decide the calculation methodology: there are two basic approaches – stochastic or historical.

Stochastic processes: if a piece of market data is assumed to be a normal distribution then we can ascribe different probabilities to different values. For example:

1 % probability of 140,
5 % probability of 155,
50 % probability of 182 and so on.

This removes the need for a large amount of data but ignores correlation between different market data.

Historical data: we go back over a certain period of market data, apply every day-on-day change in all market data to the set of trades under examination and for each day we get a different total value. Suppose we call them V_1, V_2, ... V_{200} for 200 different dates of data (which give 199 differences). We then take the 1% worst value and say that we are 99% confident that the loss due to market data will not exceed that value. This method suffers the drawback of being totally dependent on one period of history. If, for example, we took the last two years, we are assuming that future market changes are likely to mimic data changes only from the last two years.

4. The calculation: the heart of any VaR calculation is the valuation of the trade or portfolio under consideration with one set of market data. The task is then to vary the market data in enough ways and enough times to produce realistic probability measures for the risk.

The more scenarios considered, the more realistic the market risk output. Therefore, market risk managers are always seeking better hardware to run their processes, more market data and faster computational capabilities. Usually this reaches a point where more calculations do not significantly alter the output risk and then the increase in the number of iterations can cease.

11.1.2.2 Problems with VaR

The use of VaR as a measure of risk has become less fashionable. Stress and scenario testing are taking over because VaR does not predict how much you will lose if an event occurs. VaR is very dependent on correlation between various market forces. This gives rise to two problems. Firstly correlation tends to vary considerably. Secondly in crisis situations correlation tends to be very high.

11.1.3 Instantaneous measures of risk (sensitivity analysis)

The market risk control department may want to see how an instantaneous change in underlying price affects the value of a trade, book, department or the entire financial entity. The most common measure of instantaneous risk is known variously as DV01, PV01 and delta – equivalent terms denoting the first order derivative, that is the change in value given a small change in underlying.

DV01 can be measured across multiple trades by taking each underlying and changing its price by a small amount, calculating the change in aggregate value of trades.

For example: suppose aluminium has a spot price of 2230 dollars per tonne. The DV01 of aluminium would value the book with current prices (say it is 5 030 440 dollars) Then aluminium price would be moved to 2231 and the book value recalculated (say it is now 5 037 625). Then the DV01 of aluminium is 7185 dollars (5 037 625 – 5 030 440).

The DV01 can be analysed for each underlying to give a feel for where the market risk is distributed.

In addition to DV01 there are other first and second order risk measures such as time decay (theta), rate of change of delta (gamma), correlation between market forces, default event risk, volatility (vega) and interest rate risk (rho). These are described in Chapter 10. The market risk control department will allocate limits to each of these risk measures and analyse them on a regular basis to determine if and where there have been any breaches.

Apart from some foreign exchange and interest rate risk common to most products, linear products only have one exposure to risk – the underlying spot price. Derivatives, such as options, have several risks known collectively as "the Greeks".

Dependency upon one set of prices: these sensitivity measures give some idea of how much exposure exists, given current market prices. Market risk control generally works from reports produced overnight and so they are a maximum of one day behind the current situation. Of course, as prices change the sensitivities change with them, so delta might be 0.5 at spot 450 but 0.7 if spot moves to 475. The risk calculation will try to provide a realistic measure of how much is lost if prices move by a given number of standard deviations from their current position.

11.2   NEED FOR RISK

Trading cannot be undertaken without risk. Any trade or asset held by the institution is at risk. The success of any trader or trading department is measured by how they make use of the capital they are provided with for investment and trading while keeping within their risk limits.

A firm engages in trading a variety of products in multiple asset classes. The primary responsibility of the market risk control department is to know the amount of exposure and where that exposure lies. Then, in the event of an emergency, senior management will have enough information to make important decisions. Additionally, the institution will be protected from one individual or one desk bearing too much risk and endangering the entire company.

11.3   ALLOCATION OF RISK

Risk is divided into layers within the trading organisation. An example might be:

- individual traders
- trading desks
- division or department
- company wide.

Mindful of the regulatory limits, the board of the firm will decide the total amount of risk available. They will then allocate risk to each division and the managers of the division will allocate it across the trading desks. Each desk head will allocate his allotted risk according to the trading strategy of his individual traders.

For instance:

Overall risk: 1 billion
Interest rate division: 100 million (risk to interest rate changes)
Linear products desk: 10 million
    Jenny (deposits): 1 million
    Karen (futures): 4 million
    Linda (swaps): 5 million

11.4   MONITORING OF MARKET RISK

Once the risk limits have been set, the market risk control department will monitor them. It does this over different periods of time – daily, weekly and monthly – and for each of the layers of the organisation described above. Various calculations might be performed.

Illiquid products: sensitivity analysis is possible when prices are easily available, but when a product is illiquid, it is very hard to give it a realistic measure of risk. Generally more risk would have to be allocated to illiquid products as it would cost more to trade out of them should that be necessary.

New products: when a new product or asset class is traded by the company, the market risk control team must become acquainted with it, so that some reasonable predictions can be made as to its risk profile. The problem with new trades is that there is little empirical risk data about them other than that derived from simulations. The trade has not yet been subjected to real market forces. Market risk control is generally wary of new trades. It might:

- assign a high risk to them;
- limit their trading until the market is sufficiently mature and more experience is gained as to their behaviour.

The latter policy may not suit the traders, who know full well that the opportunity to really profit from a new trade is a direct consequence of their competitors having less knowledge of the product. Any advantage they might have will be reduced if the trading is limited in size or diversity of product.

11.5   CONTROLLING THE RISK

Periodically, perhaps once a week in normal circumstances, the head of market risk will meet the head of each trading desk to discuss his market risk profile. The purpose of this dialogue is to continually review the limits to make sure they are fair and reflect the current trading environment and also to discuss any breaches.

If a limit has been breached there are various courses of action that might be taken.

Take steps to repair breach: breaches of limits are often just taken as a "heads up" warning. The first response may simply be to increase the limit on a temporary basis. Longer term the trade or trades causing the breach might be reversed to reduce the risk. The trading manager might, however, argue that this is expensive and cause the loss of the expected profit from the trade.

Exception to limit: this might be granted for a fixed time in order to allow the trader to cash in on an expected profit or because of particular adverse conditions that are expected to be only temporary. Exceptions are generally recorded to prove that market risk control made the trading team aware of them. Obviously, too many exemptions will defeat the purpose of putting limits in place.

Changing the limits: the internal allocation of limits between traders might be altered to allow the one who is over the limit to take some risk from another who is under the limit. Alternatively, the trading manager might ask for extra risk to be granted. In this case, another desk or division would have to give up some of their risk to make up the difference. The reallocation between departments may require intervention of senior management in cases where risk will not be relinquished voluntarily.

Posting reserve: the traders might be so keen to keep their current positions that they will post money from their profit and loss account into a reserve account to cover the additional risk. This effectively reduces the risk because, if the money were needed, it would be taken from the reserve which is free of exposure to market risk.

Do nothing: the trading manager might provide reasons why the breach should be allowed, promising to take remedial action and ask for time to put this in place. The control department should return to review the situation after the time has expired.

11.6   RESPONSIBILITIES OF THE MARKET RISK CONTROL DEPARTMENT

Staff in the market risk control department are officers of the financial entity. They provide independent assessment of the market risk to which the institution is exposed and are accountable to the board or senior management.

Requirements: aside from good sources of market data and sufficient calculation resources, market risk departments are very dependent on reliable trade valuation, which, as mentioned, lies at the heart of the process. They must be fully versed in the specifics of the valuation model and know its expected behaviour for extreme values. They must also understand the trades they are testing. Perhaps an analogy could be made with a pharmaceutical company that must understand the components of a drug it is testing and the workings of the human body upon which the drug will act. They must test in a variety of conditions, especially for the unusual and more extreme states.

Relationship with front office: ultimately, all the revenue for the trading section of a firm comes from the front office. That means all employees are dependent on the success of the traders for their jobs, including those in the market risk control area. In addition, it is the granting of risk to trading departments that allows them to generate revenue. Hence there is a possible conflict of interests between market risk control and front office. The problem is compounded in good times, when the pressure of a successful trading desk making large profits for the organisation may lead to a relaxation in the risk limits themselves or the application of them.

In theory, there should be a three-way professional tension involving the board or senior management who allocate risk, traders who use the risk and market risk control who monitor and report on the risk. Generally, the balance of power between traders and risk control varies according to the risk appetite of the organisation.

11.7   LIMITATIONS OF MARKET RISK DEPARTMENTS

It should be clear that market risk control departments do not prevent disasters from occurring. The expectation is that, should something unusual happen, they will be able to provide the necessary data on the risk profile of the organisation at various macro and micro levels so that the extent of the damage can be assessed.

Also, they cannot possibly measure every possible disaster. Nobody can determine how much or in what way the future replicates the past. Market risk control lives in the world of the unknown, but uses the theory of probability to give some feel for exposure to risk. Understanding the limitations of market risk is very important in order to put an appropriate level of credence on its measurements.

11.7.1   Everything correlated

Market risk allocates risk on an asset-by-asset basis. Interest rate traders are given so much interest rate risk; commodity traders, commodity risk and so on. Most of the measurements of risk (with the exception of scenario testing) also consider each risk type separately. This means there is an implicit assumption that one type of market risk is not connected to other types of market risk. This assumption is not always correct – we have observed several episodes in the recent and distant past that have caused markets to react in concert across the range of asset classes. This means that in times of crisis markets are ultimately correlated to each other.

11.7.2   The tails

As mentioned, the change in asset price follows a mathematically described pattern, known as a random variable. Two or more random variables can be modelled together assuming some level of correlation between them. So we could investigate the relationship between oil prices and USD/EUR exchange rates. These models are often quite informative. But when we reach the extreme case, known mathematically as the tail of the curve, different factors come into play and cause the standard model to become less reliable. A lot of economic and mathematical work has gone into predicting tail behaviour, such as the various copula models used in credit derivatives. It is the tail that is most interesting to market risk control which is very concerned with what may happen in extreme cases.

11.7.3   The human factor

Risk analysis is a mathematical exercise; valuations do not have emotions. However, an important point to bear in mind is that the drivers for the valuations are the various input data, and that input data comes from prices set by human beings reacting emotionally as well as intellectually to events around them. Although the human factor in market risk cannot be precisely quantified, it should be taken into consideration and studies on past crises can reveal trends in human and hence market behaviour.

11.7.4   Balanced approach

A conservative approach would assume the worst on every occasion. This might prevent unexpected risk being incurred but could paint an overly bleak picture and restrict justified trading and profit-making potential. An optimistic approach, on the other hand, might falsely represent the true state of risk. When conveying risk information to management and regulatory authorities, the market risk control department should state the methods they adopted in arriving at their risk forecasts. They might also give a range of risk outputs according to more and less conservative measures to allow their readership to decide how cautious they would like to be in their interpretation.

11.8   REGULATORY REQUIREMENTS

11.8.1   Basel II

The regulatory authorities adopted a set of rules known as Basel I (later superseded by Basel II). Some of these incorporate controls on levels of market risk. Here we shall briefly outline the three pillars of Basel II and then discuss one market risk limit arising from them known as capital adequacy ratio.

1st Pillar – Minimum capital requirements: this sets rules that are more closely aligned with a bank's actual risk of economic loss (including capital adequacy ratio set at 8 %).

2nd Pillar – Supervisory committee: "Supervisors will evaluate the activities and risk profiles of individual banks to determine whether those organisations should hold higher levels of capital than the minimum requirements in Pillar 1 would specify and to see whether there is any need for remedial actions."[1]

3rd Pillar – Market discipline: "Leverages the ability of market discipline to motivate prudent management by enhancing the degree of transparency in banks' public reporting to shareholders and customers."[1]

11.8.2   Capital Adequacy Ratio (CAR)

A financial entity has an amount of capital. The regulatory authorities allow the institution to have a maximum amount of risk at any given time, this risk being linked to the capital by a value known as CAR.

$$CAR = Capital/Risk$$

Basel II set the CAR at 8 %. As this did not prevent the credit crunch in 2008, many governments are currently pressing regulators to review these rules.

A value of 8 % means that for every 100 dollars of capital, the institution can have a total risk of 1250 dollars ($100/1250 = 0.08$).

One of the issues with calculation of CAR is the precise quantification of risk. Some products have greater susceptibility to market risk than others, and so some sort of weighting has to be applied to each product. For example, cash is nearly risk-free and so has less weighting than mortgage loans, which in turn are less risky than uncollateralised loans.

The reason for the CAR limit is to give some confidence that the institution will be able to repay some of its debt should market forces act against it.

11.9   SUMMARY

Trades are subject to market risk. Managing this market risk is essential to prevent widespread losses when the market changes adversely. The market risk control department sets appropriate limits for trading, monitors market risk and reports breaches to ensure that the firm has control over its market risk. In some senses the market risk department can be thought of as the biggest and largest trader within the bank – controlling all other traders and sometimes (though rarely) initiating large trades itself.

---

[1] Quoted from the second Basel accord (Basel II), issued by the Basel Committee on Banking Supervision.

12

Counterparty Risk Control

As soon as a trade is executed with a counterparty, an exposure to counterparty risk is created. Counterparty risk is when, for whatever reason, the counterparty will not fulfil their contractual obligations. The department concerned with vetting counterparties is generally called the "credit risk" department – not to be confused with credit market risk (i.e. risk to changes in credit spreads).

12.1 REASONS FOR NON FULFILMENT OF OBLIGATIONS

The non fulfilment of the counterparty's obligations manifests itself in non settlement or delayed settlement.

Non settlement: non settlement could be because of:

1. Company default: after executing a trade, the counterparty has ceased to be a trading entity and can therefore no longer settle the trade. This would usually arise because of some legal change of status, such as filing for Chapter 11 of the US bankruptcy code or going into administration.
2. Court order: a court order freezing the company's assets would make settlement impossible.
3. Dispute: a counterparty might refuse to settle a trade pending resolution of a dispute regarding an individual trade, or because there is outstanding litigation between the two companies involved in a trade, even though it might not be related to that trade.

In these scenarios, absolute non settlement is unlikely. Some redemption of promised assets is usual, but these would be subject to delay and reduction in amount. For example, a creditor owed money by a liquidated counterparty at a senior subordinated debt level may only receive 40 % of the full amount and might have to wait months or even years for payment.

Delayed settlement: delayed settlement could be due to:

- ambiguity in the trade contract
- the contract not being clear as to exactly when settlement is due or the terms of settlement might have been misinterpreted by one or other counterparty leading to a delay in expected settlement.

Mistakes in settlement process: many settlements fail and need to be reprocessed. There are a variety of reasons for this – see Section 8.5.

12.2 CONSEQUENCES OF COUNTERPARTY DEFAULT

If a settlement is delayed, not paid in full or completely missed, this will have many consequences for the company expecting it.

The first likely consequence is loss of money. Losses caused by counterparty defaults reflect badly on traders, managers, risk departments and the entire company. Many trading desks have collapsed because counterparties failed to pay their debts, even though the trading strategy was sound and correctly implemented. A counterparty default can, in one event, cause more damage than several other risks over a long period of time.

The asset that was expected to arrive on a certain date will not be there and steps will have to be taken to replace it or to manage without it. For example, if a consignment of gold bars from counterparty X was due by Wednesday and was supposed to be shipped to counterparty Y on Thursday, a delay of even one day might result in complete loss of the second trade or penalties for late delivery.

Much trading depends on managing expected changes in asset holdings, including cash transfers. When these fail to happen, trading is thrown out of balance, hurried decisions need to be made and more costly firefighting measures are required.

12.3   COUNTERPARTY RISK OVER TIME

Like many other types of risk discussed in this book, counterparty risk is time dependent. The longer money is owed, the more chance there is that it will not be paid. Counterparty risk control departments take this into account and generally measure risk and allocate trading limits as functions of time. These take the form of time intervals (known as buckets).

For example: Cautious Bank has the following trading limits with Adventure Finance.

Time Period	Limit (EUR)
Under 3 months	10 million
3–6 months	5 million
6–12 months	3 million
12 months–5 years	2 million
Over 5 years	1 million

12.4   HOW TO MEASURE THE RISK

Delayed settlement is primarily due to operational processes failing to work for one or both of the counterparties to a trade. The assessment of delayed settlement risk is mainly dependent on estimation of these risks (see booking, confirmation and settlement sections).

Here we consider the risk of non settlement.

The amount at risk is comprised of:

- the total exposure to a given counterparty;
- the probability of the non settlement by that counterparty;
- the amount lost in the event of non settlement.

The first of these can be measured fairly accurately by investigating all the outstanding trades with a particular counterparty. The total exposure is dependent upon the size and nature of the trades and not on the characteristics of the counterparty.

The latter two do not depend upon trades, they are hard to measure and vary between different counterparties. To arrive at an estimate of these amounts, the credit worthiness of the counterparty must be examined. Counterparty risk control departments employ various models. The most common are based on ratings allocated by rating agencies, such as Standard & Poors, Moodys and Fitch. A counterparty with a high rating (AAA, AA+ etc.) is by definition less likely to default.

In addition, the amount of loss in the event of default (also known as the recovery rate) is estimated by ratings agencies. This is usually based on historical recovery rates of companies similar to the one under consideration.

12.4.1 Expected loss

$$\text{Expected loss} = (\text{Probability of default}) \times (\text{amount lost if default occurs on one unit}$$
$$\text{of exposure}) \times (\text{size of exposure})$$

The two key factors to be estimated are therefore probability of default and amount lost should default occur. The latter equals one minus the recovery rate where the recovery rate is the amount of money recovered on default. If, for example, one holds a bond that defaults, the issuer may still pay 40 % of the bond's notional upon default and so the loss would be $(1 - 0.4) = 0.6$ of the exposure.

Historical values do not however predict the future. Some counterparty risk departments use adjustments to historical values based upon factors such as economic considerations.

One approach, which has been found to be unrealistic, is to use credit default swap rates to build an implied default rate curve for a counterparty. This is useful for deriving a risk neutral measure for trading but provides a biased estimate for predicting future default rates. It is very similar to deriving future interest rates by using current interest rate trade prices. The bias comes because the traded forward instrument comprises the estimate of future rate plus a reward for taking risk. This extra reward component means that typically the risk neutral measure over estimates the future value.

12.4.2 Credit exposure

Now let us consider the credit exposure created by one trade. The exposure is defined as the amount the company that is owed money (or other assets) would lose if the counterparty defaults on the trade in question.

By considering the exchange of assets over the life of the trade, we can derive this exposure in each of the reporting time buckets.

Take the case of a simple loan. Cautious Bank lends JPY 200 million to Adventure Finance at 4 % annual interest rate for nine months with the only repayment being at the end of the contract. Here there are two asset flows:

First settlement date: Cautious Bank pays Adventure Finance JPY 200 million
After nine months, Adventure Finance pays Cautious Bank JPY 206 million (4 % APR
  means 3 %[1] of 200 million in nine months.)

In between these two flows, Cautious Bank has a credit exposure because it is owed money. The time and amount of money is known. The counterparty risk control department will now say that in the 6–12 months bucket, there is an exposure of JPY 206 million. Total Exposure = sum of all expected flows.

Now let us consider two cases where the exact exposure cannot be known. Firstly, Cautious Bank transacts a two-year swap with Adventure Finance. Cautious pays 5 % and receives LIBOR + 75bp, with quarterly payment dates, notional of deal GBP 10 million. The exact

---

[1] We assume an actual/actual day count convention to simplify the calculation.

cashflows in a fixed-float swap cannot be determined in advance – we don't even know which side will end up owing money. Therefore the counterparty risk department will apply some sort of limit to where interest rates might be over the course of the trade – say between 0.5 % and 3 % – and will then calculate the maximum amount which could be owed between this range. Then each payment date would have a credit exposure that would be aggregated into its time bucket.

A harder case would be where Cautious Bank buys a call option on France Telecom shares. The current price is 65 cents and the strike is 63 cents. In the event that the trade is in the money at maturity, it will be exercised but the amount owed to Cautious could be limitless (see Chapter 4 "Derivatives"). It would be absurd for the counterparty risk control department to apply an infinite credit exposure on this trade, so it makes some estimate of the likely future price of the France Telecom shares and uses that to determine the exposure. As time goes on, this estimate will change and the exposure will change with it.

Note that the seller of an option has no counterparty risk except for delivery of the premium.

12.4.3   Potential future exposure (PFE)

Above we described how to calculate credit exposure. A more sophisticated approach, where exact credit exposure cannot be determined, is by using potential future exposure (PFE). PFE offers an alternative to the traditional credit exposure measures of mark-to-market and collateral management. It is measured by calculating an upper bound on the confidence interval for future credit exposures and so takes into account future as well as current positions.

Future credit risk predictions are more useful as relative rather than absolute values of risk. They can highlight books or portfolios that are particularly exposed to counterparty risk when compared to the total positions of the firm.

There is no easy means of reducing potential future counterparty exposure, even when it has been highlighted by calculation. Most firms still use collateral management as the best means of containing the risk.

A further means of preparing for counterparty risk is to reserve against it. What key factors affect the future mark-to-market value? At what time in the life of the deal does potential future exposure reach a maximum?

If a trade has price volatility of say 10 % per annum, then as time goes on there is a possibility that prices will move further and further away from their current value and increase counterparty risk. However, because the remaining life of the trade is shortening the risk of default is declining. These opposing effects will put an upper limit on the likely drift of counterparty risk.

12.4.4   Netting

Counterparty A is owed money by B arising from one trade. Because of a separate trade, A owes money to B. One might think that the expected flows could be netted (i.e. taken one from the other) in order to reduce the overall counterparty exposure. But credit risk departments are averse to such netting, when the two trades are independent: A will still owe money to B from the second trade, irrespective of B defaulting on the first trade.

If the cashflows are bound together in the same trade (such as a swap), then only the net effect will contribute to the exposure.

When netting is not allowed and the company owes money to its counterparties, trades are given a zero credit exposure (but not a negative exposure).

12.4.5 Back-to-back

One exception to the netting rule is a back-to-back trade. Here an equal and opposite trade is executed with the same counterparty to offset part or all of the obligations of the first trade. There are many reasons why a new back-to-back trade may be transacted, rather than just simply agreeing to cancel the first trade:

- The back-to-back reduces but does not remove all the exposures.
- The first trade was done on an exchange prohibiting cancellations.
- The legal risk of cancellation is too great.
- The operational processes do not handle cancellation.

When a back-to-back trade is executed, it is linked to the original trade. The counterparty risk control department may agree to net the positive and negative counterparty exposures to produce a reduced or zero exposure. It is important to be sure that the back-to-back trade is exactly the same as the original trade in all its trade details. Even a small deviation might cause residual counterparty exposure.

12.5 IMPOSING LIMITS

In order to control counterparty risk, the counterparty risk control department imposes a maximum limit for each counterparty and each time bucket with whom the company trades or is likely to trade. This will be based around the estimates of default probability and recovery rate. The smaller the chance of default, the higher the limit.

Then the current trading portfolio is analysed to see how much credit exposure exists with each counterparty in each time bucket.

A trader wanting to transact a new trade with a counterparty will first need to check that the new trade does not cause the credit limit to be breached.

Example: Cautious Bank has trading counterparties A and B. The current exposures are (in millions of EUR):

Time period	A	B
Under 3 months	3	20.7
3–6 months	2.76	30.4
6–12 months	4.3	29.9
12 months–5 years	5.5	17.6
Over 5 years	0	10.4

If the 6–12 months limit were 4.5 for A and 50 for B, a new trade causing exposure greater than EUR 0.2 million would be in breach for A, but the bank could trade up to EUR 20.1 million with B in the same time bucket.

12.6   WHO IS THE COUNTERPARTY?

Very often one legal entity has many trading companies. When considering default risk, it is important that exposures to the same legal entity are aggregated together, even if the trades causing those exposures were transacted with different companies. This is because, in the event of default, all money owed by that legal entity would be under threat of non settlement.

Apart from trading in different countries under different names, the legal entity may own several other companies under a complex business structure. Counterparty risk control departments have to know the structure of all trading counterparties and whether the default of one has any legal consequences on any of the others. This knowledge is complex and subject to changes of which the counterparty risk department must keep abreast.

12.7   COLLATERAL

Many markets and financial entities insist on the posting of collateral in order to facilitate trading and give more confidence in a counterparty's ability to settle its obligations. Collateral is the deposit of assets by the party owing money for the period when money is owed. Collateral usually takes the form of a percentage payment of outstanding debt and can be adjusted up or down on a regular basis, depending on whether the amount of outstanding debt rises or falls. This collateral is often known as margin. We are familiar with this concept on credit cards. At the end of every month the cardholder is invited to pay off all, or a percentage of, the debt and have the rest rolled over to the next month.

12.7.1   Example of a collateral agreement

A common form of collateral management between professional counterparties (e.g. banks) is the following.

1. Both parties agree the list of trade types to be covered (e.g. interest rate products, equity derivatives, etc.).
2. The parties agree a valuation methodology for each asset type.
3. Each day the trades are marked-to-market and the net value of all positions is compared to yesterday's value and the change in value is paid by one party to the other.

The aim of the above is that, if the posting of collateral takes place at the valuation time, then there is no counterparty risk at that point. As deals evolve and move further in (or out) of the money the counterparty risk is eliminated by this posting (payment) of collateral. Of course to be effective this requires a netting arrangement between the counterparties over these trades. However the posting of collateral does not eliminate counterparty risk – spotting that a counterparty is failing typically takes several days to establish so a PFE over that period can give an indication of the residual risk.

12.7.2   Advantages of collateral in general

1. Sign of intent: the counterparty is expressing his intention to settle the debt. He is also made more aware of the size of his debt when he has to make a contribution towards it. He is less susceptible to the debt growing without his knowledge when he has to post regular margin payments that will increase if his debt increases.

2. Reduces exposure: the actual collateral reduces the credit exposure and allows a greater amount of trading with that counterparty.

3. Early warning device: should the counterparty be experiencing repayment problems, the regular margin payments will be an early warning. If the counterparty cannot pay the percentage collateral, he will certainly not be able to repay the full debt. The company trading with the distressed counterparty has time to investigate the problem and take steps to reduce its effect when given such a warning.

12.8   ACTIVITIES OF THE COUNTERPARTY RISK CONTROL DEPARTMENT

The following are some of the activities in which a counterparty risk control department of a medium to large firm might be engaged.

12.8.1   Set policies for estimating exposure

A calculation methodology will be agreed for each trade type, usually based on the expected flow of assets as described above.

Where the exact asset flows cannot be determined (like in the examples above for swaps and options), the counterparty risk control department will need to have calculation policies and look into the actual market data to set boundaries.

For complicated structures it may have to calculate credit risk on a trade-by-trade basis and will therefore have to expend time understanding each trade.

12.8.2   Assign limits based on credit worthiness

One of the key activities is to research the credit worthiness of each counterparty and assign a trading limit. This limit will then be divided amongst all the trading departments of the institution. This could be on a fixed basis (equity gets 60 %, structured trading 10 % etc.) or on a first come, first served basis or by some other means agreed by all the trading managers.

When a trader wants to deal with a new counterparty, the counterparty risk department will need to arrive at a sensible limit. This is often smaller than would otherwise be the case until the counterparty has become more trusted through trading over time. The counterparty risk department may also be involved in the due diligence process, which is a regulatory requirement of trading with new counterparties. Some of this research may be shared or fully undertaken by researchers in the credit trading area of the institution.

12.8.3   Measure exposure

Having formulated a methodology and rules for its implementation, the counterparty risk department will then measure credit exposure and report it on a regular basis (daily). It will monitor trading with each counterparty and alert traders and managers when limits are being approached. Ideally, the traders will be able to view the utilisation of counterparty limits so that they do not miss trading opportunities. For example, if a trader knows that only 25 % of the limit is being used, he can more readily trade than if the utilisation is approaching 100 %.

One graphical method of representing this is shown in the graph in Figure 12.1.

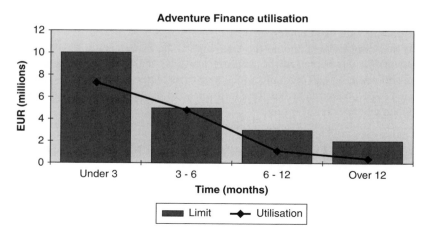

Figure 12.1 Counterparty limit and utilisation

The bars show the exposure limit over time with counterparty Adventure Finance. The line is a plot of actual utilisation. In this example the trader is within the limit for every time bucket although he is very close to the limit for the 3–6 months period.

12.8.4   Deal with breaches

Accidental breaches may be due to human error or reporting issues, such as the trader not being aware of the exact utilisation before he trades (perhaps because another trade had just been executed, which was not yet accounted for in the credit exposure).

These might involve a warning to the people concerned. Deliberate trading over the counterparty limit might be a disciplinary offence as it puts the institution at risk.

12.8.5   Policies for new trade types

Counterparty risk control must accommodate new business by formulating and testing credit exposure calculation on new trade types. This again requires a full understanding of the asset flows and their probability of occurrence.

12.8.6   Maintain legal data

As discussed, the legal structure of all the counterparties is very important. This has to be established and maintained by the counterparty risk control department.

12.8.7   Managing margin payments and receipts

Formulating collateral agreements is another task of the counterparty risk control department. This may involve careful negotiation with credit officers of the counterparty concerned. As trading is a fundamental activity of the financial entity and the main means of generating profits, anything that can promote trading while protecting the institution's assets is a boon.

The processes for paying and receiving collateral margin are usually operated by the middle office, but counterparty risk control has to oversee them and investigate when problems arise.

12.8.8   Interface with management

Although limits are set to minimise the effects of counterparty non settlement, the counterparty risk control department may advise management on how to deal with tolerated credit exposures. The setting of the limit itself is a balancing act between allowing trade and protecting assets, and therefore needs to take into account the institution's appetite for credit risk.

12.9   WHAT ARE THE RISKS INVOLVED IN ANALYSING CREDIT RISK?

12.9.1   Correlation between counterparties

Assuming a company has correctly gathered its counterparty data and understands the links between the various parent and child companies, there is still a hidden risk that once one counterparty fails, it will pull down others with it. For example, a hedge fund might require the support of a major investment bank for its funding. The counterparty risk department will have to weigh up the benefits of investigating the funding of its counterparties against the extra research work involved and the cost of not knowing the information.

12.9.2   Added complication of credit risk

Counterparty risk is often a separate operation from the department trading credit products. In reality, the trade on a credit product has dual credit risk – firstly, to that to which the trade refers; and secondly to the counterparty of the trade. To get a true picture of counterparty risk, knowledge should be shared between the two departments.

12.9.3   Insufficient consideration of counterparty risk

Even if the counterparty risk control department is functioning correctly and setting sensible limits, its success at containing risk is contingent on the attitude and support of management. The managers are under pressure to deliver profits by promoting trading, so until a company has suffered a major reverse, they may not strictly enforce its reports and recommendations, seeing the counterparty risk function as being overly cautious or anti-trade.

12.9.4   Sudden counterparty changes

If a limit has been set according to current counterparty rating information or by any other means and that limit becomes fully or nearly fully utilised, there is very little room for manoeuvre should the counterparty suffer a reverse and the limit needs to be revised downwards. New trading with that counterparty can be restricted, but closing down existing trades might be expensive. If there is a credit trading desk in the organisation, sometimes it will be asked to cover the exposure by buying credit protection on the counterparty.

There are occasions when a counterparty fails suddenly and spectacularly, such as Lehman Brothers in 2008. The whole market was caught by surprise, but a good counterparty risk department should be able to identify the outstanding exposures and perform a damage limitation exercise.

12.10   PAYMENT SYSTEMS[2]

A payment system is a set of mechanisms for the transfer of money between economic agents. These agents may be the counterparties to a trade or intermediaries for payment or delivery of funds (i.e. money) or financial assets.

Many payment systems have been established between banks and are known as interbank systems. These include CHIPS in the United States, RIX in Sweden and CHAPS in the United Kingdom.

A payment system consists of:

- institutions providing payment services;
- various forms of money;
- means of transferring them;
- message instructions and communication channels;
- contractual links between parties.

The banks themselves could act as intermediaries or counterparties.

Benefits of payment systems: having a safe, secure and electronic means of transferring money brings many advantages to all participants in financial (and other forms of) trading. The sheer volume and value of payment system transactions justifies their use over any sort of manual system which would not be able to cope.

Risks associated with payment systems: a typical payment involves a payment leg (which is the monetary payment itself) and a delivery leg (transfer of ownership of a financial asset). Sometimes the delivery leg can also be a monetary payment as in a foreign exchange transaction. In the case of a loan, there will be two payments in the same currency but at different times.

In any expected payment there are two clear risks – credit risk and timing risk. Credit risk is the risk of loss on outstanding claims on participants in transactions which includes the counterparties themselves and any payment or delivery intermediaries. The nature of credit (or counterparty risk) has already been discussed in this chapter.

Timing risk is the risk of unavailability of funds or items for exchange at the due time. When the item not available is the settlement medium itself the risk is known as liquidity risk.

Whereas credit risk involves the possibility of a loss, timing risk involves a possible cashflow shortfall. The timing risk is usually due to technical problems with either the payment system itself or the way the payment has been entered into the system. It can be very costly – involving expensive borrowing to cover the shortfall – and it can be totally unexpected.

Example: here we present an example payment through a payment system and describe the risks that could arise.

Suppose a hedge fund bought five million pounds of shares in Air France from an asset manager. The hedge fund banks at Barclays and the asset manager with HSBC (see Figure 12.2).

---

[2] Material in this section was taken from "The Nature and Management of Payment System Risks: An International Perspective" by Borio and Van den Bergh, published by the Bank for Internal Settlements.

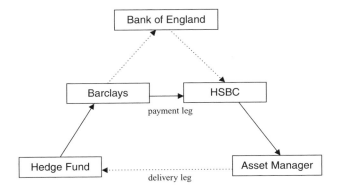

Figure 12.2   Intermediate payments and their risks

We have the following **credit risks**:

- hedge fund on asset manager in case funds are transferred before receipt of shares;
- asset manager on hedge fund in case shares are transferred before receipt of funds;
- Barclays on hedge fund in case the payment leg (to HSBC) is made without the fund having sufficient funds;
- HSBC on Barclays in case funds are transferred to the asset manager without funds in Barclays account or before receipt of final funds from the hedge fund in the Bank of England account;
- Bank of England on Barclays in case it transfers funds to HSBC without sufficient funds in Barclays account.

And we have the following **liquidity risks**:

- Barclays on the hedge fund in case the funds are not available at time expected;
- HSBC on Barclays in case the funds are not available at time expected;
- asset manager on HSBC in case the funds are not available at time expected.

12.11   SUMMARY

Any trading entity has a chance of default. If default occurs it will not honour its debts, leaving its counterparties with potential losses. The management of counterparty risk enables a firm to see where it has counterparty exposures and to keep them in line with the chances of default helping to control an important trading risk. The counterparty risk control department is charged with measuring and controlling this risk. Here we have explored some of the methods by which they may achieve this and looked into a common method of settlement known as payment systems.

13

Accounting

As in any other business, the finance department of an investment bank, hedge fund or other company involved in trading needs to keep fair and accurate books and records. The finance department will use standard accountancy practices. It is beyond the scope of this book to explain such practices; we will discuss how trades manifest themselves in the accounts during and after their lifetime.

Our discussion will cover the balance sheet, profit and loss statement and other financial reports.

13.1   BALANCE SHEET

The purpose of the balance sheet is to provide the management, current investors, potential investors and regulatory authorities with a "snapshot" of the company's assets and liabilities at a particular point in time. The items on the balance sheet relate to a given date typically stated on the balance sheet.

The balance sheet is divided into fixed assets, investments, cash and debtor categories. From the sum of these values plus the original capital value of the company, the profit and loss can be deduced. An example is shown in Table 13.1.

We shall now discuss each of the items on the balance sheet

13.1.1   Fixed assets

This would include any property owned by the company, fixtures and fittings, hardware, intangibles such as software, and other fixed items that are not subject to variation except for depreciation over time.

13.1.2   Investments

All live trades would feature in this item. Investments need to be marked-to-market for each financial accounting report; this gives a snapshot of their value for accounting purposes.

13.1.3   Cash

All currency holdings by the company would be converted into the equivalent in the reporting currency using the foreign exchange rate at the time of the report and aggregated to be shown as a single total cash figure. The Bank of England treats gold as a currency for these purposes. Table 13.2 is an example for a company reporting in euros.

The total value of EUR 70 million would show on the balance sheet item cash. As foreign exchange rates fluctuate, the cash value will change and this will affect the overall profit and loss.

Table 13.1

Item	Current value (millions, EUR)
Investments	150
Cash	70
Debtors	30
Fixed assets	50
Total	300
Capital	240
Profit and Loss	60
Total	300

13.1.4 Debtors

The mark-to-market value of a trade is the present value of the trade derived by using current market prices. Receivables that are not subject to mark-to-market fluctuations but which represent amounts owed by the company are represented in this item.

13.1.5 Creditors

Similarly, if the company owes money to another party this will be shown in the creditor entry.

13.1.6 Capital

This represents the original capital contributed to the company as adjusted by any profit or loss of prior periods.

13.1.7 Profit and loss

Profit and loss is generally expressed as revenue less expenses. In trading terms it can be thought of as the total net worth of the assets minus the capital value of the company.

13.1.8 Events that affect balance sheet items

Many activities of the company will impact the balance sheet. We will confine ourselves to explaining how trade lifecycle events affect the balance sheet. For this example we will assume the trade involves a purchase so that money is paid out initially and is paid back after maturity.

Table 13.2

Currency	Local amount (millions)	FX rate (1 EUR is)	EUR equivalent (millions)
EUR	46.35	1	46.35
GBP	6	0.8797	6.82
USD	14	1.4226	9.84123
ZAR	3	11.2066	0.2677
Gold	10 000 oz	USD 959 per oz	6.7223
Total			70

1. Funding for a trade: if the trader does not have sufficient funds to transact a trade he will have to arrange funding by way of an internal loan from the treasury department or from external sources. Suppose the loan was for 1 million euros. Then the accounting for the funding of the trade would see the **cash** item increase by 1m and the **creditor** item increase by 1m.

2. Trade executed: once the trade has been executed, it will make a contribution to the investments item of the balance sheet. The initial value of the trade would be the trade cost (net of commissions). If the trade cost 1m euros then **cash** would decrease by 1m and **investments** would increase by 1m.

3. During life of trade: the trade will be marked-to-market at regular intervals. If the trade is worth, say, 1.1m then the investments item will increase by 0.1m. This will lead to a profit and loss increase of 0.1m.

4. Maturity of trade: at maturity the trade will no longer be subject to mark-to-market variations. The amount of the final settlement will be known and this will be debt the counterparty owes. Suppose the trade is worth 2.3m on maturity. The **investments** item will decrease by 2.3m and the **debtor** item will increase by 2.3m. There will be no impact on profit and loss as the profit and loss impact will have been accounted for previously throughout the life of the trade.

5. Final settlement: upon final settlement, the counterparty should pay the full cost and so the **debtor** item will decrease by 2.3m and the **cash** will increase by 2.3m. Once again, there will be no impact on profit and loss as the profit and loss will have been accounted for previously throughout the life of the trade.

6. Effect of loan: the loan will have to be repaid with interest. This is typically a known amount and will usually be deducted from profit and loss as an expense each day, if using accrual accounting to calculate a daily profit and loss figure.

Suppose the 1m loan was extant for 100 days with an interest rate of 3 % per year. Then the total interest owing is $100/365 \times 0.03 \times 1\,000\,000 = 8219$ euros per day.

So the total accrual per day is 18 219 euros which will be shown as a decrease in the **cash** item. The **creditor** entry will increase daily over the life of the trade until it is settled from cash.

7. Illiquid trade: if the trade is illiquid it may not be possible to mark it to market. Until recently this situation was rare but due to adverse market conditions some products that used to be traded regularly became illiquid.

One technique to deal with illiquid trades or prices is by using a proxy. Suppose one grade of oil is liquid and a derivative grade is illiquid. Trades on the illiquid grade could be valued by adjusting the price according to price fluctuations on the liquid grade.

When it is impossible to derive an independent valuation, the middle office may allow the trader to revalue himself. There may well be conditions attached to this valuation such as the trader being required to obtain three external bids.

13.2 PROFIT AND LOSS ACCOUNT

13.2.1 Introduction

Profit and Loss (usually abbreviated to P&L) is the amount of money made or lost by the company. Every trade will make a contribution to P&L. In addition, aggregated P&L reports will be required at various levels within the organisation such as

- trading desk
- trading division
- entire company.

With respect to trades, P&L consists of different types depending upon how it was derived and whether it is real or virtual as explained below.

13.2.2 Realised

Realised P&L is actual P&L no longer subject to uncertainty. For example a trade bought at 500 and sold at 600 has made a realised P&L of 100.

13.2.3 Unrealised

Unrealised P&L is a potential P&L. It is derived from the actual value of a trade were it to be exchanged today even though there may be intention for such an exchange.

13.2.4 Accrued

Accrued P&L arises as a result of a known income or expenditure that is shared out over the period of time for which it applies rather than being accounted all in one go on one particular day. For many events, accrual is a fairer way of dividing the P&L.

If, for example a bond coupon period fell between two tax years, it is fairer to account part of the coupon in one tax year and the rest in the other than having to pay the full tax in either year.

Examples of accrued P&L are:

- interest accrued for the period of the loan;
- bond coupons accrued from one coupon payment date to the next;
- transaction fees that are accrued from start date to maturity of the trade.

13.2.5 Incidental

Incidental P&L might arise from fees, taxes or tax rebates and other costs associated with trading not accounted in the categories above.

13.2.6 Worked example

Now let us take a look at a trade and see how it affects P&L throughout its lifecycle.

Suppose 20 equity call options are purchased each for a premium of 8000 euros with a maturity of five years. (All monetary amounts are in euros.)

The cost of purchase is 160 000 plus a broker's fee of 5000.

Trade Date
The options are worth the same as the price paid. The broker's fee has zero accrual

Unrealised P&L:	0
Realised P&L:	0
Accrued P&L:	0
Total:	0

After one year
The mark-to-market price of each option is 9000.

Unrealised:	20 000 (1000 for each of the twenty options)
Realised:	0
Accrued:	-1000 (one fifth of the broker's fee)
Total:	19 000

After two years
Fifteen of the 20 options are sold for 10 000. The rest have a mark-to-market of 8500.

Unrealised:	2500 (500 for each of the remaining five options)
Realised:	30 000 (2000 for each of the 15 sold)
Accrued:	-2000 (two fifths of the broker's fee has accrued)
Total:	30 500

Maturity
The remaining options were exercised and netted a total profit of 17 000.

Unrealised:	0
Realised:	47 000 (17 000 plus the already realised 30 000)
Accrued:	-5000 (the full broker's fee)
Total:	42 000

13.2.7   Individual trades

The true P&L of a single trade will be the comprised of

- the difference between price sold and price bought;
- less the cost of funding;
- less taxes and fees associated with transaction;
- plus any income generated while holding the trade such as equity dividends or bond coupons.

This will be of interest when the trade is distinct due to its size, complexity or usefulness to the person trading it. In low volume trading desks every trade can be monitored individually; with higher volumes this becomes impractical. For example a collateralised debt obligation (CDO) is traded infrequently and reported individually whereas a desk might do tens of foreign exchange trades per day and is only interested in their net effect.

Of particular interest to managers is a single trade showing a particularly high loss, which could trigger alarm bells within the organisation.

Compliance officers and auditors may also be interested in individual trades with high profits or sudden changes in P&L. An unusually high profit might be caused by the counterparty agreeing to take a loss on the trade due to money laundering. A sudden change in P&L might indicate a change in calculation methodology or very different market data inputs either of which could be because of a defective monitoring process.

Even when trades are aggregated for P&L reporting, they may need to be broken down and reported at the individual level for audit or compliance purposes.

13.2.8 Who is responsible for producing P&L?

The P&L report is one of primary concern to most stakeholders in any financial entity. Traders are directly measured by their ability to generate P&L. Not only are they tracked individually but also as part of the desk and division to which they belong. Trading managers need to justify their existence by producing profitable trading desks. Senior management need to convince investors and shareholders of their competence by returning trading profits.

The middle office is responsible for compiling daily P&L. In order to do this they need to take accurate mark-to-market valuations of the trades. This is not always possible – there may be conflicting sources of price data or missing price data. It is the traders who are closest to the market and who might feel they can obtain the best market prices but the middle office must be wary; traders have an obvious motivation in using prices that present the P&L in the most favourable light. There is often a clear conflict of interests and there is a risk that middle office will be unduly influenced by the people who generate the revenue that pays their salary and bonus.

Traders will have their own idea of P&L and will argue their case if the official P&L produced by middle office is very different.

The finance department will aggregate P&L figures given by middle office for the more general P&L accounts and other reports that they produce on a longer period basis such as every month and every year.

13.2.9 Risks associated with reporting P&L

1. Inaccurate reporting: there are two potential risks here. One is simply that the number being reported as the P&L is inaccurate. This could be due to poor input data or calculation errors. Assumptions may have been made which are ignored or forgotten when the P&L is reported giving the value more credence than it deserves.

A second issue arises when the P&L cannot be accurately determined. If the trade under consideration is not currently traded in the market and the market data used in its valuation is illiquid then it is hard to derive a current fair value. Various assumptions will have to be made and their validity is open to interpretation.

2. Over reliance on P&L: important though it is, P&L should not be taken in isolation. A large proportion of current P&L will come from unrealised positions each one of which carries market risk. If market conditions change a huge potential profit could be wiped out. The P&L figures should always be read with the size of market risk in mind to arrive at a more realistic interpretation of the true state of affairs.

3. Short term P&L: imagine a company selling billions of pounds of insurance and receiving premium payments. After some time there may have been a lot of money generated and very little paid out so the P&L appears very healthy. It's time to reward the staff – the company pays them out of its big profits. Then the next day disaster happens and the insurance needs to be paid. This is very similar to what happened in the credit crunch. Too little attention was paid to trades which had made money but carried residual risk. When rewarding traders on a yearly basis there is always the danger that they will over represent the short-term profitability of their trades and ignore their overall longer term value. P&L must assess and account for all facets of the trade right up to its maturity.

4. Over reliance on the market: deriving fair value by marking-to-market is only good if the market gets it right. Recent events have shown that markets are imperfect and can make big mistakes. Although there are few alternatives to mark-to-market for determining unrealised P&L, the people using P&L figures to make business decisions should always take market imperfection into consideration.

5. Rogue trading: in theory the daily production of trade reports should make it very hard for unexpectedly large positions to develop. In practice we have seen several instances of rogue trading. Sometimes this is a malicious attempt to defraud, other times it is over enthusiastic trading without proper supervision. Again undue emphasis on P&L to the neglect of other reported figures such as positions and exposures can lead to undesired consequences. Also there is no point reporting trade positions and values if no process is in place to act upon them. The surveillance camera is only effective if someone is monitoring it.

13.3   FINANCIAL REPORTS FOR HEDGE FUNDS AND ASSET MANAGERS

Here we present some of the additional financial reports required by specialist finance companies such as hedge funds and pension and other asset managers.

13.3.1   Overview

Hedge funds and asset managers attract investors who are prepared to deposit money with the hope and expectation that it will be well managed and make a return on investment in the future. The asset manager must keep careful account of how much has been invested, when and by whom.

13.3.2   Fees

To pay their costs and make profit for their shareholders and partners, hedge funds and asset managers charge fees to investors. They can be any or all of the following:

Management fees: a global macro fund might charge 1.5 % per annum management fees. This means any investor pays this fee regardless of the performance of the fund.

Performance fees: if the fund makes profit, the hedge fund or asset manager may take a share in the form of performance fees. This could be something like 10 %. If the fund loses money there is obviously no fee payable. The performance fee provides an incentive to the fund manager.

Entry and exit fees: there may be a cost for an investor to join or leave the fund. This may be due to an additional administration overhead or to promote stability of investment within the fund.

13.3.3   Reports

In order to manage these investments, hedge funds and asset managers are required to produce extra reports:

Subscription and redemption: this documents all investments added and withdrawn from the fund.

Assets under management: this is a report of the current assets in the fund.

Performance: the fund manager must produce regular performance reports for investors. This is usually once a month but interim reports are sometimes required on demand or in special economic circumstances to give actual and potential investors due warning.

The performance report has to be externally audited to ensure that investors are being given a fair representation of the state of the fund.

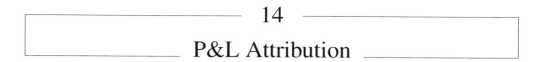

14

P&L Attribution

As discussed earlier, reporting the daily P&L is an important activity of the trade lifecycle. In addition to knowing today's P&L however, many participants would like to know how the gain or loss in P&L actually happened. A special report known as P&L attribution or P&L explained can provide this information.

Once the P&L has been calculated and compared with the previous period's calculation, it is instructive to piece together the factors that caused the changes in P&L.

14.1 BENEFITS

Reporting the P&L attribution has at least three benefits. For simplicity, we will assume the P&L is calculated daily and the P&L attribution reports between two consecutive trading days.

14.1.1 Catches mistakes

The P&L attribution puts the trade's P&L in context with other trades and with the same trade done the previous day.

In context with other trades: various mistakes in booking will be detected by putting a trade in context with its peers. For example, if a new trade was erroneously entered with 10 times more notional, then it will have an abnormally large P&L compared to similar trades.

In context with previous day: suppose a piece of market data was incorrectly used in the P&L calculation today. Then the P&L between today and yesterday would show a much higher or lower jump than expected, alerting the reader to a possible problem.

14.1.2 Reconciliation

P&L is the headline measure of how an individual trader, desk or division is doing, but the trader's personal calculation of P&L may be different from the "official" P&L calculated by middle office and used in many other parts of the organisation.

Much time can be spent each morning with traders, managers, middle office and control functions arguing over differences in P&L. The P&L attribution can drastically reduce this time by pinpointing from exactly where the P&L was derived, leading to all parties understanding the process and the trade and market inputs that lead to it.

One investment bank had three members of staff spending an average of three hours per day on investigating P&L differences. An attribution report would therefore have saved 15 expensive man hours per week!

14.1.3 Better understanding of the trades and the market

Aside from identifying problems in the trade booking and valuation process, P&L attribution is a very useful tool for traders and management to see where they are making and losing money. A trading strategy often evolves from a view on the direction one or many pieces of market data are going to take. P&L attribution quantifies profit broken down by market data groups, allowing strategies to be tested and revised.

At higher levels within the organisation too, the P&L attribution identifies which market forces are making the greatest impact on P&L. This is useful for identifying risks and capitalising on prevailing market conditions.

14.2   THE PROCESS

P&L attribution can work at any level in the P&L process, namely for individual trades, trading books, desks, divisions or company wide. The process works by calculating a series of values at the required level of aggregation and reporting each one separately as it goes. The P&L attribution is always run between two reporting dates such as yesterday and the day before, last Friday and the Friday before, last month end and the month end before.

A typical set of reported values might be:

- difference in present value
- contribution by new trades
- contribution by amended trades
- contribution by deleted trades
- contribution by trades maturing between the two dates
- cash entering or leaving
- market movements
- theta.

14.2.1   Market movements

This consists of considering all the market data that the trade or aggregation of trades is dependent upon. Each one is then taken in isolation and the changes in that market data between the two dates are applied to the trade or aggregation of trades to see its effect on present value. Examples of market movements might be interest rates, foreign exchange (FX), bonds and equities.

The analysis of market movement and other impacts is nonunique. For example, suppose yesterday to today's P&L change is broken down as follows:

(i) date change with yesterday's market data
(ii) change in market data (say interest rates moves, then FX, then equity, . . .)

This will give different answers to that of changing market rates first and then changing the date. Neither is correct or incorrect and the difference is often not large – consistency in approach is more important.

14.2.2   Theta

Even if market data remained exactly the same between the two reporting dates, the trade will change value due to the effect of time. This time effect is known by the Greek letter, theta.

Table 14.1

trade id	P&L 25-Mar-09	P&L 26-Mar-09	P&L Change	A New	B Deleted	C Amend	D Cash	E Unexplained	F MktMovement
bn6226	23 534	22 556	978	0	0	0	0	298	680
bn450f	−2206	−2115	−92	0	0	0	0	−28	−64
bn521rr	−0	34	34	−0	0	0	34	0	0
Crt	−11 742	−11 742	0	0	0	0	0	−0	0
fwc13	−720	0	−720	−720	0	0	0	0	0
fwc1146	876	0	876	876	0	0	0	0	0
fwc147	434	0	380	380	0	0	0	0	0
fwd342	434	0	434	434	0	0	0	0	0
cds_a4d	664	726	−62	0	0	0	0	−1	−61
cds_b33	0	393	−413	0	−393	0	−20	0	0
cds_c222	0	1178	−1178	0	−1178	0	0	0	0
cds_d2	1098	1201	−103	0	0	0	0	−1	−102
luy	−107	−106	−1	0	0	−1	0	−0	0
is_33	−661	−543	−118	0	0	0	0	−0	−118
repo3343	−17 210	−17 206	−4	0	0	−4	0	0	−0

(Figures in thousands of euros.)

14.2.3   Unexplained

The difference in present value between the two dates should be explained by the sum of all these stages. Any differences are called "unexplained". Some unexplained is always likely because the underlying calculations will use assumptions that will cause differences when valuations occur on two different dates. High unexplained is often a symptom of trade booking or market data errors. It is therefore useful to examine trades or aggregations of trades with high unexplained and try to deduce where the problem has occurred.

14.3   EXAMPLE

In Table 14.1 we present the P&L attribution in two stages, although it would most likely be displayed in the same spreadsheet with the two tables combined into one running from left to right across the page.

Suppose we drill down to look at all the trades in one book and calculate attribution between two business dates (25 and 26 March 2009).

First, we have the trades and the P&L values for both dates plus the change in P&L. Then we see the contribution to the change in P&L of new, deleted and amended trades together with cash transfers.

Then we have the unexplained P&L and the change caused by movements in market prices. The sum of A, B, C, D, E and F equals the change in P&L.

Now we break down the market movement into its constituent factors and show in Table 14.2 the total market movement for cross-reference back to the first table.

This particular group of trades is subject to market movements in **bond basis deltas.** This can be explained by taking an example of five year bonds in Vodafone trading at 180 basis points spread to the underlying interest rate but the five year credit default swap in the same company trading at 200 basis point spread. The basis (difference) is therefore 20 basis points. Someone who holds bonds and CDSs is paying 20 basis points. Now the impact on P&L caused by a change in the basis is defined as the bond basis delta.

Table 14.2

trade id	MktMovement	BondBasisDeltas	cdsDeltas	FX	IRDeltas	IRVegas	RecoveryDeltas	Theta
bn6226	680	332	260	0	79	0	0	8
bn450f	−64	−31	−24	0	−7	0	0	−1
bn521rr	0	0	0	0	0	0	0	0
Crt	0	0	0	0	0	0	0	0
fwc13	0	0	0	0	0	0	0	0
fwc1146	0	0	0	0	0	0	0	0
fwc147	0	0	0	0	0	0	0	0
fwd342	0	0	0	0	0	0	0	0
cds_a4d	−61	0	−62	0	2	0	0	−1
cds_b33	0	0	0	0	0	0	0	0
cds_c222	0	0	0	0	0	0	0	0
cds_d2	−102	0	−102	0	2	0	0	−1
Iuy	0	0	0	0	0	0	0	0
is_33	−118	0	0	0	−117	0	0	−1
repo3343	−0	0	0	0	−0	0	0	−0

Credit default swap (CDS) deltas: this is the change in P&L caused by a change in the credit default swap rate.

Foreign exchange: the change in P&L due to a change in foreign exchange rates.

Interest rate deltas: the change in P&L caused by a change in interest rates.

Interest rate vegas: the change in P&L caused by a change in interest rate volatility.

Recovery rate deltas: the change in P&L caused by a change in recovery rates.

Theta: this is explained above.

14.4   SUMMARY

P&L attribution is a very useful technique for understanding P&L and catching errors in some of the booking and valuation procedures. Here we have shown how the process might work.

Part III
Systems and Procedures

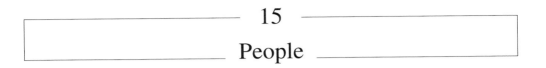

15

People

When looking into the systems and procedures of the trade lifecycle, the best place to start is with the people behind them.

A financial entity has many business activities relating to the trade lifecycle. Note that not all institutions employ all the business functions: the range and size of the organisation will dictate when specialists are required and when the same people carry out more than one function. For example, a small hedge fund might have the same person looking at market and credit risk control, manage without independent model validation and have one of the partners acting as the compliance officer.

We can divide the business functions into three broad sets:

- revenue generation
- activities that support revenue generation
- control.

We shall now discuss the various business functions.

Revenue Generation

15.1 TRADERS

The simplest form of trading is to start the day with a given amount of money and no other assets, transact trades throughout the day and finish in the evening with (hopefully) more money and no other assets. This would mean the business having no overnight risk to manage and the traders could be assessed by how much profit they brought in. Although this form of trading might exist for some very limited products, generally traders have to deal with a variety of products and assets and manage the risks associated with them.

Trading varies between the high volume and instant decision-making spot trades, to complex structures requiring weeks of preparation and scrutiny. The type of person who trades will vary according to what is being traded – different skills will be required for different markets. Some trading is very mathematical, some relies on economics and business, but all of it requires the courage and clarity to make firm decisions.

Traders bear heavy responsibility because somebody is trusting them to make return on the capital they are being given without subjecting that capital to undue risk. They are constantly involved in the present, while trying to predict the future.

Traders need to know their products and their market place; they must look out for economic and market indicators. They need to analyse a lot of information and form a view as to the direction of prices. Having formulated or been given a trading strategy, they must decide how best to implement it, while at the same time taking advantage of sudden opportunities. Conversely, they must be able to deal with reverses and trade out of risky positions, without leaving them overexposed to changes.

Broadly speaking, traders will require:

- sufficient systems and staff on hand to service their requirements;
- few bureaucratic constraints imposed upon them;
- as little time as possible spent on clerical activities, such as entering data into systems;
- fast and accurate calculations;
- the ability to manipulate input data and parameters to assess their effect on trades;
- warning of events and price movements of interest to them;
- knowledge of when they are approaching some limit on their trading activities;
- timely and accurate reporting of their profit and loss (P&L);
- easy access to market data.

15.2 TRADING ASSISTANTS

In order to maximise the time a trader can devote to his trading activities, many firms employ trading assistants. These assistants have full front office access to trading systems and sit side by side with traders on the desk. Assistants can be used in different ways:

- administrative – running processes, booking details, liaising with other departments;
- analysis – gathering data and running reports, testing theories and back testing potential or real trades;
- programmatic – developing trading tools in a rapid application development (RAD) environment. The trader specifies what he requires, the programmer puts together a quick spreadsheet or primitive system and then it is refined and improved or simply discarded;
- advisory – some trading desks have more senior and experienced staff on hand to advise or approve trades. These people are a second pair of eyes to catch errors and make suggestions; they may not be actively trading themselves.

15.3 STRUCTURERS

The job of the structurer is to put together structured and hybrid deals which are among the most complex in the financial industry (see Chapter 4 on derivatives). The structurer may trade himself or leave the execution of the structure and its components to the trading desks.

The structurer may require sophisticated valuation techniques and may have his own call on quantitative analysts and programmers. He will need access to market data for indicative and historical prices across various asset classes. He will need good communication with the sales force and the trading desks across all products and assets because his job may encompass many of the traded products in the organisation and some that are not yet traded.

He will also need the services of legal counsel to check his potential trades which might be very specific and unique. One of the key features of his work is to explain the complicated structures to clients, managers and risk control. He may need to work with them to thoroughly test and approve his ideas.

Typically, the structures take longer to be put together than simpler trades and many may be discarded without ever being transacted. It could be that the structurer only needs to put on two new structures a year to make his quota of profit, but for that he might have to try 20 structures – each one taking two weeks to construct and test.

15.4   SALES

The sales desk brings business into the firm. Salesmen inform clients of trading possibilities and encourage them to order trades, which will be executed by the traders. They put traders in touch with potential clients and advertise the products on offer. Salesmen need a good understanding of the trades and how they might benefit their clients. To attract new business, they need to know who to approach and in which organisations. To maintain existing business, they need to develop good relationships with their clients.

Activities That Support Revenue Generation

15.5   RESEARCHERS

Financial entities employ researchers to provide more information to the traders and sales force. The research might be general background information or be more specific. It may be produced periodically or at the request of a particular trading department. Some research papers are kept private within the organisation, while others are published. The reason for publishing is to enhance the company name and reputation – a good individual piece of research, or a reliable researcher whom people read for advice, will bring in clients and enhance the appeal of both the product being researched and the institution. When a new product is being marketed, it is in the interests of the institution promoting it to encourage others to participate in order to create a viable and liquid market. Research is a tool for advertisement and creating product awareness without compromising competitive business advantage; it therefore has both external and internal faces.

15.6   MIDDLE OFFICE (PRODUCT CONTROL)

Middle office, as the name suggests, sits in the middle between the traders and other business functions. It has both support and control functions. The aim of middle office is to ensure that the trade is correctly booked and all its requirements, such as an appropriate and reliable source of market data, are available so that the trade can begin its journey through the processes of the lifecycle. Middle office is sometimes referred to as product control, emphasising the control aspect of the function. The elements of middle office responsibilities can be broken down into:

15.6.1   Trade

A trade protocol will have been agreed between management, legal counsel, salesmen, traders and various control functions. Middle office will be the first to catch any new trades not adhering to the protocol. Middle office also checks that sufficient trade details have been supplied to allow successful booking of such new trades. It must also ensure that existing trades are being adequately monitored.

15.6.2   Data

Product control must ensure it has a complete and accurate supply of static and market data every time a valuation is required. The most usual time for valuation is overnight and so data must be present every evening. The price data used should be a fair indication of prevailing market conditions and may well be from a different source to that used by the traders, hence arriving at a different valuation. The valuation derived by product control is the official one and will be used in the books and records of the financial entity. In the event that price data is missing, erroneous or stale, product control must decide how to proceed. There are various data discovery and data engineering methods described in Chapter 20.

15.6.3   Implementing trade changes

The changes that might occur on a trade are described in Section 8.7.

The middle office is responsible for implementing these changes. Some require regular daily activities such as fixings. Others are irregular depending on the trade, the underlying asset or the market.

15.6.4   Reporting

Once executed the trade becomes both an asset and a risk to the organisation. Middle office must report the trade both in isolation and in aggregation with other trades to all business functions which need to know. The number and range of reports will vary according to the particular organisation concerned. The preparation, compilation and distribution of the reports are the responsibility of the middle office. Most organisations require daily, monthly and yearly reporting.

15.6.5   Valuation

One component of the suite of reports is the valuation. This is often done with particular mathematical models. Although middle office need not understand all of the intricacies of these models, it does need to know the input requirements, the running parameters and have some sense of how to interpret the results.

15.6.6   Responsibility

We do not live in a perfect world. Many organisations have to "make do" with incomplete systems which have problems or require workarounds in certain circumstances. It is essential that product control is well aware of these flaws, is able to justify the outputs in relation to inputs and knows how to act when problems arise. It bears a huge responsibility for the accuracy of the official records and is acting to preserve the integrity of the institution externally to investors, auditors and regulators and internally to management and the finance department.

15.6.7   Liaison

Middle office is the supplier of reports and information to many business functions. As such it must interact with people at all levels of the business. As well as regular reporting of current activities, it needs to respond and inform when errors or irregularities occur. It must also help to plan and design processes and reports for new business activities by defining the business requirements.

15.6.8   Processes

Due to their widespread responsibilities, middle office is required to operate a range of processes. Many of them will be performed by computer systems. Thus middle office is usually a major customer of the information technology (IT) department. Middle office needs to understand its requirements and communicate them to IT, test systems thoroughly and then operate them correctly. A key feature of computer systems is their need to be enhanced. New versions of existing systems must be thoroughly tested before their release to ensure that they continue to work as before, the only difference being the enhanced functionality. Middle office must approve any new versions before release.

15.6.9   Security

Middle office provides security to the financial entity by monitoring trading activities. It is therefore usual for middle office staff to be present at all times when trading might occur.

15.6.10   End of day

A consolidation of all the day's activities occurs towards the end of the working day. This involves the middle office checking that all trades are fully booked and that the data for overnight valuation and reporting has arrived. As in any retail bank, shop or hotel, the end of day is the time for cashing up. The principle is that the earlier a mistake is noticed, the lower the cost of fixing it.

The end of day P&L is reported by middle office but there is usually a daily discussion with the traders to allow them to comment or complain about anything they feel is unfair in the way the P&L has been derived. However, middle office has the final say in what constitutes the official P&L.

15.6.11   End of month

It is common in investment banks and hedge funds for middle office to prepare extra reports at the end of each month. These often require external checking of trades and data to ensure the fair valuation of trades for shareholders, investors and regulators. Middle office has to represent the interests of the financial entity in this process.

For some data such as volatility surfaces, it is too time consuming to gather realistic market data every day so data suppliers, such as Totem, conduct a thorough price study once a month for end of month reporting. This involves them asking, say, 20 market makers for their prices, disregarding the top two and bottom two and taking an average of the middle 16 to arrive at a representative set of market data.

For end of day, the middle office will have used data supplied by the traders. But at end of month, this is corrected to the independent value. If the traders have (deliberately or otherwise) used skewed values, these will be corrected by means of a provision.

For example:

A trader's P&L comes out as EUR 1 million using his implied volatility data.
At end of month, using the independent market data it is revised to EUR 700 000.
So a figure of negative EUR 300 000 is added to his accounts as a provision to correct the P&L.

He now carries that provision for the coming month until the next time the independent market data is used.

It generally takes somewhere in the region of three to four working days each month to derive and verify the end of month valuations and to report them to the relevant audience.

15.6.12   Summary

Having such a broad range of tasks to perform, middle office requires many different types of people including accountants, operators and administrative personnel. They need a good understanding of the products, together with careful application of the operating procedures. They need to spot when something looks amiss and pay careful attention to detail to ensure the numbers add up correctly. Apart from running reports, they should have an intuitive feel for expected results and be able to investigate problems to identify and fix them. Additionally, they require interpersonal skills to communicate with many internal and external people.

15.7   BACK OFFICE (OPERATIONS)

The back office is sometimes known as operations or "ops". Where traders agree and execute deals, it is the back office which does all the real exchange of assets, documentation and money. It is responsible for processes involving confirmation and settlement of the trade. These tasks require interaction with counterparties and custodians and sometimes with members of the exchange upon which a trade was executed. These activities are explained in Chapter 8.

Before any money is allowed out of the company, back office staff must be entirely satisfied that all payment details are correct. They must diligently process and check payment and reception instructions. As the people that sign the company cheques, they must be highly trustworthy and their activities must be clear, transparent and above suspicion.

Apart from paying counterparties, the back office department may have to pay commission to brokers and intermediaries, taxes to government agencies and fees to bodies such as exchanges.

Where custodians are not used, back office staff must account for all money received into and paid from nostro accounts. They must register holdings in bonds and shares and take possession of documentation and physical assets. Where custodians are employed, they must be supervised and accuracy checked to ensure that the company's interests are being properly managed.

Confirmation, as discussed in Section 8.3, involves close liaison with the counterparty and possibly with traders and middle office to ensure trade details are correctly recorded.

15.8   QUANTITATIVE ANALYST

The quantitative analyst (quant) is responsible for developing mathematical models for the valuation and risk management of trades. These could involve an ad hoc spreadsheet taking a few hours to put together, or a fully documented library comprising several man-years of effort. Quants very often have several roles.

15.8.1 Short-term pricing

A potential new trade may present itself to the trading desk. Before executing, the trader may want the quant to provide a rough and ready valuation of the price and sensitivities to market data movements (risks). This involves making sufficient assumptions to enable a speedy calculation, but not assuming so much that the validity of the results is compromised. Traders like to play around with different scenarios, so rather than provide one simple set of valuation results, the quant is likely to deliver a mechanism where the trade can be priced with a variety of different input data and parameters, usually by means of a spreadsheet.

15.8.2 Long-term model development

When a sufficient number or size of a particular type of trade is being transacted or the exposures caused by trades reach a certain volume, a reliable and comprehensive model is required to measure and protect the company from trade risk. The model will be customised or expressly written for each asset class and each type of trade within that asset class. Common features across asset classes or trade types may share core components of the same model.

For example, there may be an equity pricer for basic equity trades and a gold pricer for basic gold trades. But options on equities may share the same model as options on gold with variations to cater for the individual properties of equities and gold.

Outputs from models should be homogenous, so that trades valued under different models can have their results aggregated or compared.

Major new models require careful analysis of the requirements, efficient implementation, thorough testing and complete documentation. Quants often build their own testing tools, which are kept separate from the system incorporating the model.

Quants need to be aware of the operating constraints of the model they are developing, answering questions such as:

- will there be a sufficient supply of liquid market data to run the model?
- will the model run within an acceptable time period?
- can an existing model be adapted to serve a new trade type or does a new model have to be developed from scratch?

15.8.3 Tools of the trade

1. **Spreadsheets:** spreadsheets are universally popular with quants and traders because of their complete flexibility and uniformity. It is rare to find a quant who is not able to build and maintain a spreadsheet.
2. **Algorithms:** some quants are required only to develop algorithms for the models. Programmers then incorporate the algorithms into systems. Even with pure algorithms, the quant would be expected to provide thorough testing and assist in the system integration of his models.
3. **Programming:** quants have varying levels of programming skills. Depending on the organisation and the distribution of quants and programmers, quants may be required to write full or partial systems for their models using a programming language.
4. **Libraries:** a common and effective division between the work of quants and that of programmers, is to have the quants write libraries for their models. These libraries are self-contained pieces of functionality which have published interfaces for required inputs and

expected outputs. The programmers then integrate these libraries into the valuation systems, without having to know what goes on inside the model (the "black box"). Advantages of this approach are the clear separation of responsibilities, the ability to plug a testing tool into the library and the parallel development of the library and the system – as long as the interface is agreed and known, both sides can develop independently.

15.8.4   Role of quantitative analysts

Although we have listed quants as a support to the revenue generators, they can sometimes produce revenue themselves, such as when the valuation libraries are sold commercially. Generally, however, firms do not want their models known externally because they give away a competitive advantage.

Quants have three major clients for their work within the financial entity:

1. **Traders:** we have already described the activities that traders require of quants. Many mathematical trades come to fruition only as a result of a close partnership between traders and quants coupled with ongoing risk management.
2. **Market and counterparty risk control:** the risk control staff may work with or directly employ quants to develop models for accurate assessment of the risk due to market forces or exposure to counterparty debt. As they require heavy processing with lots of input data, they may also need mathematical techniques to improve efficiency.
3. **Official valuation:** quants will develop pricing and sensitivity models, as described above, to be used for the official trade valuations in order to ascertain profit and loss and to identify the risks to which a financial entity is exposed. Middle office is generally tasked with running these processes, but the reports generated are used by management, finance, market and counterparty risk control departments and external groups, such as regulators and investors. The models used for official valuation are very often identical to those used by the traders. However, the process and its required input data and parameters are not controlled by the traders.

The nature of quant work is often very academic. Quants need to take a standard mathematical approach and adapt it to suit the requirements of the trade under consideration. This requires the quant to arrive at a balance between the academic and commercial worlds. For instance, precision is a very important mathematical discipline, but in a commercial environment, compromises may have to be made due to the imperfect nature of the "real" world in which trading exists. Also there is usually a time delay between the use of commercial models and their incorporation into published academic papers.

15.9   INFORMATION TECHNOLOGY

Information Technology (IT) is a vital part of any modern financial entity. The people who design, build, operate and service these systems constitute a large and important group in the organisation because of the reliance on computer systems to perform a large number of trading processes. We shall break the IT function down into front-line support, infrastructure, architects, project managers, programmers, operators and testers and explain the human side here. Chapter 18 is devoted to IT systems.

15.9.1   Front-line support

These people are the financial paramedics. When a process fails, their job is to diagnose the problem quickly and accurately. They usually sit close to the users of the systems they are supporting. The diagnosis may be:

- user error – trying to use the system in an inappropriate way;
- hardware problem – the machine itself has a problem;
- data error – bad or missing input data;
- system error – the system is not performing the way it should.

Front-line support will advise the user where he has made a mistake, attempt to fix a hardware problem and point out why data may be invalid. In the case of a system error, they may fix it or implement a workaround to keep it operational while the problem is handed over to the people who wrote the system.

This team needs to be thoroughly acquainted with the operational requirements of the system, both the hardware and data. They must know how the system is used and, to speed diagnosis, know where to look for errors.

Having a front-line support capability benefits both the IT department and the users. More efficient use can be made of programming skills and time; programmers will not need to waste time solving user problems which may often be nothing to do with the system itself. The immediacy and availability of the front-line support instils a sense of security for the users – knowing that help is at hand when required.

If the system is third-party – supplied by an external vendor – front-line support will have to develop a relationship with the vendor. They will need to learn the system, communicate problems to the vendor, track progress with fixes and help in deployment of new versions.

15.9.2   Infrastructure

IT infrastructure staff are responsible for the computers and operating systems which support the operations running the trade processes, but not the trade processes themselves. These would include networks, cables, hardware provided by exchanges for electronic trading, personal computers and servers. They are the computer mechanics and they need a good knowledge of the machine requirements of their users and the software they are running.

IT infrastructure may also be responsible for implementing policies to preserve the integrity of the users' machines. This involves monitoring and controlling the software downloaded to machines and eliminating potential threats from viruses or hackers. They may also keep machines standardised, so that users can operate the same system in the same way from multiple locations and ensure everybody is running from the same operating system and using the same version of software.

15.9.3   Architects

For larger developments an architect may be employed. This could be for the design of a process, a database or an entire system. The architect needs a good understanding of the current and future requirements of the system he is designing. He will ensure that the technical specification is properly implemented throughout the development stage, showing prototypes and interfaces to the users on the way to the finalised system. He will also have to keep pace with updates to the specification – these are common in the constantly changing world of finance. A well thought through design, however, should cope with anticipated changes without major alteration to the system (see Chapter 18).

15.9.4   Programmers

Programmers write in-house systems and processes for users throughout the financial entity. Programmers range from the very technical (who have little contact with their clients), to the very application-focused (who interact daily with users). For a detailed description of the tasks of programmers, see Chapter 18.

15.9.5   Project managers

IT serves most other business functions and, as such, sits in the middle of the organisation. Project managers sit in the middle of IT itself. They have to oversee all the computer systems used in the trade lifecycle. A more detailed description of what they need in order to do this is in Chapter 18, but here is an outline.

15.9.5.1   Business knowledge

In order to provide an IT solution, a project manager must understand the business and its requirements. Only then can he design and manage the processes that will be built to satisfy them. The project manager must speak in business language – he is the representative of IT to the user community, which has little technical knowledge. The project manager must be able to discern and define the requirements, even when he receives only a vague outline from the user. An analogous example from the domestic appliance industry might be a washing machine user who may state that he wants clothes cleaned at an affordable price, all the other requirements being left up to the manufacturer.

15.9.5.2   Knowledge of data flow

The basic functionality of any IT system is to put data in, press a button and get data out. Understanding the flow of information throughout the firm is the basis of providing a good solution. This entails detailed knowledge of the data and the way the data is passed around.

15.9.5.3   Technical knowledge

When a solution has been agreed, the project manager will have to budget for it in terms of resources, costs and time. Estimating the time a project will take is one of the hardest aspects of project management, as it often depends on external forces. Experience will improve the estimation, as will keeping firm control of the system requirements. Any increase in functionality expected (known as "scope creep") will have a negative impact on delivery time.

15.9.5.4   Management

The project manager must control the project or projects with which he is charged. This means estimating timescales, budgeting staff and costs, monitoring and updating on progress, managing developers, as well as cajoling and encouraging, to ensure completion by the deadline. A project manager must also manage the expectations of the users. It has been said that users never appreciate a good system, but will quickly detect a bad one!

15.9.5.5 *Communication*

The project manager is in a unique position in terms of the amount of interaction he has with other business functions and his own staff. Because it is necessary for him to cross several business functions, he will develop an overall view of the processes being used across the organisation. He will also see competing priorities and pressures on limited resources which must serve many masters. His task is not to judge between them but, by appreciating what is required and the business gain achieved by each process, he will be able to advise managers of the best way forward and may be able to arbitrate between different business functions to provide a common solution, eliminating duplication. The project manager will require good communication skills and a diplomatic manner to be successful in these tasks.

15.9.6 IT operators

Operators may be required for individual processes or to control the overall trade system. Their job is to run and monitor everything and provide early warning of problems to the users affected and IT support.

Common tools employed for this task are:

1. **Heartbeat:** the system might continually report its status in various categories. For example:
   - green – everything OK
   - yellow – warning (action may be required)
   - red – error (action is required).
   The operator can monitor the heartbeat and take appropriate action.
2. **Diagnostics:** log files, performance meters, outputs from systems are all types of diagnostic tools that inform the operator about the health of the system.
3. **Statistics:** over a period of time, performance statistics can be gathered which show areas that might require improvement in efficiency or accuracy.
4. **Spot tests:** the operator might be required to make random, on the spot tests on any part of the system to ensure it is operating correctly.

15.9.7 Testers

An IT system needs thorough testing to ensure it works correctly. Programmers are notoriously bad at testing, partly because testing requires a different mentality to programming and partly because they have no motivation in finding faults in a system they have created.

Testing requires great attention to detail and a clear communication of any problems found, so that they can be reproduced and fixed. We will discuss this further in Chapter 19.

Control

15.10   LEGAL

The legal department represents the legal interests of the financial entity in many areas, but here we confine the discussion to those impinging on the trade processes. Firstly, the legal team must ensure that the trading process and the trades themselves conform to the laws of the jurisdiction in which they are transacted. They must examine the more unusual and complicated trades to ensure that the full extent of the obligations entailed are known. This is of particular relevance to insurance-type products such as credit default swaps – it is easy to sell insurance and receive regular premiums without being fully aware of the liabilities.

Lawyers may be required to arbitrate trading disputes between counterparties or between a financial entity and an exchange. An acceptable and speedy resolution to a dispute saves money, preserves the company's reputation and ensures that trading with the counterparty can be sustained.

The legal department must also act to remove or reduce the possibility of the firm being sued. In the event of any sort of litigation, the legal department would have to prepare a case and instruct barristers.

The legal department clearly needs a good understanding of trading practices and how they relate to the relevant legislation.

See Chapter 24 for more on legal issues related to trades and trading.

15.11   MODEL VALIDATION

Many larger investment banks have a team known as model validation. Its primary task is to check the models developed by the quants. This involves building a testing mechanism which is usually completely separate from the system which is used in the trade process to call the mathematical model for valuation or risk measurement. This test harness will attempt to stress the model to ensure it withstands a wide range of acceptable data inputs and rejects unacceptable inputs.

Model validation will also probe the theory behind the model, to make sure it is mathematically and commercially realistic.

Having researched the theory and tested it in practice, it may issue guidelines for use (such as limits on parameters or input data or warnings about the meaning or accuracy of results). It will check that the system in use for official valuation is producing the same results as their own test when given the same data inputs and parameters.

As well as acting as a second pair of eyes in one of the least accessible areas of the financial entity (due to the complicated nature of mathematical models), the model validation team will also impose a release control mechanism. This means that any time a new version of any pricing system is released into use it must undergo a series of tests to ensure that the changes in it have not inadvertently altered any valuations. This is done by a combination of regression and spot testing (see Chapter 19 on testing).

Model valuation tries to give an assurance that the model being used does what is says on the tin. However, there is an equally important question: is what it says on the tin really what is required? A sound management structure should ensure that this question is being asked. Model validation staff are often the most qualified people to answer because they are a control function, distant from the trading pressures experienced by quants. See Chapter 23 for more on validation.

15.12   MARKET RISK CONTROL DEPARTMENT

The market risk control department is responsible for assessing the risk to market forces to which the financial entity is susceptible. The details of market risk calculation are described in Chapter 11. Market risk must understand trades and how the various market data affects them. It needs to check individual trades as they are transacted and potential new trades before they are transacted. In addition, it must assess overall market risk by aggregation of many trades. A lot of its work is very mathematical, but sometimes experience and instinct play their part in detecting where the firm is vulnerable.

Market risk managers carry huge responsibilities. Market forces can lead to severe losses and yet prediction and calculation of these losses is not an exact science. It depends on the availability of market data and the liquidity of the products being traded.

A successful organisation will ensure that the voice and warnings of market risk managers are heard and acted upon. Market risk must therefore be as realistic as possible with its input data, assumptions and calculations.

15.13   COUNTERPARTY RISK CONTROL DEPARTMENT

The counterparty (or credit) risk control department analyses the firm's exposure to each of its counterparties, should they default and fail to meet their obligations. The details of the activities undertaken by the department are in Chapter 12. Like market risk, the counterparty risk function is essential in understanding and controlling the risk which trading generates.

Counterparty risk control has to balance the legitimate concern of traders to be able to trade as widely as possible, while seeking to protect the company from unnecessary losses. The appetite for accepting counterparty risk depends on the risk profile of the company's management and the prevailing financial climate. After the collapse of Lehman Brothers, a state approaching panic swept through the financial services industry and credit risk limits were slashed. This precipitated the credit crunch – nobody wanting to extend credit to anyone else.

15.14   FINANCE

As in any company, the books and records of the trading activities must be accurately produced and reported. This is the responsibility of the finance department. It is interested in producing aggregated views of trading, rather than looking at individual trades. It is generally dependent on other departments, such as middle office, for valuing the trades and collecting the trade details.

In addition, the department must monitor the financial health of the company, together with its actual and anticipated assets and liabilities. At regular intervals they must prepare budgets for all departments' future spending. At times they may have to advise on expenditure cuts and therefore need to know the value as well as the cost of all the company's activities.

15.15   INTERNAL AUDIT

Internal audit is a monitoring function deliberately designed to be independent of other business functions. It reports directly to senior management. It is in some respect the internal police force, monitoring how well the processes being undertaken adhere to the company guidelines. It also investigates and thinks through current operating processes and advises on omissions, risks and improvements that could be made. The purpose of audit is to identify risks and provide some measure of the impact of ignoring risks.

Although other departments may view them with suspicion, the purpose of audit is to protect the company's assets and ensure smooth operation of its systems. It can be a useful external pair of eyes, providing an alternative perspective and ensuring that all sections of the company are acting in the best interests of the whole. Uniquely, it gets to see all systems and processes and can advise where there is duplication.

The department operates in two ways:

15.15.1   Routine checks

These are carried out periodically or on predefined occasions, such as every time a new trade type is approved. The check will involve the testing of rules imposed by the company to make sure that breaches are being acted upon and do not go unnoticed. Examples of rules could be:

- no single trade imposing an obligation of more than a certain amount upon the company;
- no one trader having exposures greater than a certain amount;
- settlement always being carried out by at least two staff;
- no trading being conducted on mobile phones;
- all trades being booked within one hour of execution;
- failure to produce P&L reported to senior management on every occasion.

It is not generally the task of the audit department to take action itself – that is left for the appropriate member of staff in the business function concerned. Depending on the seriousness of the breach, audit will expect certain measures to be taken.

15.15.2   Thorough audit of one area

Generally auditors will from time to time pick upon a particular business function or process and carry out an in-depth investigation. For example, they might examine the commodities settlements process, compare it with other settlements within the same organisation and in other organisations and come out with a series of recommendations for improvement. These are known as audit points. The audit points are divided by their seriousness and each one is given a deadline by which it must be addressed. Audit will often carry out a follow-up check to see how things have progressed in the interim.

15.16   COMPLIANCE

The role of compliance is to ensure that people and processes comply with the law. Two of the most relevant laws to the financial services industry are money laundering and insider training. It is the responsibility of compliance to devise procedures to ensure these laws are not being broken and to ensure adherence to them.

15.16.1   Due diligence

The compliance officers must also ensure that trade with counterparties is conducted with due diligence. This means that the background of the counterparty is checked to make sure it is a bona fide institution and not a front for criminal activities. Suspicious counterparty requests, such as offering to take on trades at an obvious loss, must be reported to the relevant regulatory authority and the police.

15.16.2   External regulation

Since financial services are vital to the national and international economy, governments have imposed a system of regulation on those undertaking such services. This is to enhance confidence, protect the honest and law-abiding majority from the illegal actions of the minority and to ensure a level of competence is maintained to protect investors and clients outside the industry.

   This regulation is implemented by various bodies such as the Financial Services Authority and the Securities and Futures Authority. The compliance officer must liaise with regulators, who might request inspection of trading documents, investigate trading procedures and conduct spot checks.

15.16.3   Staff training

Compliance must educate its staff in their legal responsibilities. It might conduct periodic training sessions or provide material, such as videos and interactive questionnaires, to keep staff abreast of the latest rules and regulations.

15.17   TRADING MANAGER

The trading manager is the trader's immediate supervisor. He must agree a trading strategy with each of the traders reporting to him. He will allocate them a limit on asset holding and indicate an expected profit to be made within a given timescale. There will also be discussion about how to control risks. For leveraged trades such as options, there will be a limit on exposure.

   For example, a manager has a desk with six traders. Two are tasked with short-term and arbitrage-type trading, two do medium-term swaps and two do longer-term trading based on economic fundamentals. The expected returns and associated risks are spread across the desk and the manager can monitor the situation.

   There will be an implicit understanding that should the trader lose more than a certain amount of the assets entrusted to him, he will be asked to leave. This might be something in the region of 40 %, but will depend upon the volatility of the market and risk appetite of the institution for which he is trading.

   The trading manager is the first point of control on the activities of the trader. He should monitor the type and size of trades and ensure that limits are being adhered to. Quite often the trading manager is himself trading, and so he has to combine the two disciplines.

15.18   MANAGEMENT

The management bears responsibility for the financial entity and is accountable to shareholders and investors. Managers must decide priorities, resolve conflicts and ensure the well-being of the institution, by understanding and controlling the risks. Generally, they will set trading limits to ensure that potential losses are contained.

15.18.1   Balance

There is always a need to balance the pursuit of extra revenue through trading, with controlling the risks that trading brings. The appetite for risk will determine where this line is drawn. Risk comes in many forms and once the general risk appetite is determined, an exploration of where to allow and where to prevent risk can be applied to define a management policy for the running of the institution.

15.18.2   Board of directors

The board of directors is the highest decision-making body in the financial entity. The composition of the board can give an insight into the balance of power between revenue generation and control. If senior managers of control functions, such as counterparty and market risk, sit on the board alongside the trading management, it indicates control is considered of high importance. Most support functions, such as IT, will report to the trading management at subboard level.

15.19   HUMAN RISKS

Inevitably, a trading organisation relying on human beings is going to be subject to human risk. Here we list some of the common risks.

15.19.1   Too much knowledge in one person

If an individual is particularly good at his job because of his greater knowledge, experience or application, it is often tempting to give him more responsibility and a greater share of the overall burden of work. Other people do not see the need to study his area of expertise, because they know he can be relied upon. This causes a knowledge risk, where an area of the trading lifecycle is left solely in the hands of one individual. If that individual should leave the firm or become ill, there will be nobody to replace him. Although it may seem like a waste of resources, it is always important that every area has sufficient back-up. Too many organisations have failed to recognise their over reliance on one person until it is too late and he or she has departed.

15.19.2   Not enough knowledge

This is one of the greatest risks to any organisation. Sometimes the management of a particular trading area becomes convinced that a type of trade or trading strategy is foolproof and certain to bring in risk-free profits. Trading commences but suddenly the lack of proper understanding is exposed to great cost. It may seem absurd that financial entities specialising in financial products with strict internal and external controls should be able to engage in trading that is misunderstood, but it happens surprisingly frequently. Even when controls and procedures are in place, if the fundamental behaviour of the product is not known, these will be of little benefit.

It is not just in trading that a lack of knowledge can be risky; the trade lifecycle is a chain of processes and is therefore only as strong as it is at its weakest point.

Although training is often provided, particularly to junior staff, there is a tendency to consider a new product as a modification of existing products or to borrow techniques from one asset class into another. These assumptions can lead to incorrect processing and added risk. All new trades and structures should be thoroughly understood and the information disseminated to *everybody* involved in the trade lifecycle.

15.19.3   The wrong people

Each business function has its particular demands and responsibilities. Personality and outlook play a part in how well an individual suits his business function. Examples:

- Back office must be diligent, calm and responsible while dealing with large sums of money.
- Market risk must speak out and not be afraid to challenge the traders when they see potential problems.
- Trading managers (especially ex-traders) must sometimes suppress their entrepreneurial tendencies and take into account advice from control functions.

Since large amounts of money are at risk, a trading environment can be very stressful. It is essential that this is considered when selecting individuals to fill the business functions.

15.19.4   Not enough investment in people

There is sometimes a tendency to believe that computers can solve all the problems and only minimal staffing levels are required in some business functions. If things are going fine, this may well be the case. But for the unusual, the unplanned or the unlikely, computers will not be able to step in and sort out the problem. Appropriate levels of staffing must be maintained. The balance between humans and machines is hard to gauge, but broadly speaking, computers should deal with the ordinary and expected and human beings the more specialist or unusual circumstances.

Whenever computers are running processes, it should never be assumed that they have performed the task correctly on every occasion – even if a process has run successfully 200 times in succession, there is always a chance of a problem on the next run.

15.19.5   Incentive

People need to be compensated for the time and effort they spend doing their jobs. Extra incentives to perform well in the form of annual bonuses are a feature of the financial services industry. Bonuses do, however, lead to problems. They are meant to be performance related and foster greater individual and group attainment. In some areas such as sales and trading, contribution to the overall revenues can be assessed and divided reasonably fairly. This is much harder to achieve in support and control functions. Here the bonuses may not be allocated meritoriously because the contribution of staff cannot be compared. An unfair bonus distribution weakens morale, enhances stress and leads to decisions being made with an eye to the effect on bonus, rather than for the overall good of the firm.

One major investment bank has recently put up base salaries for control and support staff to be equal to comparative jobs in other industries, while decreasing the bonus pool. It remains to be seen whether there is a positive or negative effect on productivity, but certainly many staff would prefer a stable salary rather than a variable bonus.

15.19.6   Short-term thinking

Allocating bonuses, fixing budgets and deciding strategies have traditionally been annual events in the financial sector. This leads to all tasks being driven around a yearly cycle. At the end of the year, the balls are thrown up in the air and everything starts again. Many activities require longer term planning and execution, especially IT projects.

The pressure on management strategies to think no more than one year ahead trickles down through all levels and all business functions. Although a longer term position may be more appropriate, such considerations are sacrificed for short-term gain.

There are obvious risks in working to short-term timescales. Trades are often designed to post profit quickly, while long-term negative effects are overlooked.

Longer term trading could be safer and more profitable, but does not receive sufficient consideration because nobody will be around to draw bonuses from it.

15.19.7   Conflicts and tensions

In any commercial environment there are bound to be tensions and the stress of investment banking can accentuate them. However, some tensions arise from the very nature of the business functions and these are important to ensure trading is conducted with an appropriate level of control. When one or other side gains too much power, there could be risk to the business.

1. Trading versus control functions: the most obvious tension is between traders and the control functions. Counterparty and market risk control departments are responsible for reducing risks. If they refused all trading, there would be no risk, but of course then there would be no business and no one to pay their salaries. Since traders are the revenue generators for everybody, there may be a tendency to allow traders more freedom than would be the case if the control functions were financially supported from elsewhere. Similarly, a member of product control, objecting to the trader's view of the current market price, may be afraid to raise an objection, knowing that his career and bonus depend on keeping the traders happy.

Recently it was disclosed that a senior member of market risk sitting on the board of a major investment bank had raised objections to the risky nature of the trading activities and very soon afterwards was removed from his post. After the credit crunch it became clear his warnings were correct and major damage would have been avoided had they been heeded.

Conversely, in a cautious environment, genuine trading under reasonable controls can be thwarted by over zealous control functions. The senior management must allow healthy debate between all sides and monitor the situation continuously to ensure a fair balance is maintained.

2. Trading versus trading: support staff are present to create and enhance the traders' ability to generate revenue. The better the level of support, the greater the chances of the trader making money.

However competition between trading desks can lead to duplication of resources. Traders often want their own support services and systems. They want staff at hand who know their business and can adapt to their requirements quickly. If resources, such as IT developers, have to be shared between trading desks, the traders may worry they will lose control. In order to increase their power and importance, some traders insist on having their own highly focused systems even when a wider scope may be more advantageous to the institution as a whole.

The support staff themselves may prefer working for one business area; serving two masters may not be ideal and requires strong management to ensure priorities and resources are fairly distributed.

3. Trust: finance is a complicated industry. Some business functions perform very specialised jobs and their skills and knowledge are not shared by other business functions. This means that there must be trust between the various departments in order for systems and processes to be designed and run effectively.

Traders invest a great deal of trust in quants to provide suitable models. The trader may have some knowledge of the underlying model, but he will not have the time to understand all the details, nor should he. His time is better spent on trading, leaving the quant to work on the models.

Another example is the business managers entrusting the IT project managers and staff to build reliable systems. IT is very often seen from the outside as a mysterious and expensive operation. A manager of a business function requiring a new process to be written will have to agree a budget and scope for the project and then entrust the rest to the IT department.

Investing too much trust in any department or person might give them too much scope to make errors before they are caught and dealt with from outside. Too little trust will stifle productivity, cause resentment and waste time. The best way is for a balance to be struck where the specialist is trusted sufficiently to do his job without undue interference, but there are enough checks and balances to deal with problems as they arise and before it is too late.

15.19.8   Communication

We have discussed a very wide range of business functions all acting upon some part of the trade lifecycle. In order for all the pieces to work together there must be communication. This communication must operate at all levels:

- peer to peer within the same business function;
- employee to manager within the same business function;
- peer to peer across different business functions;
- manager to manager across different business functions;
- peer to peer between trading counterparties;
- to external regulators and investors from within the organisation.

Mistakes are very common where communication is missing or inadequate. Also, the wrong media for communication might cause the message to be lost. For example:

- Sending an email to a trader warning that he is approaching his trading limit might be ineffective when he receives over 1000 emails a day.
- Leaving a phone message for back office to investigate a missing settlement might not get delivered and the settlement never be received.

- Too many interdepartmental meetings might lead to key staff not attending because they are wasting too much time and thereby important discussions and communications might be missed.

A modern financial entity employs people from all around the world. Language may be an issue. Even where everybody is expected to speak a common language, nuances and expressions often communicate beyond words and these can be misinterpreted by non-native speakers of the language. Clear written documentation is sometimes less ambiguous, but this too relies on people reading it and it can be time consuming to produce.

15.20 SUMMARY

The processing of the trade lifecycle requires a wide range of people to work harmoniously together. Human beings are a major cause of problems in the lifecycle and so an analysis of the part they play and how they fit together can lead to a better understanding of the risks and a more successful operation.

16

Developing Processes for New Products (and Improving Processes for Existing Products)

16.1 WHAT IS A PROCESS?

We consider a process to be an activity performed on a trade or related to the existence of a trade. Examples of processes are:

- book trade in a system
- calculate fair value of a trade
- settle a trade
- stress test a trade under different scenarios of market conditions.

Processes run the entire business of trading. These occur at all stages of the trade lifecycle. They can be automated by computers, operated by human hand or a mixture of both. Later in this chapter, we will discuss the building and running of a brand new process, but before that we will describe a common situation in many financial entities.

16.2 THE STATUS QUO

There is an old joke about a man who is asked how to get from Liverpool to Birmingham: he answers, "if you want to go to Birmingham, don't start from Liverpool!" Many organisations have a complete tangle of existing processes and anyone trying to rationalise them would be better off starting again from scratch. Let us try to understand why processes very often turn into a tangled and disorganised mess and in doing so, we will see how difficult it can be to build and maintain processes for a trade lifecycle.

16.3 HOW PROCESSES EVOLVE

Stage 1 – toe in the water: a typical foray into the trading of new products or trading in new markets begins with a trader and a spreadsheet, possibly with some client enquires. The trader analyses the market and the products, working out where he can make money, either by trading for himself or through fees charged to the client. He puts together sample trades with sample market prices and starts a virtual book. He trials the book for a limited time and if successful, he seeks approval from his manager and the risk control functions. If they are happy, he begins transacting real trades under tight limits. Then some rudimentary processes are implemented, probably cloning those already in existence for similar products and "tweaking" them to cope with any differences. If the trade is not covered by the existing processes, a new process is built quickly and bolted on top. Figure 16.1 shows the evolution of these processes.

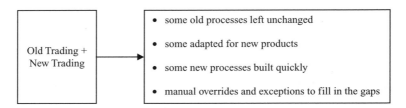

Figure 16.1   Evolution of processes

Even though each new trade might require much more human work because it involves an entirely new process or adjustments to an existing process, the volumes are low enough for the institution to manage.

Stage 2 – ready to swim: there comes a point when the original trading concept has been tested and deemed worthy of more extensive trading. The limits are adjusted and greater volumes are expected. Then the processes have to be upgraded. Sometimes it is a requirement to have working processes in place before the green light for further trading is given – then there is real business pressure to upgrade.

While a human being can be trained relatively easily to do something unusual or different from his previous experience, a computerised system requires programming and extensive testing. Some systems are easy to change because they have been designed to be flexible; others are more fixed and inflexible. Also, many processes feed systems outside the direct control of the financial entity and are therefore tied to the requirements of the external system.

As explained in Chapter 18 on IT systems, there are different approaches to developing systems. These range from a rapid application development (RAD) designed for speedy implementation, but not meant to last long; through to a fully integrated, robust solution taking years to build, but lasting for decades. The RAD approach is more common in front office and risk control; the fuller system, for the back office and finance areas.

Now we are ready to swim, more robust systems are required and those responsible for processes have to make a decision – to extend the current processes or implement new ones. It may be impossible to extend what is there and too time consuming or costly to implement a full system, so again there may have to be a compromise.

Typically, front office and risk management will have a new process, while the back office and finance processes will be adapted to fit those already in existence.

It is not uncommon to find a person in some business functions employed solely to work around the limitations of an automatic system. For example, there may be a back office settlement system designed for spots and futures. As the system cannot cope with options, someone has to book exercised options as futures after the exercise date, so that the system can process them.

Another example is a very popular data provider who developed a system based around the old DOS operating system. As greater functionality was added to the system, it became too costly to replace the original user interface with something more modern. It has now reached the point that they employ hundreds of people to train and help users work with the existing system, instead of rewriting it from scratch.

Stage 3 – training for the Olympics: eventually the trading of the new product is entrenched in the organisation. There is a perception that the current processes are operationally risky or not robust enough to cope with the trading volumes. Then a decision is taken to build fully satisfactory processes and systems. This involves designing and building a proper platform and infrastructure. By now the needs of the particular products are fully understood, the weak processes have been exposed and all of the accumulated knowledge and experience can be harnessed into building processes that will last well into the future.

16.4   INVENTORY OF CURRENT SYSTEMS

With our introductory look at how processes evolve, we can see the type of processes that might arise. Depending on the individual organisation, any of the following issues could be encountered.

Redundancy: a process has been superseded by another process that may be cheaper or more efficient to run. The users of the original process are not aware of the new one and so the institution is incurring greater cost or more risk by operating two processes to do the same function. Even if everybody has stopped using the old process, it may continue to be maintained, because nobody is sure that it is no longer used – this will add to cost and divert resources. (See Chapter 21 on reporting for an example.)

Partial duplication: sometimes a new process almost does the work of an old process, but not quite. This means that both processes have to be maintained when a simple rationalisation might lead to more efficiency. The reasons for partial duplication are lack of awareness or nobody being in sufficient control of the whole operation to be able to make the decision to merge them.

Legacy systems: many systems have run so successfully that there has been no incentive to change them. Even though the environment around them has moved on, they have been left alone with the maxim "if it ain't broke, don't fix it". The problem is that as time goes on, they become harder to maintain because fewer people possess the technical expertise that was used to build them. Sometimes new circumstances arise which were not envisaged at the time of implementation. This leads to a desperate search for a workaround or alternative solution.

A classic example is the old Cobol mainframe, which stored only two digits to designate the year, because storage space for data was at a premium. This was no problem in the 1970s and nobody thought the systems would still be in use 20 or 30 years later when the date changed to 2000. This created what became known as the millennium bug.

Planning: take three cities:

- New York has a near perfect system of streets and avenues numbered logically making orientation around the city very easy.
- Paris has 12 beautifully straight avenues converging at the Arc de Triomphe.
- London has a maze of streets with no logical order, frustrating natives and visitors – it takes taxi drivers up to four years to acquire sufficient knowledge to get a licence.

What is the reason for these differences? New York was planned from the outset; central Paris was demolished and rebuilt; London evolved without any planning.

Looking back, it's amazing to see how processes became so entangled and complicated. To plan effectively, one needs:

- thorough knowledge of what will be required in the future;
- sufficient budget to execute the plan;
- agreement of all involved to discontinue their existing processes and adopt the new ones when they are ready.

There can also be a tendency to over engineer a solution, either to give it more functionality than will ever be needed or to take into account every possible contingency "just in case". This can lead to a waste of resources or for the solution to take too long to be completed, hampering the advancement of the business.

Politics: much investment is expended in certain systems and processes and, even when everybody knows they have failed, it is politically too costly to abandon or replace them. Many people spend much of their working lives using substandard systems to save someone higher up in the organisation losing face.

It worked elsewhere: many processes are copied between business areas or from one financial entity to another. This may well be appropriate, but careful investigation should be made and each case treated according to its own circumstances. Even slight differences may cause greater operational risk or time wasting. The clever designer will combine past experience with local knowledge to build the most effective solution.

Consolidation: sometimes the business takes the view that it is better to consolidate two existing processes into one, in order to save the cost of rebuilding. This can work if it is carefully managed and if the two processes are doing very similar tasks and working with the same or similar format of input and output data.

Consolidation can, however, be far from smooth because processes are made to do tasks for which they were not designed. Maintenance and enhancement is then hampered because, even though the original design may have been simple, it has now become entangled. Very often a consolidated process is unintuitive to the new or inexperienced user – this leads to a greater risk of mistaken use or failure.

16.5   COPING WITH CHANGE

All businesses change over time, none more so than in the financial sector. Processes designed for one time have to be adapted and modernised. This can be achieved by incremental enhancement or by rebuilding from scratch. The degree to which a process can be enhanced depends largely on its design. If, for example, a process was built for any asset class and happened to be used for interest rates, it may be easy to enhance it to incorporate foreign exchange. But a bespoke commodity system may be very hard to change for any other asset class.

The popular method – but not always the best one – for dealing with change is to use a spreadsheet to cope with an unusual trade. This will require another spreadsheet to feed from the original one and so on, until the one unusual trade has evolved an entire alternative system of spreadsheets. This involves far more human effort and much greater audit and other risks than those arising from trades booked through established processes.

Dependency on IT: for fixing actual problems in the computerised processes, one would expect to make a call to the IT department. However, sometimes regular processes become dependent on IT, even though they do not have faults. This is because the process involves accessing the database or some other media beyond the control of the users. Instead of building a user interface to control and run the process, the system has been left partially or fully operated by the IT department. This can be costly and inefficient. It also takes control away from the user, making him unnecessarily dependent on others, which will hamper his ability to perform his daily tasks.

16.6   IMPROVING THE SITUATION

Whether a process is run manually or automated by computer, careful planning is required to improve it. The status quo should not be assumed to be the only option available. It may well be possible to improve the current situation without resort to building new computerised systems, by reorganising or rationalising those that already exist. We discuss computer-run processes in Chapter 18 on systems. Here we look at how to go about improving processes in general.

We assume that an institution has a set of processes making up the trade lifecycle and activities relevant to it, and that someone has been tasked with improving the current situation. He may be a project manager, a business manager or some other coordinator, but here we shall refer to him as the auditor.

16.6.1   What would the ideal set of processes be?

In order to evaluate the strengths and weaknesses of the current set of processes, the auditor needs to take a fresh look at what is required, without being influenced by what is there now. This will clarify what the processes' objectives are and show how well the existing systems are satisfying those requirements.

This consideration should take into account:

- purpose – what are we trying to achieve?
- audience – who requires these processes?
- times – ideally when should processes start and by when should they finish?
- data – what data should be used (and what data does not need to be used)?
- systems – what systems do we have available for running these processes?
- human resources – which staff are available, what skills do they have, what are they good at, what are they not good at?

16.6.2   Understanding the current processes

Before any new processes can be considered, it is important to understand what is currently in existence. Questions which might arise from this investigation are:

16.6.2.1   Where are the bottlenecks?

A bottleneck occurs when a process takes so long to complete that it prevents other processes from running smoothly. The reason why it is finishing late could be either because it is taking a long time to run or because it is starting late.

16.6.2.2   What are the time consuming processes?

Even if a process is not a bottleneck, it could be taking longer than is necessary. This might place an unnecessary burden on human or other resources.

16.6.2.3   Where are the dependencies?

A thorough understanding of the dependencies of current processes is vital before any improvements can begin. Dependencies can be upon other processes, data or particular members of staff.

16.6.2.4   Where is there duplication with other processes?

Duplication could be within the same business area or in a completely different area. The person auditing the current processes needs a wide enough mandate to investigate all relevant processes if he is to spot duplications. Duplication could be partial or total. It should be possible to completely remove a totally duplicated process. Sometimes two processes may seem to do the same thing, but they may draw data from two different sources and therefore the removal of one of them might not be so simple.

16.6.2.5   Where are the weak points?

The weak points in a process – or chain of processes – may be obvious, but sometimes they require a subjective opinion from someone with experience of how processes should work. Some points to consider are:

- too much reliance on one person
- too many errors
- too many failures to complete
- too important to be run the current way – an important process may need better protection or more people knowing how to operate it.

16.6.2.6   What is not needed?

Sometimes an institution may be paying for resources that are not required, either because processes have evolved to the point where they are no longer needed or because they were purchased for a contingency that was never used. Examples are:

- hardware – machines not being used
- networks
- software – systems or libraries
- people – consultants or external contractors
- data – third-party supplied data
- trading services – for example, barges to store crude oil that the company no longer deals in.

16.6.2.7   What are the overall requirements?

It is easy to get lost in the minutiae of processes and fail to see the wood for the trees. While it is important to look at each individual process, the aim of the exercise is to consider the overall purpose of all the processes.

For example, it could be that a process has been run for a long period, even though it actually achieves nothing – the original reason for having it has long since been lost. The process may seem perfectly reasonable at a micro level, but viewed from a higher perspective, it is obviously completely useless.

In order to put the processes in context, the overall picture must be understood. Then the underlying requirements on people, data and systems can be mapped. Also, the overall purpose can be reappraised to ensure that it still remains valid. In other words, does the current set of processes really do the job for which they are intended?

16.6.2.8   Methods of understanding

The above may seem like a reasonable approach in theory, but actually conducting a process audit can be very difficult in practice. Here are some suggestions.

- Survey the staff. Question the people responsible for tasks in the lifecycle and find out who does what and when.
- Follow the data. Data enters the processes, is processed and then leaves in the form of reports. By tracking the data from source to sink, one can build a view of all the processes operating on it.
- Flow diagram. Processes are essentially workflows: joining the dots between workflows and building up a flow diagram gives a good visual indication of the current situation and reveals gaps where undiscovered processes may be operating.
- Constraints. Knowing the full extent of the constraints under which the current processes are being operated will further enhance the audit.
- Documentation. When all else fails, read the manual! Documentation of current processes may exist and be helpful. There is, however, the possibility that the document is out of date, in which case it can provide an incomplete or inaccurate picture.

16.6.2.9   Recommendations

Having looked at how things should work in an ideal world and how things are operating in practice, the auditor can assess the shortfall (also known as a gap analysis) and come up with suggestions or recommendations. The purpose is to facilitate decision-making. Therefore, as much relevant information should be gathered as possible and then condensed into the most pertinent points for the decision makers. Table 16.1 shows an example report.

The report can refer to appendices for the full background to each recommendation.

16.7   INERTIA

One of the biggest obstacles to changing existing processes is inertia. Staff grow used to their current modus operandum and know how to work around any idiosyncrasies and problems,

Table 16.1

Recommendation	Benefits	Cost of new process
Combine all commodity trade booking into one process	Reduce mistakes. Save 3 man-days per week	Training and testing time – no new systems to develop
Automate confirmation generation for swaps	Confirmations will complete $\frac{1}{2}$ day quicker than at present	3 months for development and delivery of new system

however inefficient they may be. They are suspicious that new processes may bring new and unknown dangers, make their working day longer or more complicated or make their jobs redundant.

There is also the cost of change, which involves staff having to learn the new process, test it thoroughly and deploy it within the organisation. Usually these steps have to be undertaken while still preserving and running the old process (which cannot be switched off until the new process is fully functional). This inevitably leads to more work and to the complication of having to run two processes simultaneously.

It often helps when implementing a new process to explain to the people concerned what the benefits are – easier operation, fewer mistakes, less stress, being able to leave work earlier in the evening etc. Since the staff concerned are going to be the ones switching off the old process and starting the new, it is much easier if they understand why the processes are being changed.

Another method of overcoming inertia is the involvement of management at a sufficiently high level. Once convinced of the benefits of a new process or processes, the management can enforce a smooth transition.

When to change: timing plays a big part in the progression to new processes. Often processes change when new leadership of a business area takes over or when people used to the old methods leave. Sometimes a substantial loss to the business caused by a failure of the current processes leads to a sudden demand for radical overhaul. In other cases, change happens gradually – one process here and another one there – until eventually everything that needs changing has been replaced.

16.8 SUMMARY

However good or bad the current set of processes is, there is always going to be some level of operational risk associated with them. The more accurate the information about the current processes, the easier it is to assess the risks and know how to contain and reduce them.

As well as running a business that is seeking to optimise revenues and profit, the business management must understand their costs and how, if necessary, to reduce them. They must also know, as far as possible, the risks of taking on more of the same business or expanding into new business areas.

17

New Products

Trading is continually evolving in the financial industry. An organisation must be able to keep up and in order to do so must have procedures for transacting new products. By new products we mean new trading types or new asset classes; not transacting more of existing trade types.

17.1 ORIGIN OF NEW PRODUCTS

The desire to transact new products might come about for a variety of reasons.

Opportunities: traders and structurers are always seeking ways of making money. Sometimes they or someone else in a financial entity may spot a new opportunity. This could be through a modification to an existing trade or a completely new type of trade.

As the world of commerce evolves, so does the financial industry serving it. For example the new breed of weather derivatives has arisen recently to fulfil a need to insure against adverse weather.

As trading matures in any existing area, the market becomes well understood and well populated leading to a reduction in profit making opportunities. This sometimes has the effect of pushing businesses to look for greener pastures.

People joining the organisation: it may seem a cliché but the biggest asset of a financial entity is its staff. Being a service industry with very little physical infrastructure such as plants and machinery, a finance house distinguishes itself from its peers by the skills and application of its employees.

To grow a new business area staff with specialist skills are often deliberately targeted from outside. This could be traders, salesman, structurers, quantitative analysts or anyone else who can provide a revenue generating advantage. Together with the revenue generators, support and control staff may be recruited if those currently within the organisation do not have sufficient expertise to handle the new products and cannot be taught to do so in sufficient time.

Clients: a client expects a bank to service its requirements. If this entails something new then the bank may have to embrace it in order to satisfy the client and maintain its reputation.

A complicated structure put together for a client may not directly lead to new trading but, if there is a sufficient quantity of such structures being requested or a common component can be extracted from the structure and traded as a standalone instrument, this can lead to the birth of a new trade.

Keeping up with the Joneses: being a very competitive industry, it is essential for a financial entity to keep an eye on the activities of its peers. Stakeholders in a bank or asset manager will ask questions of managers who are not embarking on business that can return them profits.

Due to high turnover of staff and much interaction between the front office of different financial entities, it is difficult for new business ideas to remain secret. Also, in many cases it is to the advantage of a company promoting new business to build a market place for the new product. It can still retain its competitive advantage by understanding the product better than its rivals or by bringing in more business through a greater connection to clients wanting it to trade the product on their behalf.

17.2   TRIAL BASIS

17.2.1   Why trial?

It is rare for an organisation to be fully ready to embrace a new trading type. Trading a new type of trade therefore incurs additional risks and costs. The benefits of the new trade may still be uncertain and so the organisation is reluctant to commit itself until more is known.

The risks arise from having less knowledge of the product and how it might behave. Models for validation may have to make more assumptions to cover for this lack of knowledge and the product is likely to be relatively illiquid in the early days of trading. Market risk control will have to assign more risk to the trade to cover the greater uncertainty.

Operational risks are higher because processes have not yet been designed for this trade. More processes will have to be run manually and a workaround to existing processes designed to fill any gaps between what is available and what is required. This is likely to be more expensive in terms of labour and introduce a greater susceptibility to errors.

To contain the risks and limit the costs, permission might be granted for a new trade to be transacted on a trial basis for a short period of time such as one month. If successful the trial might be extended or trading on the new product fully adopted.

17.2.2   Features of the trial

Here are some of the possible features of a trial period for a new trade.

1. **Limited quantity of trades:** the trader is only allowed to trade up to a certain number of trades during the trial.
2. **Limited size of trades:** the notional size of any one trade or the trades in aggregation may be limited.
3. **Limited risk:** the amount of money at risk from the new products will be limited.
4. **Limited counterparties:** the organisation may be reluctant to jeopardise or restrict current trading lines with good counterparties and so may opt for new trading with selected counterparties only. In addition it does not want to deal with counterparties who are not able to transact and settle the new products.
5. **Limited direction and scope of trading:** examples are:
   - The organisation may insist that only purchases are allowed on the new trade.
   - For options they may allow calls but not puts.
   - For credit derivatives they may only be permitted on investment grade names.

17.2.3   Advantages of the trial

Controlled environment for testing: in the same way that an engine manufacturer tests a new design first by computer simulation and then by building a working model, so the management of a financial entity may want a controlled test of a new product before committing resources and risking the firm's capital to full trading. The trial period gives them an opportunity to evaluate the product and if it loses money, the downside will be limited.

Opportunity for improvements: while the trial is running mistakes can be rectified and experience gained in how to trade and manage the new products. Also, it is much easier for designers and implementers of new processes and systems to learn from a working example than from abstract ideas.

Due diligence: it may be necessary for due diligence imposed by the external regulators or internal procedures that the trial be conducted before full trading is allowed.

More data to be available: as more participants enter the market, prices become liquid. Having a trial increases the chances of the product being liquid when full trading commences. Liquid products are generally seen as being advantageous for a variety of reasons explained elsewhere. See Chapter 6 for an overview.

In addition, the presence of an independent data source for market prices is very helpful for middle office in particular and reporting in general. As products become more liquid, independent data providers can include them in their daily or intra-day publications.

Wait for exchanges and systems to catch up: exchange traded products are generally regarded as less risky and many institutions prefer dealing on exchanges rather than OTC. They may therefore wait for a product to become available on the exchange before trading it.

In addition, an institution relying on a third-party vendor for its systems may need to give the vendor time to catch up with developments in the market place before a system incorporating the new products will be ready.

17.3   NEW TRADE CHECKLIST

Whether or not a new trade is transacted on a trial basis initially, there are various stages that have to be completed for trading to start.

17.3.1   Management approval

Firstly, there must be a sound business case for the new trade. A manager with sufficient authority in the organisation will need to grant approval on a trial or full basis to the new trading activity. He will have to be satisfied that there is sufficient understanding of the product that it can be traded successfully and the risks associated with it can be managed. There must also be sufficient control and support for the product available within the organisation.

17.3.2   Legal and regulatory approval

Lawyers retained or employed by the institution will have to check the new trading activity is legal and that the institution fulfils any legal responsibilities arising from the trading. In particular they will have to agree documentation with every intended counterparty for the new trade.

If the new trading activity falls outside the current regulatory registration, the regulator will have to be informed and grant permission.

17.3.3   Trading limits

The trading management will set trading and risk limits as for any other product. They will generally be more cautious with new products especially if there is no trial period.

17.3.4   Risk control limits

Market and counterparty risk control will need to study the new product and ensure they have sufficient expertise to set limits and test to ensure they are not being breached on a regular basis.

17.3.5   Models

Where the new trade is reliant on a mathematical model for present value or sensitivity analysis, this will need to be available and have been checked by model validation (see Chapter 23). It is often the case that the quantitative analysts are the first to become familiar with a new product and they must convey their understanding to other business functions such as managers, risk control departments and middle office.

17.3.6   Trade lifecycle processes

In order to transact the new trade all key stages of the trade lifecycle must be supported. This could start on a rudimentary basis with the expectation of more comprehensive integration later. Staff processing the new trade must be educated to ensure they can deal with it correctly. Very often spreadsheets are used for the new trade and they are signed off as exceptions until proper systems are developed. Such spreadsheets carry their own risks as discussed in Section 18.10.

17.3.7   Middle office can book and mark the products

Middle office must be satisfied that they can properly represent the new products in the booking system and that they can obtain mark-to-market prices for them. They must be capable of showing the new products in overnight and periodic reporting.

17.4   NEW PRODUCT EVOLUTION

There is a story that in the 1950s a professor of mathematics at the University of Oxford was asked if it was true that he was one of only three people in the world who understood Einstein's general theory of relativity to which he replied – "who is the third?" Whether there were two or three people who knew it then, there are thousands who know it now. Knowledge in mathematics and many other disciplines starts with the discovery or invention by a few and is understood over time by the many.

The same is true in the commercial world for new trading which might involve these stages:

1. A single quantitative analyst or a small group of traders develop a product.
2. It is tested and refined.
3. Counterparties are sought to build a market place. Bid/offer spreads start wide.
4. Gradually spreads tighten as larger volumes are traded.
5. Research papers are published to stimulate a greater market participation.
6. Pricing and risk management models become more standard and less esoteric.
7. Existing systems are modified and enhanced to obviate the need for exceptional spreadsheets and processes.
8. Legal documentation is standardised.

9. Risk controllers lose some of their natural caution towards the new product and reduce the risks allocated to those approximating the true risk.
10. Eventually the regulators catch up and include the product in their controls and procedures.
11. The product becomes standard and derivatives upon it start being developed.

So, as a new product evolves, first the lighter and easier and then the heavier and more established processes are adapted to work with it until it becomes another standard product.

17.5   RISKS

As mentioned above, new products carry additional risks because of being relatively untested. There are fewer people with knowledge and experience and so a heightened human risk. Processes may treat the new risk type as an exception, excluding it from some of the standard operational risk controls and causing a greater possibility of processing risk.

Early participants in the new trade may misunderstand how to trade it and lose money. The trade may be too illiquid to get out of positions causing losses when market conditions reverse. Assumptions underlying the initial trade development may turn out to be unfounded or wrong.

A costly infrastructure may be developed for the new trade that is wasted if the trade fails to reach its projected market volumes.

17.6   SUMMARY

There are several advantages to entering into new areas of trading but the risks must be considered. The new trade must be well understood and the right level of support and control applied to it. Long-term planning for its eventual integration into the mainstream may well be required.

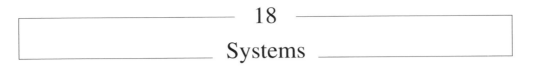

18

Systems

Definition: we define a system as a process run on a computer. We may also refer to a system as a suite of programs performing many tasks. Systems are built by the Information Technology (IT) department or by an independent software vendor.

Origin of a new system: there are three basic reasons why a new system would be required:

- The current process is being run by hand and it would be better if it was fully or partly automated.
- The current system needs improvement.
- A new process is needed.

18.1 WHAT MAKES A GOOD SYSTEM?

A good system is cheap, simple, efficient, reliable, robust, extendable and accurate.

Minimise cost: obviously cost is a major factor when evaluating systems. A cost–benefit analysis needs to be undertaken before deciding when to build.

For example, the cost of a new settlement system may be USD 100 000 per year. Currently settlement staff spend about 10 man-days per week performing activities related to settlements. An estimate would need to be made of how much this can be reduced by using the new system.

Simple: a simple system is easier to extend and maintain. More people understand it and clarity leads to greater confidence in its performance.

Efficient: an efficient system uses the minimum set of input data and resources and runs in the quickest possible time. This reduces dependencies, making errors less likely.

Reliable: a reliable system has a high probability of always working – that is, producing accurate results, putting them in the correct place and delivering them by the expected time.

Robust: a robust system will be able to run normally even in adverse conditions. Examples of adverse conditions might be:

- an inexperienced person running the system;
- someone spilling coffee on the machine running the system;
- a train strike preventing staff reaching the office;
- poor or missing input data;
- unusually heavy usage of the system.

The importance of having a robust system will vary according to the likelihood of adverse conditions. If it always runs with the same set of conditions, then the process may need only to cope with these.

Interface to other systems: the cheapest and most efficient system may not be the best if it fails to interface smoothly with other processes in the trading lifecycle. A poor interface might increase risks or mean an additional process has to be built to act as a transition, inflating the costs.

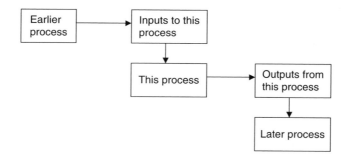

Figure 18.1   Inputs and outputs to a process

An interface is the connection between one system and the next in the trade lifecycle. The outputs of an earlier process become the inputs to a later process (Figure 18.1).

18.2   IT PROCUREMENT

Dedicated IT team: very often a dedicated IT team works directly for the business area, responding to its needs and is available for building systems using an informal approach. The allocation of resources and priority of work is established by the business manager in conjunction with the head of the IT team.

Use of firm wide IT department: when a system is required using resources shared with other business areas or the system is big in terms of cost or time, a more formal approach may be adopted in which the in-house IT department is procured to build the system.

External software vendor: sometimes a business area might invite bids from external software vendors for a particular system. This is because the firm may not have sufficient IT resources to build the system itself or it feels it may be cheaper to go externally. (See later for a discussion of buy versus build.)

18.3   SYSTEM STAKEHOLDERS

Commission of a project: once the decision has been made to build a new system the planning stage can begin. Various people will be appointed to oversee the planning and later the development and deployment. They will act as a steering committee for the system – in effect making it a project. The job of the steering committee is to oversee the project and provide general guidance and direction.

Sponsor: the sponsor is a representative of the department paying for the project. If it were an external project being developed by a software house, the sponsor would be the client. The sponsor wants to ensure he is getting value for money and the users are getting what they require.

Senior user: the senior user is a representative of the person or desk that will ultimately be operating the system to be built. Their needs are the driver for the project. In some cases there are various users and each will have a delegate representing them on the steering committee. An example would be a new project to monitor and report credit usage being built for traders, managers and the credit risk control department.

IT manager: the IT manager is responsible for the delivery of the system to the users. In conjunction with the project manager, he will allocate resources for all stages of the project.

He has a more hands-off role in the process. He monitors and informs on progress and helps out if there are problems.

Project manager: the project manager coordinates the project. He has a hands-on role and is the interface between the steering committee and the IT development team. His role will be discussed later in this chapter.

18.4   THE IT TEAM

Depending on the size of the project, a team which may include the following specialists will be brought together. Some of these people are described in Chapter 15 but we describe them here in the context of a project team. We have already mentioned the project manager. In addition there may be:

Business analyst: the analyst understands the way the business is run and, in particular, the requirements of all the users of the system. He also has some knowledge of the way systems are implemented and hence can help the design and advise on the development of the system. Nowadays, many programmers are expected to fulfil the role of business analysts themselves in order to reduce the costs and layers of communication within the project. When the development is out-sourced, either to a different location within the same organisation or to an external systems provider, the business analyst will be required to provide the necessary liaison between developers and users.

Designer: the designer of the system is somewhat analogous to the architect of a new building. He formulates an overall structure for the project and then ensures that the development conforms to that goal at all stages. He is the one person with the entire system in mind and is therefore the focus for all decisions in the development of the project. For smaller projects, the designer is very often one of the developers. Although more than one person may be involved in the design, it is usually advisable to have a single design owner, so that the development proceeds in an orderly and efficient manner – a train can only have one driver.

Developers: any project will need a team of developers and this could range from one to a hundred, depending on the size of the system. The design of each project will be different, but most projects have at least three levels (see below), calling on different development skills. Often, though, the same developer will work on more than one part of the system.

Tester: testing is an oft-overlooked part of the development process. Many institutions employ specialist testers, others rely on a combination of developers, project managers and users to test their systems. So important is testing to the release of new systems that we will look at it in isolation in Chapter 19.

Support and maintenance: once the system has been deployed, it will require support and maintenance. Support is fixing actual problems in the system; maintenance means small-scale changes or tuning to keep the system working normally even when conditions change over time. Very often support and maintenance are carried out by the same team of people. In big organisations, the support team is split between first and second-line support.

First-line support: the support staff are readily available to the users at all times when the system requires support. They may not fully understand the intricacies of the system and they may not be programmers, but they will have a good idea of troubleshooting. If they cannot fix the problem, they will try to provide a temporary solution or workaround. They will then communicate with the person or team most likely to be able to fix it, explaining the problem in technical terms and possibly supplying a real set of circumstances in which it occurs to make the job of fixing easier.

This is similar to a general practitioner (GP) who is the first port of call for a patient with a medical complaint. Either the GP will treat the patient himself or he will select the most appropriate specialist for onward referral. He will then write to the specialist using medical language to accompany the patient's own description of the problem. In addition, the GP may perform some medical tests on the patient and will pass these to the specialist.

The system does not work in a vacuum – it may use dedicated hardware, networks, communication devices and other systems. Any of these could be affected by the system which has the problem, or they may go wrong for other reasons. The first-line support must therefore be experienced in identifying the source of the problem. It could be

- an actual system error
- user trying to use the system in an invalid manner (user error)
- data error
- hardware error
- another system or process malfunctioning.

Second-line support: this will most likely be the programmers who wrote the original system, as they are best placed to find the solution. The first task in fixing a problem is to diagnose exactly why and when it occurs. Once located, the fault can be fixed, taking into account any ramifications caused by the fix on other parts of the system.

Any fix will have to be retested and then re-released back to the users. The second-line support is more remote from the users. As changes to the actual system generally involve a lot of overheads, they are often grouped into batches known as releases (see the section on change procedures).

Technical author: documentation is a useful, and sometimes essential, addition to any system. The employment of a technical author is more unusual with in-house systems, but common with external vendors. His job is to write any documentation relevant to the use of a system, in the same way as a manual is provided with operating instructions for a washing machine.

18.5   TIMELINE OF A PROJECT

Now we have mentioned the main players in the project team, let us look at the stages of the project lifecycle. These stages apply to both formal and informal development. Even small projects should include elements of each stage, in order to produce a well-built system.

Plan: users, management and IT come together to decide what needs to be done and by when.

Design: the user requirements are converted into a technical design to guide the development.

Development: the process of building the system.

Testing: ensuring that the system does what is required.

Deployment: making the system available to the users.

User documentation: written notes or a full document explaining how to use the system.

Support: fixing problems found in the system after it has been released.

Enhancement: changing the system because of new user requirements. Enhancement could be a small addition or a full-scale further phase of the original project.

18.6 PROJECT MANAGEMENT

There is ongoing project management from planning through to deployment and beyond. The project manager is the human face of the system and users expect to be able to talk to him about their requirements and concerns.

The same people might well be working on more than one project simultaneously. For example: one project is in the design stage, two are being developed, one is being tested and four have been released and are in use. Coordination of all these activities is another aspect of project management. IT staff must be fully utilised but not over burdened and there must be sufficient back-up of expertise to cope with sickness and holidays.

18.7 THE IT DIVIDE

Trading is a familiar activity. We earn money, we spend it, we make investments, we have bank accounts, we earn interest, we pay interest, we borrow money to fund the cost of buying a house and so on. Anyone working on the trade lifecycle for any period of time will come to learn some of the language of trading and will have some idea of how trading works.

This does not apply to information technology. People can work in investment banks and use IT systems every day for 30 years and leave without any real idea about how IT works. The technical language and professional discipline of IT is a world apart from any other financial activity. This void of understanding leads to what we will call the IT divide – the gap between those inside and outside of IT.

The risk due to this divide is that the users fail to get what they really want and a lot of resources are wasted producing the wrong solution or one that fails to deliver everything that it might have done.

Trust: the job of the head of IT in a financial entity is to spend money. He has to procure hardware, software and, most expensive of all, IT professionals, to service the business needs of his bosses. The business has to trust him to spend wisely.

At lower levels there must also be trust. In our experience, few users know exactly what they want out of a new IT system, but they can tell immediately what they do not want. It falls to the IT staff to examine the current and future requirements and devise a solution. Users trust IT to satisfy their requirements.

When a system is in use, users must also be confident that support will be on hand to fix problems. When enhancements are requested, the project manager must give honest predictions as to the cost involved, so that priorities can be set and competing business needs taken into account.

If too much trust is given to IT this can lead to wilful or accidental abuse but insufficient trust may impair the ability of the IT department to do their job.

Bad scenario: Project manager Elaine and developer Fiona sit down with the user Georgina for a meeting to discuss a new system. The IT people leave thinking that Georgina wants a similar system to one they built the previous year for an equivalent user in another asset class. Georgina leaves sure that the IT people know her requirements and will come back with a solution.

Three months later, Georgina has heard nothing and asks Elaine how things are going. Elaine says she is not sure but will ask Fiona and update her. Fiona claims everything is fine and it will be ready within a month.

A month later Fiona tells Elaine that she is having problems with one part of the system and may need some help. Harriet is brought in and together with Fiona they manage to come up with something to show Georgina.

The next week Georgina takes a look at the system and immediately sees that it is unusable, pointing out a fundamental flaw in the basic functionality. Elaine and Fiona evaluate her feedback and realise the system will need a major redesign.

It takes a further three months to deliver the second attempt. When it arrives, it is better than the first attempt, but has annoying deficiencies which Georgina has to spend much of her time working around.

Georgina has waited eight months for an inadequate solution and lost confidence that IT will ever deliver something from which she can really benefit.

Good scenario: project manager Leanne and developer Michelle meet the user Nina. After the meeting they write down a functional specification listing all the required functionality and Nina approves it.

Michelle writes a technical specification with timeframe for each part of the development process.

Michelle spends two days building a simple prototype and shows it to Nina.

Michelle evolves the prototype as she adds more functionality. She meets Nina weekly to discuss progress and ask any pertinent questions.

When the real system is ready it becomes the focus of discussions and the prototype is discontinued.

Upon delivery Nina receives a system she is expecting and it does what she requires. She is never left in the dark and there are no last minute surprises. For the sake of a little extra documentation and a couple of days expended on a prototype, everybody is kept informed and any time the system diverges from what is required it can easily be brought back on course.

Communication: communication is the antidote to the IT divide. Regular and informative communication will iron out problems and make everybody feel they are involved. The mystique of the IT world is dispelled for outsiders and the IT people understand they are delivering real solutions to real people. Communication also applies within the IT department itself. With any project there are likely to be many people doing different things simultaneously and regular communication is the only way to ensure everybody is pulling in the same direction.

IT in the centre: the essential task of IT is to improve on the manual processes in existence and create systems for new processes not in existence. Since the role of IT is intrinsically bound by the processes in the trade lifecycle, IT is inevitably in the middle of the financial entity – communicating with all departments involved in the lifecycle. Therefore it often falls to IT to carry out the planning and rationalisation discussed in Chapter 16 on processes.

Being located in the centre of the business functions also means that anyone controlling IT has a lot of power in the organisation. It is often the case that the success of a business depends upon the IT systems operating within it. Although it is not always easy to quantify the benefit a good IT department brings to the firm, it is very apparent how much damage is caused when the systems are not adequate!

18.8   TECHNIQUES AND ISSUES RELATED TO IT

Prototype: a prototype is a small-scale model or representation of a complete system. In IT projects, the prototype is often an approximation of the eventual user interface, but with little or no working functionality. This gives the user an idea of what to expect and how it will look.

The prototype can play an important part in the process of communication between the programmer and the user. A picture says a thousand words and a prototype is several pictures. It is both a sample of the finished system and a pictorial view of the functional specification. It can be static: a one-off attempt by the programmer to capture the requirements of the user to ensure the ship is heading in the right direction before going out to sea. Or it can be dynamic: evolving through the lifecycle of the project to enable ongoing communication and approval. Some prototypes are themselves developed and they become the finished product.

A prototype is not always appropriate, especially for short projects where the time spent on producing it is an unnecessary or costly distraction.

Also, as mentioned, a prototype generally demonstrates the user interface of the system, but this is by no means the whole system. A perfectly satisfactory prototype does not guarantee a perfect system – it could be that the underlying functionality is missing or wrong. Programmers and users must discuss all levels of the system, including those beyond the scope of the prototype.

Application Programming Interface (API): at the end of the project there is only one computer system so how can many developers work simultaneously on the system and not get in each other's way? The solution is known as an API. It defines the borders between one piece of work and another. The most efficient means of utilising many developers is to break the system down into modules or components. Each developer works on the module or modules best fitting his expertise. Towards the end the modules are bolted together to become the finished system.

From the outset, programmers must know what each module can do. If they require functionality in a module written by somebody else, they will need to know the way to call it and what to expect back from it.

If each module is designed with its own API known to all the developers, then the modules can be developed independently of each other and in any order. Although it will be impossible to test a function within a module until it has been written, at least the caller of the function will be able to write the interface to it.

The modular approach is similar to an electronic circuit. Individual components or black boxes make up the circuit. Only the person who built it knows what is inside, but everybody knows what goes in, what comes out and what it does.

The concept can be extended to the development of libraries of functionality. These can be developed by completely different departments or purchased from software vendors outside the organisation. A common example is a library for valuation.

The API for the library consists of function calls and a brief description of what each one does. In Table 18.1 we give a very simple example not in technical language. (A real API would be in standard technical language understood by the provider and user of the library.)

Programmer creativity: the programmer may seem like a scientist, producing technical solutions to business problems, but actually he is more of an artist. There are generally several ways of writing a computer program – the programmer will use his experience and

Table 18.1

Function	Description	Inputs	Output
ValueSwap	Values a trade which is an interest rate swap	Trade, market data	Value
RiskSwap	Returns risk for an interest rate swap	Trade, market data, risk requirements	Matrix of risk numbers
BondCashflows	Determines the cashflows for a bond	Bond	Vector of cashflows

individuality to create a solution. Although he may be constrained by a detailed design and have to conform to a preplanned API, there is plenty of scope for creativity. This may be why the profession attracts people from a wide range of academic backgrounds – English literature, foreign languages, history and economics, in addition to the less surprising mathematics and computer science.

This creativity has the advantage of allowing innovation and originality in the production of a system perhaps making it faster or more accurate or enabling the system to be completed earlier.

The risks caused by such creativity are that other programmers will not be able to support a particularly unusual style or that the style causes the development to take longer without any real gain in functionality. Programmers are often searching for an elegant solution that is aesthetically pleasing, because this provides more job satisfaction than a simpler, more straightforward approach. The same criticism is applied to mathematicians who are forever searching for a shorter and neater proof to a difficult problem – although there is more justification here because a short proof is more easily understood and remembered.

Generic versus specific: if you want to devise a transportation system for the city of Cardiff you will look closely at the city and find the best solution for its local needs. Now, if you want to extend it to Edinburgh, you can either build a completely different system suited only to Edinburgh or take the common features of all cities and build something generic and then add something specific on top to cope with the individual features of Edinburgh.

The designer of a computer system must ask himself to what degree is the functionality he is building generic and what is specific? This depends on how extendable he wishes the system to be. If he is building a bond system purely for fixed and floating rate notes, does he factor in the capability to handle asset-backed securities, even though they are not currently being traded? If he does he may delay the project writing unneeded functionality; if not, the system may be harder to enhance later when the new trading commences.

An entirely generic solution might be designed to cope with every possible trade in every possible asset class. It may have a pyramid architecture (Figure 18.2) with completely generic

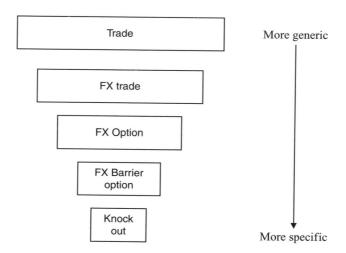

Figure 18.2   Pyramid of trade objects

modules at the top providing common functionality. Every time a new product is required, a specific module is built for it and slotted in at the bottom of the pyramid. This is a very flexible and future-proof method of design, but it takes a long time before anything tangible comes out of it, because much abstract foundation has to be laid before real products are incorporated.

An entirely specific solution, however, applies to one set of circumstances and is not extendable to any other situation. It is fast and direct but soon becomes inefficient if additional functionality is required.

These are two extremes – the best course is generally somewhere in the middle, guided by the particular environment in which the system is being developed.

Change management: once a system has passed the testing phase it is released to the users. Very rarely does the first version remain unchanged throughout the lifetime of the system.

Once released the system may undergo changes caused by:

- bug fixes;
- ongoing maintenance to remove weaknesses and make it more efficient;
- enhancements requested by users;
- changes caused by events outside the system itself, such as a new data feed, upgrade of hardware, users in a new location etc.

These changes must be managed. Every new release is in effect a new system and so it should be thoroughly retested and subject to the same controls and procedures as the original system (see Chapter 19 on testing, in particular, regression testing). Then it has to be redeployed. Sometimes this can be done piecemeal – users taking the new version when it is convenient for them to do so; other times the new version must be adopted simultaneously throughout the organisation.

The set of files constituting the new version is called a release. It is important to know which release any particular user is trying in case he experiences a problem. It could be, for instance, that the release has been superseded by a version which already fixes the problem encountered or that releases after a certain date exhibit the problem and those before do not. Here we describe some features of change management, so that the reader has a feel for how to manage a working system.

For most commercial programming languages, a system is developed by means of a set of source files. These source files are written in such a way that a compiler can turn them into instructions understood by the computer.

The process of making a release involves taking the set of source files and building them into the released files. At this point the release files have no means of being mapped back to the source files and vice versa unless they are given some sort of tag identifier.

As source files are changed they are given versions and stored in a repository system, known as source control, which can track changes and identify which source files were built together into one release (see Figure 18.3).

Identifying the source files constituting any given release is vital if debugging is required. The programmer must assemble the same set of files that went into the release in order to ensure he is working with the same system that had the problem.

Release documentation should be maintained. The release and its contents, together with the build number, should be documented (the source code system can tag the files that made

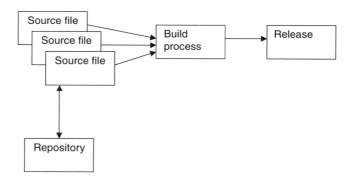

Figure 18.3 Build and release process

up the release). Suppose, as in Table 18.2, there are six source files (in reality there would generally be a lot more than six) called A to F, then:

Table 18.2

Release	Contents	Source code versions
1.001 Build 83	First release	A (1.41), B (1.27), C (1.01), D (1.93)
1.002 Build 87	Works with new data format	A (1.42), B (1.27), C (1.01), D (1.93), E(1.01)
1.003 Build 88	Fixed bugs 23, 28,30	A (1.43), B (1.28), C (1.03), D (1.93), E(1.01)
1.004 Build 102	Gamma risk added, fixed bugs 25,50,51	A (1.45), B (1.28), C (1.04), D (1.94), E(1.02), F(1.01)

In this case, if one user has a problem with release 1.003, the files in build 88 would be retrieved from source control and checked.

Not all input files and procedures need to be built into a release. Some database processes and tables, for example, have a direct effect on anyone using them as soon as they are changed. Although this can be a boon because it bypasses the release procedures and allows instant impact, it can also be dangerous if it is unmanaged and the users are not prepared.

Risks: if the versioning history of the source files is lost it may be impossible to recreate an older version and fix a problem, so care should be taken to choose robust source control. The ability to go back to previous versions should be tested properly and not left until a crisis when it is actually needed.

A cumbersome release procedure can waste time and cause extra problems. If files built in different versions are released together they may not work together. If the support team cannot identify the release that is causing the problem, it may be very hard to track it down.

Having different users on different versions is a recipe for trouble. They may get different results or publish reports with different formats. It is confusing and embarrassing if a financial officer or senior manager receives different reports depending upon who prepared them. Controlling user releases is often beyond the remit of IT who are responsible for building them. It is often up to the users' managers to impose an orderly and concerted move to a new version when it has least impact on daily business.

18.9   SYSTEMS ARCHITECTURE

Let us look under the bonnet of a typical system and examine its major components. Many systems use what is known as a three-tier architecture comprising user interface, business logic and data repository.

18.9.1   User interface

This is the means by which the user communicates with the system – passing instructions to it and getting results back. A good user interface will be:

Simple and easy to use: the best user interfaces are simple. The functionality should be arranged so that the most regularly used is the most accessible. The user interface should be a dialogue with the user – as if he is talking to the system and it is talking back to him.

Intuitive: even if user documentation is provided, the user will expect to be able to operate the system in a logical way. Unusual or counterintuitive screens or buttons may alarm him, such as red lights flashing when really the system is behaving normally.

Consistent: the user interface should be internally consistent. This means that if there are several screens, they all look and feel similar: if there is a row of buttons at the top of one screen for the principal operations, then it should be the same on all screens; if yellow means a user input area, this should apply everywhere.

The user interface should also be externally consistent to other systems in the user's environment. It would be hard for someone to use an alphabetical filing system for interest rate future trades and a by-date filing system for interest rate swaps.

Written for the user: like any speech or book, a user interface should be written with the user in mind. The developer should spend time watching and learning how the user operates and try to mimic his behaviour within the user interface. For example, traders like everything to be visible on the screen without having to keep scrolling right or left to see different types of data. Any poorly designed screen or part of a screen irritates the user and reduces his chances of using the system successfully.

Friend of the user: just as everybody likes to adjust the car seat before driving, so different users like their user interface configured in different ways. Where there is choice of screen order, colours, menus etc., there should be the ability to save these for each user and retrieve them when that user starts up the system. A customised system helps the user feel at home with it and makes the system more consistent with other systems he uses.

Extra layer of validation: the user interface provides a useful extra layer of validation between the user and the underlying system. It can check all the user's inputs to make sure they fit a valid type and range of input and catch errors before they reach the processing stage. Moreover, the user interface can guide and train the user to input the correct values.

Not every system requires a user interface. Automated jobs, for example, are run by the system without user involvement. However, even these systems generally provide activity reports detailing successes and failures – another type of user interface: communicating about how the system has performed.

18.9.2   Business logic

This is the main processing layer of the system. Inputs and instructions are received via the user interface and then processed, the results being passed back to the user interface. This layer is hidden from the user and written in the most efficient manner for the machine to accomplish its task. Therefore the user inputs that are expressed in the user's way of communicating with the system are turned into inputs required by the processor. For example, the user might supply a trade date and a maturity date, the processor turns this into a single number representing the time span between the two dates in years. (Trade Date 16 June 2007, Maturity 16 Dec 2010 becomes the single number 3.5.)

After processing, the outputs are converted into the language and style understood by the user. This means it is possible to have the same layer of business logic but many different user interfaces. For example, the same risk engine might plug into one user interface for middle office, another for the traders and a third for the market risk department.

18.9.3   Data repository

The third layer of the three-tier architecture is the place where the data is stored.

Usually it is a database or file system especially designed for persistence and retrieval of data. Data storage needs to be implemented in a manner making retrieval fast and accurate. The database developer needs to know the scope of the data used by the system and the sort of queries likely to be required.

In system terms, the entity being used in the system is defined by its data. For example, a fixed bond is defined by the properties of the bond stored in the database. If a property is not saved because the designer of the database left it out of the database, that bond cannot be properly represented in the database and therefore can never be stored.

The way data is stored in the system underpins the entire design. Since the database is at the lowest layer within the system, any changes to it mean most of the layers above are affected. Adding to a database is generally simple, but replacing what is already there is much harder and should be avoided.

The design of an effective system begins at the database layer and the designer needs a thorough grasp of the entities for which he is designing.

In addition to these three tiers there is often a core system layer that lies at the heart of the whole system (see Figure 18.4). Communication and control is handled from here. The developers of this part of the system need to consider volume of traffic, connectivity to other devices and many of the more technical sides of the IT solution

18.9.4   Example

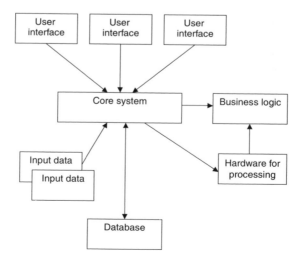

Figure 18.4   Example of a system layout

18.10   DIFFERENT TYPES OF DEVELOPMENT

Not all IT projects are developed the same way. We divide our discussion into three major types of development.

18.10.1   Rapid application development (RAD)

This method of development usually involves one programmer sitting close to the user, most likely a trader. The development is quick and easy but not meant for heavy or prolonged use. In an RAD environment, the developer can become an extension to the trader. Having an RAD developer on hand either allows the production of a solution beyond the technical capabilities of the trader or allows the trader more time to concentrate on his trading and risk management. A lot of RAD development is done on spreadsheets because of their flexibility.

RAD is particularly appropriate when

- the trader wants to try out a new idea;
- there are insufficient resources to build a more durable solution and business is being inhibited as a result;
- the trader has limited spreadsheet or other development skills;
- the complexity of the trades requires a more sophisticated method of representing them;
- a new business or product is being evaluated.

18.10.2   Dedicated IT team for a business function or area

Some desks or divisions in financial entities have heavy use of IT resources. They may therefore have a dedicated IT team to work for them. This means that the IT team can become acquainted with the business and develop a closer relationship.

An example of such an arrangement might be the exotics FX team of an investment bank having an IT team that builds risk management tools for it. In developing these tools, the IT team gains specialist FX exotics business understanding, making it well placed to develop a full risk management system. Just as the trading desk works closely with other business functions like middle office and sales, so the IT team can extend its system to cover the needs of these areas. Quants may work alongside the IT team in such a structure.

The focus and driver for the IT requirements is the trading desk itself. The trading desk has many support and control functions so it makes sense for the IT providers to be in the same place.

A system developed by this team might take an RAD as a prototype and develop a more durable technical solution around it. The systems developed are more robust than RAD but nimble enough to respond to changing business requirements. The users of the systems do not necessarily expect a polished finished product, but they do want something reliable and accurate that is tailored to their specific needs.

18.10.3   Independent IT division

Many financial entities have an independent IT division not working directly for any one business area or department. It forms a common resource shared by all business areas. The IT resource costs are divided amongst the various profit centres according to the time and materials spent on each or as a flat fee.

Generally the IT staff in this division will be more technical and build more robust solutions, often spanning many business areas or encompassing the whole firm. These systems are more for generic business activities, such as a confirmation system taking in all asset classes and products.

Sometimes this division produces libraries or modules that can be used by other IT teams. They may, for example, develop a generic web browser for garnering information from the Internet which could be applied in different ways by the commodities and interest rate IT teams.

The developers here may not have so much business knowledge and therefore will rely on business analysts or colleagues in IT departments closer to the business areas such as in the first two divisions described above.

18.10.4   General comments

Having the ability to divide IT teams into these three methods of working can mean the correct level of skills and resources is dedicated to each system. As an RAD system gets greater usage, it moves on to the dedicated desk IT team to turn it into a more wide-ranging solution. As the institution matures in its trading patterns, more robust and general systems may be required to be built by the independent division, freeing up the more dedicated teams to work on more business focused projects.

The risks of having multiple development teams is that systems fall into gaps between them. An RAD system might become too heavily depended upon because of its popularity with the users or because there are insufficient resources to turn it into a better system. Similarly, the management might see working systems developed by the desk-based IT team and fail to appreciate their weaknesses or the advantages to be gained by building a fuller system. Timing issues might prevent one development taking over from another so that systems are left in use beyond their sell-by date.

Conversely, there might be duplication of resources. The dedicated desk team might over-reach and spend too much time on a robust solution that could have been better handled by the independent IT division. Programmers with specialist skills might be unnecessarily duplicated across the various teams. Professional pride might prevent one IT team communicating properly with another or there might be disagreements about who is responsible for functionality and systems lying in the grey areas between the teams.

Spreadsheets: many financial entities use one or many spreadsheets to handle some of their system requirements. The advantages of using a spreadsheet-based solution are:

- complete flexibility;
- easy to convert disparate inputs and outputs;
- easy to plug into other systems;
- familiarity to all users in the financial entity so minimum of training and customisation required.

The disadvantages are:

- lack of control over what the user is doing;
- inability to audit what has been done;
- very difficult to keep control of different versions. Each user can customise his spreadsheet, effectively making it into a completely different system;
- even with password protection, security can be an issue.

18.11   BUY VERSUS BUILD

One of the first questions that need to be answered when planning a new system is whether to buy it from a software vendor or to build it in-house. Here we present a brief overview of the pertinent issues.

Buy a vendor solution: this places the onus of development and support on the third-party vendor who will normally charge a yearly subscription. No in-house development will be required. In theory this approach should be cheaper. If 10 clients are using broadly the same system, the vendor can charge approximately one tenth of the cost (plus profit) to each client and can maximise his core expertise of delivering software while leaving the client to concentrate on his own business.

The following points however, need careful consideration before choosing this route:

- there will be an internal use of resources to evaluate a solution, test it and use it when it is purchased. There is also the configuration of the system to make it work in-house. This will involve both accepting input data from market and static data suppliers and feeding outputs to downstream reporting systems. Although the vendor will sometimes offer to configure his system at minimal cost, there are usually hidden costs associated with changing to any new system. Also, new vendor releases may not come at a time suited to internal resources for testing and deployment being available.
- a vendor solution is (in principle at least!) less responsive to changing requirements and is inflexible. If new features are required the client will have to await their inclusion in the vendor's next version of the product. The client becomes dependent on a release and priority cycle beyond his control. Also, there is a danger that if the request is particularly bespoke to one client, it will either be given low priority or there will be an additional charge for that client. On the other hand, if a client seeks a market advantage in a new piece of functionality, he may not want his competitors, who may share the same vendor product, to know.

In-house development: this requires technical expertise within the firm and knowledge of the complexities of that part of the business. An in-house solution is much more able to respond to the business requirements and priorities. However communication and understanding between the providers (programmers and quantitative analysts) and the users (traders, structurers, middle office, risk control etc.) is of paramount importance. It can also be an expensive solution, as the business must pay the full cost of development, gaining none of the economies of scale outlined above with a third-party vendor solution. On the other hand a "90/10" approach of achieving smooth processing of 90 % of the products with 10 % handled by exception can be quick and economic.

Mix of in-house and vendor: very often a client will want to develop his own analytical engine, for example, but to plug it into a generic framework. In practice, the development effort in producing a valuation algorithm is less than that of integrating it with a user interface, database and other components of the business solution. Also the valuation is where the competitive advantage resides, so it makes sense to buy a platform and plug in the in-house analytics.

Sometimes, the converse is true. The institution has its own software infrastructure, but it lacks the expertise to develop its own models or wants to use externally validated pricing algorithms. So it will choose to buy an analytical library and maintain the other components in-house.

18.12   SOFTWARE VENDORS

The vendor's perspective: the supplier of software to financial entities will not, in general, be offering a shrink-wrapped product that can be taken out of its packaging, plugged in and run. The core of the product might be generic, but each client will have his own requirements. The vendor must understand the general market for which he is supplying software and link this to a specific appreciation of his client's needs. These may be due to the operating environment, the internal and external feeds connected to the system or the particular type of business the client transacts.

Apart from competing with other vendors, the vendor may also have to prove he can deliver a better solution than the in-house IT department. This can be both a technical and political challenge. The technical challenge is to prove that the vendor has sufficient business knowledge to overcome the inherent assumption that in-house IT knows more about the business of its own company. The political challenge is the possible loss of face caused to an IT department when the business seeks to employ an external vendor, with the implication that it cannot deliver what is required.

The fast changing environment of finance demands that vendors continually keep abreast of the business they are serving. They need to be able to release new products and enhancements and satisfy urgent requests for change.

The procurement process of a large financial entity can be bureaucratically burdensome and cashflow can be a problem for a small software vendor because it is often paid many months in arrears.

Despite these problems, many software vendors offer a quality solution designed and developed by people experienced in the financial industry. They can employ economies of scale to compete effectively against large IT departments, who are themselves often located a long way from their business clients. Moreover, they can invest in proper software techniques and testing to deliver a better quality product.

The financial entity's perspective: an effective relationship with a software vendor can bring rewards to a business inside an investment bank or hedge fund. It can specify exactly what is required and does not have to compete with other business areas for a share of IT resources. The financial entities are often much larger than the vendors and can exert their spending power to guarantee prompt and reliable service.

When procuring third-party resources, the business is free from the shackles of internal IT policy and timescales. It may also be cheaper than paying towards internal IT costs.

Another major advantage is that software vendors are known for better quality products. Since their reputation depends on supplying paying clients without the embarrassment of delivering faulty goods, they generally invest in quality control.

Vendors are specialists and gain plenty of experience about their products from the market place. Periodic review of vendor products can help a business ensure their own IT provision is keeping up with market practices.

The financial entity must be careful, however, to guard its competitive advantage by ensuring that any specific request it makes to a vendor about a sensitive area of business is not distributed to competitors as part of a general software release.

18.13   PERFORMANCE

The performance of any system depends upon the skill of the software developers in optimising the implementation and the platform upon which the system is to be run. The platform is the hardware encompassing issues such as the power of the computers and the speed of network cables. Improving hardware is often a better way to reduce cost than optimising software.

18.13.1   Hardware constraints

As well as developing software, the system designers need to consider the hardware on which it will be run. Historically, systems were run on large mainframe computers where the resources were concentrated on the mainframe server with nothing more than a terminal on the user's desk. Then the PC was invented with enough power to run applications. Now there is a trend back to server-based applications via web interfaces operated by the user.

Financial entities often require heavy use of computer power and have adapted to the change in hardware available, by using a blend of server and client run applications. Often it is cheaper to buy more hardware than to spend time optimising the software.

18.13.2   Grid computing

A technique has been developed to make the most of all hardware available, be it PCs on user desks or common servers. It is called grid computing. When a system can split its processing into many tasks, these tasks are distributed to all the available machines. A queuing system may be devised whereby the next available machine is handed the next task in the queue. The machine processes the task and informs the controlling program when finished. The results are either passed back to the controller or, more efficiently, stored in a common repository such as a network file or database. A separate process aggregates all the results at the end when all the processing has been completed. A variation is to distribute the tasks according to the power of the machines – more intensive processes going to the more powerful machines.

At quiet times, such as at night and weekends, grid computing can take advantage of the huge number of machines that would otherwise be sitting idle.

The danger of grid computing is that because of the requirement to have the process sitting on a user's machine, there may be conflicts between the software used for the grid processing and that needed for the user's everyday activities. Even if the grid computing is clever enough to segregate itself from the rest of the user's machine, it could still be affected by user activity, such as the machine stalling or being rebooted.

Floor infrastructure departments who are responsible for the software on users' machines are sometimes resistant to grid computing being applied to personal computers or commonly accessed networks. Nevertheless with careful management, it can still be an advantage to have grid computing for systems requiring heavy processing, even if limited to common servers and a few user machines.

18.14   PROJECT ESTIMATION

One of the hardest tasks in IT is estimating the parameters of a project. Projects have three main parameters – cost, time and functionality. It takes a great deal of experience and judgement to accurately estimate how long a project will take, how much it will cost and what it will contain when completed.

Cost: the amount of human and machine resources dedicated to the project plus additional costs such as data licences and third-party supplied software and systems.

Time: the time taken from conception to delivery.

Functionality: what the system is capable of doing which is of benefit to the user.

Generally it is possible to control two of these three features – very rarely all three, but poor management can limit control to only one.

If a limit is put on the time a project may take and the cost in the form of allocated resources, in most cases an amount of functionality can be estimated but very rarely guaranteed. Similarly, with a required set of functionality and a known timeframe, the resources may be subject to variation or the resources can be constrained and then the time taken is left variable. With extremely good project management and a dedicated team of developers, a constrained cost and time can produce the required functionality although in our experience this is rare.

Sometimes the timeframe is constrained and even to produce less than the expected functionality requires more resources than were originally allocated. On other occasions, a project must have a set of functionality for which both the time and the cost go over budget.

Anything can happen in the course of a project to cause delays and added cost; often these are outside the control of the project manager. Here we suggest some typical problems which are within his control, but nonetheless cause delays and extra costs.

Scope creep: as we mentioned earlier, users are not always sure of what they require until it is suggested or shown to them. As a project takes shape, they see what is being offered and take advantage of the situation by asking for more. The project manager may be reluctant to alienate the users by refusing them, or the extra functionality might seem easy to add. The process by which the required functionality of a project grows is called scope creep and it is very common in project development. To minimise scope creep, one can be very firm from the outset and get the users to agree to exactly what functionality they are being given. Any additional requests can be delivered as subsequent phases of the project, each with its own estimation of time.

User power: apart from the problem of inertia explained in Chapter 16, a user might be unwilling to move to a new system until he is convinced it is absolutely right. Even though the new system gives him more functionality than previously and is easier to use, he still wants to eke out as much benefit as possible, while the IT development team is available and waiting upon him. He knows that once he has signed off, the IT team will move on to another project and he could be left for years before he has another chance to add to the system.

This problem arises due to poor management. In a properly managed environment, users would be serviced by IT according to business priority and not by some arbitrary process of happenstance. If a user has urgent or important requirements after a project is delivered he should be given resources to deal with them, there and then.

Mythical man month: in his seminal work on project management *The mythical man month: Essays on software engineering* Fred Brooks shows how adding more resources to a project which is already late often makes it even later.

There is no easy way to correct a project which is running late. Software development is not like pulling a wagon up a hill, if it gets stuck you can't just add more horses; it is more akin to an oil painting, adding another artist will not speed the project or give you a better product – it will just make a mess. The project manager should be aware of what is happening with the development and make small adjustments when they are needed, rather than trying to make large adjustments when it is too late. The developers for their part must keep the project manager updated on progress and warn him early of problems or issues.

18.15   GENERAL THOUGHTS ON IT

Balance: imagine two systems. One is written to cope with all eventualities, full error and exception handling, bulletproofing and the near certainty that every conceivable scenario can be catered for. The other provides what is required but will fail if anything out of the ordinary occurs. Which is better? The answer is: it depends. An RAD solution might be better suited to the latter approach, a full blown system designed to last for at least 10 years might require the former. The level of security and resilience may not be mentioned in the functional specification signed off by the user. The user assumes it is proportionate to the environment in which the system is being deployed.

Another balancing act the project manager has to perform is whether, given fixed time and resources, he builds something small and safe or large and risky. Again the project manager needs to understand the system risk appetite of his users.

Everything can be done: there is very little that cannot be achieved with a good system and a fast computer. IT staff know this, but they need to make the user aware of what is easy and what is difficult. The user may choose a difficult option with only limited benefit, because he does not know how much more he could have received if he had chosen an easier alternative. The process of system development is a continual dialogue between those who need and those who can produce – the more they understand each other, the better they can work together to the advantage of everybody concerned.

18.16   SUMMARY

Systems play a major part in any trade lifecycle. This chapter has shown the role of IT in delivering and supporting systems. It has also discussed the role of IT, the view of IT looking out into the general organisation and the way IT is perceived by the users of systems. The relationship between IT and other business functions can play a big part in the success of the trade lifecycle – some ideas to enhance this relationship have been suggested. The chapter has also considered the question of buy versus build.

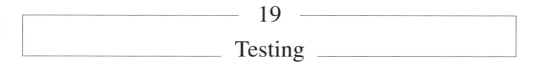

19

Testing

Testing is a key stage in the development and running of any process in the trade lifecycle. Although testing does not add anything tangible to the lifecycle, it serves to reduce the number of mistakes and improve reliability.

19.1   WHAT IS TESTING?

Testing is the activity that is undertaken to ensure that a process does what it is supposed to do. A process is designed to fulfil a business need; testing should ensure that need is fully satisfied by the process.

Testing applies to processes whether or not they are run by computers. A manual process may, however, require a different style and scale of testing because humans are better than machines at adapting to changes in operating conditions. The majority of our discussion in this chapter is related to system testing, but the ideas can be extended to manual process testing.

It is not always necessary or desirable that a process be perfect. The time spent making a process perfect might be wasted when a less than perfect system would be satisfactory for the given business process. Deciding on the appropriate level of quality is a matter of negotiation between the management, the development team and the users. It also depends upon the environment in which the process was developed and is being used.

For example, a third-party vendor supplying a confirmation system might be expected to provide a higher level of quality than an in-house developed system. This is because:

1. The vendor is more remote than the in-house developers and so the time to fix problems will be greater.
2. The vendor will probably be supplying several clients and hence has economies of scale, enabling better testing.
3. The client is paying directly for the vendor product and so has a greater expectation of quality.
4. The users and the in-house developers may be used to working in an iterative manner before arriving at the final product.

The overall acceptance of a process will be based upon whether it reaches the required level of quality. Individual testers might discover many faults with the system and log them. Then quality criteria will be applied to determine which must be fixed to make the system acceptable. This might involve the project manager, the tester and the users working together (see the subsection below on fault logging).

19.2   WHY IS TESTING IMPORTANT?

Testing is often the poor relation of the development process because it is expensive in terms of time and resources, and to do it properly requires a particular attitude and skill set.

Testing is important because it creates safer and more robust processes, reducing the cost of fixing, replacing or working around faults. Testing in a timely fashion removes uncertainty and ensures that the problems can be fixed while the system developers are still available and can remember how they built the process.

The extent of testing depends upon the importance of the process and the risks if it fails. NASA might spend several years testing their lunar spacecraft, while a simple spreadsheet may only undergo a quick rudimentary check.

The management of a particular process should balance the cost of testing against the risks of not testing to arrive at an appropriate testing level.

Testing is often a matter of cultural background. There is a story of a Japanese company supplying a component for an American car manufacturer. It was asked to ensure the component had no more than 15 faulty parts in every thousand. After some weeks, the Japanese company supplied two consignments: one containing a thousand good components and the other containing "the 15 faulty ones as per specification"!

Many financial entities do not allocate any proper testing time, leaving it to a combination of developers and users to "come out with something that works". The fast changing landscape and constant demand for new and refined processes eats into the development time. So companies are often guilty of considering testing a luxury rather than a necessity. They are then left wondering why their processes are not working properly, leading to more processing errors and longer working hours for staff to deal with the problems.

19.3   WHO DOES TESTING?

In the general commercial world, it is the responsibility of a supplier to ensure the goods he supplies conform to an acceptable standard. Systems developed for financial entities are different because they are tailored to the specific needs of the business users. So the development of such systems is, in essence, a partnership between in-house IT or external software vendors on the one hand, and the business users on the other. They have a joint responsibility and interest in ensuring the system performs the task required.

Testing can be done by staff in the IT division (internal or external) supplying the process, or by those in the business function who are going to be using it. Either side might employ specialist testing personnel or rely on their regular staff to carry out testing.

To see the different sides of testing, let us consider the analogy of a meal cooked by a team of chefs and served to customers at a restaurant. The cooks will test the meal by tasting it and the head chef might give his view on the overall presentation. The diner will conduct similar tests, although he may be more discerning and objective.

In the same way, an informal set of tests might be performed by IT developers and the project manager and perhaps a more discerning test by the users. But in reality this will leave several gaps in the overall testing required. Like chefs, developers are creative people with a vested interest in their product being successful. Unless they are very self-critical, they will find it hard to test sufficiently rigorously to uncover faults. They are also under time pressure to deliver quickly.

The users also have limited testing time and inclination. Time spent testing detracts from their daily tasks. There is a temptation to check the obvious and routine operations and sort out any other problems as and when they are discovered. On the other hand, some users are overly officious in their testing duties and are unnecessarily critical of a new process, delaying its release while changes are made and re-tested.

A very common pattern in the development process is for systems to be used before they are fully tested. Faults are discovered randomly as different sections of functionality are subject to real life processing. They are then fixed and the system is re-released. This process iterates, sometimes over months or years, until a stable system has evolved.

19.4   WHEN SHOULD TESTING BE DONE?

Every time a process is used it is being tested. A fault might not be detected until a particular circumstance or combination of circumstances arises. Therefore, a process can never be said to be fully tested.

Testing usually occurs at several different points in the development and release of a process:

- during development;
- after one section of development is complete;
- after the whole process is complete;
- when the system is given to users;
- when the system is about to go live;
- once the system is in use;
- after any changes or additions have been made.

Ideally, testing of any stage of development should be carried out as quickly as possible after the development. The advantages being:

- less chance of faults spreading through to other parts of the system;
- easier to identify where the fault lies and who introduced it;
- less chance the developer has forgotten how the part was developed;
- fewer errors when the system is shown to users;
- more time available for fixing problems;
- easier to plan the project.

Whenever a fault is discovered, there is the risk that all results produced by the system hitherto were subject to the same fault. This reduces confidence in the system and can lead to major work tracing the effects caused by erroneous results.

19.5   WHAT ARE THE TYPES OF TESTING?

There are several distinct types of testing at different stages in the development and release cycle. We start by describing the main stages of testing and go on to look at some particular types. It is beyond the scope of this book to cover all possible testing techniques.

19.5.1   Stages of testing

1. **Unit testing:** as the name implies, unit testing is the testing of a single component in the system. This testing is in isolation from the rest of the system. Often unit testing is done by the person writing the unit, although it may be retested by an independent tester.
2. **Integration testing:** when units are assembled they are tested in groups and this is known as integration testing. This tests whether the units can work together.
3. **System testing:** system testing is conducted on a complete, integrated system to evaluate the system's compliance with its specified requirements. It goes a stage further than integration

testing by making sure the software and hardware work in their designated operating environment.

4. **Acceptance testing (or user acceptance testing – UAT):** this is generally performed by the user. Its purpose is to ensure that the system conforms to the user's requirements. After successful acceptance testing, the user is said to have "signed off" the system. The system is then deployed and used.

5. **Parallel testing:** this can be part of acceptance testing and involves the user running his existing system in parallel with the new system under test. The purpose is to ensure that every activity that can be done under the old system is present and correct in the new system. One major problem of parallel testing is that it requires maintenance of two complete operating environments together with full working data for as long as the test is being run. This can be a major strain on resources. Another drawback is that the test might only ensure the new system matches the old, without testing new functionality or functionality that should have been improved.

Generally parallel testing is good for short periods of time when a new system is meant to replace the old system without significant changes or enhancements.

19.5.2   Testing types

1. **Smoke testing:** this is a quick, superficial test to ensure that one unit or a part of the system appears to be working. It is usually conducted when something is first produced or when it has been changed. If something fails during smoke testing there is no point continuing with more thorough tests until it is fixed.

2. **Black box testing:** a unit of the system is tested as a black box, meaning that input data is fed in and output results are checked without knowledge of how the unit works.

3. **White box testing:** the tester has knowledge of the internal unit under test and attempts to test most or all possible paths through the underlying programming code.

4. **Spot testing:** this is random testing of the system. Although it is not structured, it allows the tester to be imaginative and gives an overall confidence in the underlying system before more structured testing is performed.

5. **Extreme testing:** the tester designs extreme cases and tests how the system performs. This might comprise tests on hardware, such as removing and replacing the power cord, or on software, such as particularly large volumes of data, or using corrupted data files.

6. **Data testing:** data testing checks how the system copes with all manner of input data. This might include particularly large or small numbers, missing data, data set negative when it is usually positive or data arriving in an unusual format.

7. **International testing:** many systems are developed in one location for use internationally. The tester must simulate conditions in other locations, such as changing time zone and language to see if the system can operate correctly.

8. **Machine testing:** a system might be designed for all manner of hardware. The tester needs to check that it can run on all required platforms such as Blackberry, laptop, desktop and server.

9. **Depth testing:** depth testing checks that all the possible routes of functionality have been tested. For example, some screens might be four or five clicks away from the start screen. Anything released as part of the system, however inaccessible or unlikely to be used, should be part of a thorough test regime.

10. **Stress testing:** this determines the stability of the system by testing beyond normal operational use, often up to breaking point to observe where the limit lies.
11. **Regression testing:** once a set of tests has been designed and carried out, it is often desirable to be able to repeat them for subsequent releases of the system. Having a predefined set of tests, and comparing the results with those expected, is a quick and useful means of spotting problems that were not previously present. This is known as regression testing and can very often be automated.

19.6   FAULT LOGGING

A major part of testing is to record faults. Here we outline some of the salient features of fault logging. The tester will usually attempt to complete most of these, but they may be subject to changes by people such as project managers – the setting of priority being one example.

19.6.1   Types of fault

1. **Critical:** a critical fault will probably be communicated immediately to the support or development staff, but might also be logged for auditing and review purposes.
2. **Crash:** if a fault causes a system to crash it is, if nothing else, very annoying. It could also pull down other processes running on the same machine and cause loss or corruption of data. Crashes are generally regarded as unacceptable, even when there are workarounds available, and so fixing them is given a higher priority.
3. **Incorrect functionality:** here the system fails to do something it is supposed to do. This is a very wide-ranging type of fault; it could be innocuous or it could have very negative effects.
4. **Cosmetic:** although cosmetic changes might be given lower priority, they do detract from the usability of the product and are generally easy to fix.
5. **Request:** a request for new or changed functionality is not a fault, but very often the tester is in an ideal situation to make recommendations. It is helpful if there is some way for him to record them alongside the faults. This makes it easier for the development team to offer a concerted solution. The work involved in satisfying a request is usually very similar to that in fixing a fault, providing the request is for a small scale change or addition. Requests for major pieces of work should not feature in fault logs.

19.6.2   Workaround

Upon discovering a fault, the tester might, with or without the aid of the user, design a workaround to cope with the problem until it is fixed. It is helpful if some description of the workaround is provided so that priority can be assessed. Some workarounds are easy to live with; some are difficult and may cause other problems.

19.6.3   Priority

Priority can be assigned in multiple layers but broadly, faults have high, medium or low priority. Together with priority, the presence or absence of a workaround should be taken into account; an easy workaround might reduce the priority.

Faults are not always fixed in order of priority. Sometimes it makes sense for a developer working in one section of the system to fix all the faults in that area before moving on to another section. Also, the fixing of faults depends upon the availability of staff and how long the fault might take to fix. It might make sense to fix easy, lower priority faults, while waiting for a more experienced developer to become free for the higher priority but harder ones.

The number of high, medium and low faults gives an indication of the current quality of the system and its readiness for use. Of course it should be remembered that the absence of faults could indicate a robust system or, more worryingly, insufficient testing.

19.6.4   Area

A system might comprise several screens, areas of functionality or output reports. These might have been developed by different teams at different times, so it is important for the fault log to state exactly where the problem arose.

19.6.5   Fault description

If a fault is described comprehensively it is easier for the support or development team to locate the problem and fix it. The first thing someone investigating a fault will want to do is to recreate the problem, so it is good practice for the tester to state all of the steps leading up to the fault. "I pressed the Generate button and it hung" is less useful than "I entered a bond trade with the following characteristics [stated in the fault report] and when I pressed the Generate button the system stopped for at least five minutes whereupon I closed the application".

The context of the fault should also be reported: did it happen on first attempt, after 10 successful attempts etc. Sometimes one fault might be comprised of two or many faults; a good tester will think through what is happening in the system and try to identify all the individual faults.

Faults are sometimes caused by correct functionality being incorrectly documented. The tester should have a good feel for the system and its documentation to discern where the fault really lies. An incorrect document is misleading and impairs the successful operation of the system.

19.7   RISKS

Here we summarise the business and operational risks related to testing.

Too little testing: processes may not run correctly, leading to extra costs for the business. Misleading results may have undesirable consequences. The investment in developing or purchasing software is being wasted if the software fails to perform correctly.

Too much testing: resources are wasted carrying out superfluous testing and improving software beyond what is necessary.

Poor testing: there may be a false sense of security about the system if it is assumed testing has been carried out, but in reality it has either not been done at all or not been done effectively. This might lead to unexpected delays, faults or the assumption that results are accurate when they may actually be false.

Over reliance on testing: a well-tested system improves its quality and robustness, but does not make it more efficient. Underlying flaws in design or implementation may mean it is harder to extend the system in the future or it does not perform as well as it could. A well-tested system is not necessarily a good system.

Poor communication: as we have found, testing is a collaborative activity involving managers, developers, users and specialist testers. For testing to be effective, the results must be communicated to all interested parties. Developers must know and understand the faults, users must be aware of any shortcomings and managers need to build testing and fault fixing into their planning. The overall confidence in the system is highly dependent on good, effective testing.

19.8   SUMMARY

An organisation which devotes time to testing will enhance performance and reduce operational risks. There are various types and means of testing; each company will need to tailor their testing to suit the scale and complexity of their operations.

20
Data

Data, deriving from the Latin *dare* meaning to give, is used to refer to information. This definition is too wide for our purposes and so in this book, the word data will be taken to mean information required in the trade lifecycle and associated processes that originate from outside the trade itself. It may be helpful to think of the trade as the recipe and data as the ingredients – the success of the dish is very much dependent on the quality of its ingredients.

Note: data is technically a plural word but the singular, datum, is rarely used in the financial industry.

20.1   COMMON CHARACTERISTICS

The range and type of data required to process a trade can be vast. There are, however, a few factors which are common to most if not all data.

Identification: the data needs some unique identifier to distinguish it and show the user to what it refers.

Time of validity: the data provided is relevant for a given period of time. Data can be relevant for an instant and then be invalid seconds after it has been published or it could stay meaningful for many years.

Reference time: the data may refer to a given date or time or may be completely independent of time.

Value: the data has a value. This could be one item, a vector, a matrix or several dimensions of information. It could be textual, numeric or both.

Source: the data comes from a source. This could be a file, a person, an exchange or some publication.

20.2   DATABASE

A database is a mechanism for storing data. Some organisations use one database to hold all their data, while others have many. The key requirements of a database are:

Storage: it can actually store all the data required in a safe and secure manner. The data must retain its integrity – whatever is stored must be an acceptable representation of the original.

Retrieval: the retrieval must be efficient and accurate. It is useful and sometimes essential that data can be combined, filtered and sorted in the retrieval process.

Robust: the database should be available whenever it is required.

Database design is very important to the success of any process using data. The design must take into account the data to be stored and the likely retrieval queries required.

20.3   TYPES OF DATA

In considering the types of data used for the trade lifecycle, we divide them into three loosely defined groups based on the frequency of change.

Market data: this changes regularly. As the name implies, market data originates from the market. It is usually derived from recent market prices – a price being the agreed purchase cost of a trade or the price at which a trader would be prepared to enter into a trade. Examples of market data are:

- a 12-month future contract in cocoa traded in tonnes on the NYBOT commodities exchange;
- current exchange rate of GBP/USD;
- price of J Sainsbury ordinary shares on the London Stock Exchange.

Static data: static data changes very infrequently. Examples of static data are:

- industrial sector classification of Lloyds Banking Group;
- business day convention of Spanish government bonds;
- address of the Chicago Mercantile Exchange.

Semi-static data: this third group is hardest to define. It falls somewhere between market and static data and implies data which may change but not at regular intervals.
Examples:

- Moody's credit rating for Bulgaria;
- the recovery rate for British Airways bonds;
- the name of the chief executive of JJB Sports.

20.3.1   Why does type of data matter?

It is useful to split data into these categories in order to apply efficient processes for collecting and managing them.

Input: market data will need to be input at frequent intervals, static data can be input once and semi-static data need only be input upon a change.

Storage: most institutions will not delete old data, because it is useful in a variety of ways. So there needs to be room to store each bit of market data while it is in the system.

Although nowadays storing data is relatively cheap, access times will increase as the data grows and this needs to be taken into account when processes come to retrieve market data.

Expectation: processes receiving data need to know what data to expect, when it will arrive and how much of it there will be. Market data input processes might expect data for each member of the set, even if it remains unchanged from the previous day. Static data would not be expected at all: if there were a change it might require some manual intervention, as it may not be worth writing a process to cope with something so unexpected. Semi-static data would not usually be expected, but if it were present, processes would need to know what to do with it.

20.4   BID/OFFER SPREAD

A market maker facilitates trading by providing a market for the asset in question. To do this, he must be prepared to buy and sell the asset. He is not going to do that without some financial incentive to compensate him for his effort and the risk he is taking. The incentive is the bid/offer spread. For any given asset he will quote two prices: the lower is the one at which he is prepared to buy; the higher, the one at which he will sell. Hence if orders or traders come to him, some wanting to buy and some to sell, he will make a profit in this spread.

The risk to the market maker is that there will be more sellers than buyers or vice versa. This will mean he will have to raise or lower his prices to regulate the market. He needs to make a careful judgement when fixing his bid and offer prices using his professional skill. The greater the difference (or spread) between bid and offer prices, the greater his profit. However, he has to compete with other market makers and therefore his spread needs to be realistic.

It could be argued that in collecting market data, one need only calculate the mid price (the average of bid and offer) and record that as the price for that asset. However, there are at least two reasons why one might wish to store bid and offer prices.

The size of the bid/offer spread can be a good reflection of the liquidity of the market. A larger spread means that the market maker is not expecting high volumes of trade and needs to insure against a one-way traffic in the trade. Also he needs to make more money on each transaction as trading is sparse. The converse is true when markets are very liquid. In addition, at times of uncertainty in market prices, the spread will widen. For example, the single biggest economic indicator published periodically is the non farm payroll released by the US Bureau of Labor Statistics on the first Friday of each month. Just before the announcement at 08:30 Eastern standard or daylight time (13:30 in UK, 14:30 in Europe), spreads in assets directly affected by the figure will widen considerably.

The second reason for storing bid and offer prices is that these show the actual price required to trade the asset. The mid price is theoretical but cannot actually be traded. For instance a bank holding 100 million Ford Motor company bonds and wanting to sell them in the market will need to know the best offer price available, rather than the mid price.

20.5   CURVES AND SURFACES

When market data is expressed as a figure for a given unit of time (or tenor), it is often helpful to aggregate the data for all its tenors to form a curve. To the system, the curve is simply a vector of numbers, one for each period of time; to the human being operating or using the data, it is line drawn on a graph with the price on the Y axis and time on the X axis. From curves we can infer the market's predictions for the future direction of assets. The points on the curve comprise quotes for future or forward instruments.

Table 20.1 shows gold future prices as of September 2009.[1]

And Figure 20.1 shows the corresponding futures curve.

Now let us consider one of the most fundamental curves – interest rates. There are many institutions prepared to lend money for a variety of terms ranging from overnight to at least 30 years. The interest rate applied is a function of the credit worthiness of the borrower – the lender's expectation of receiving full repayment of his loan. Even if the borrower were 100 % guaranteed to repay on time, however, the lender would still charge to cover the loss in value of money over time. This market value is the fundamental interest rate and is used to price money over time using discount factors.

To determine this curve, we need to find where the market quotes interest rates for lending money, without credit risk of non payment. There are two such markets – the inter-bank market and the bond market for a very secure government bond.

The inter-bank market is where large banks lend to each other with the assumption of repayment. Similarly, US Treasury bonds are considered fully guaranteed by the security of the United States government.

---

[1] Published by Comex Gold.

Table 20.1

Future contract date	Price (USD per troy oz)
Oct 2009	997.0
Nov 2009	996.3
Dec 2009	996.5
Feb 2010	999.7
Apr 2010	999.4
Jun 2010	1001.1
Aug 2010	1002.4
Oct 2010	1001.2
Dec 2010	1005.6
Feb 2011	1006.1
Apr 2011	1009.2
Jun 2011	1012.6
Dec 2011	1024.7
Jun 2012	1039.0
Dec 2012	1055.4
Jun 2013	1073.4
Dec 2013	1092.2
Jun 2014	1112.4

An inter-bank market such as LIBOR (London inter bank offer rate) has three types of market instrument.

Money market: these are short-term loans from overnight to nine or 12 months in duration.

Futures: these are standard contracts for forward exchanges of money, where the rates are fixed today. They range from about three months to two years.

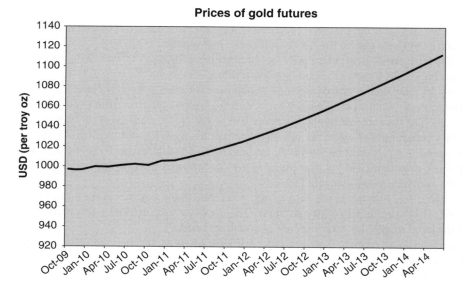

Figure 20.1   Comex gold futures

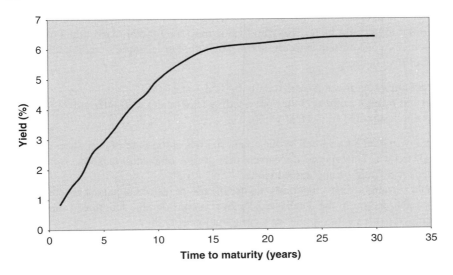

Figure 20.2   Yield curve

Swaps: these are quoted for longer periods extending up to 30 years or beyond.

By combining prices for these three sets of instruments, we can derive a yield curve which indicates the yield (or interest rate) against time (Figure 20.2).

Surface: some instruments have three dimensions – two dimensions of data for any time period. In order to look at the shape of market data over time, we need to use a three dimensional object, usually referred to as a surface. A typical example is implied volatility. Although volatility is generally regarded as a reflection of the way prices move, it can also be a source of market data. This is because premium prices of an option infer the volatility (known as the implied volatility). The typical behaviour of options is that they have greater implied volatility when deeply in- or out-of-the-money. In- or out-of-the-money is a function of price. So in order to model the market data we need three dimensions – value, price and time. By observing market data for implied volatility across different prices and times, we can construct an implied volatility surface.

It is important to recognise that future curves and surfaces generated from current market data are only a market-implied snapshot of how asset prices will move. They change as market prices change and therefore implied future prices have volatility. They are, in essence, current market data for spot and future instruments – they are not actual future prices.

20.6   SETS OF MARKET DATA

Let us consider the universe of market data required to handle all of a financial entity's trade processes and calculations. Different sets of market data can be applied depending on the business function and the type of operation being performed. Here we discuss some of these types.

Current (live): as the name implies, current market data is what is available in the market place right now. It is by definition the latest possible set of real market prices.

Official: a financial entity will usually designate a set of market data to be official and use it in order to perform its reporting and valuation. The official market data may be from a specific source or one present at a certain time, or both. For example a credit hedge fund might designate official data as:

- credit default swap prices provided daily by CMA at 17:00;
- interest and foreign exchange rates provided by Bloomberg at 16:40; and
- credit ratings supplied by S&P at 18:00.

Dealt: any market data agreed by the counterparties at the time of execution will form part of the trade details. This may be the current data at time of execution, some average of recent market data or it could be any agreed value.

Historic: certain business functions require the use of historical data. This could consist of the official data stored in the database daily over a considerable length of time or historical data purchased from a data supplier or a combination of both.

Indicative: sometimes an approximation to market data is required without precise numbers. This is known as indicative market data.

Random: many processes are concerned with simulating possible market data. One means of achieving this is to use random data. Although truly random numbers are very hard to generate, computers have randomising functions which can produce pseudo-random data.

Predicted: mathematical techniques can be applied to a selection of random data to predict averages, likely ranges and extreme values.

User selected: there are occasions when data is missing, of poor quality, incomplete or unlikely. The user will then want to input his own values. Alternatively, he may want to test out different scenarios using his own choice of market data.

20.6.1   Business usage of market data sets

Having listed the possible types of market data sets, we now see how different business functions will use them (Table 20.2).

Sales: the sales force is attempting to attract clients to the institution. It needs to demonstrate trades and their likely effects over time. Example data is generally sufficient for these purposes and so indicative data can be used. Where salesmen are concluding trades with clients, current data may be required.

Table 20.2   Business functions use of various data types

	Indicative	Current	User	Official	Historic	Predicted	Random
Sales	Mainly	Possible					
Traders	Yes	Yes	Yes	Yes		Yes	Yes
Middle office			Yes	Yes			
Back office		Likely		Possible			
Market risk		Yes		Yes	Yes	Yes	Yes
Credit risk		Yes				Yes	
Legal	Yes				Yes		
Audit	Yes	Yes	Yes	Yes	Yes	Yes	Yes
Finance				Yes			
Management		Yes		Yes			

Trading: traders are constantly looking for opportunities and seeking to maximise their profits while keeping their exposure to risk under control. They need as many different sources of data as possible in order to perform these activities. A trader will frequently want to see live, official and future data at the same time – future data being comprised of random, predicted or his own estimations.

Presenting data to a trader is a problem in itself. Most traders have their own way of working and will have many screens to accommodate their needs. The trader will want to switch rapidly between his sources. He may want to keep his live source and have real time updates on his positions or freeze it while he tests other scenarios. It is important that at all times the trader is aware of the source and time of any data he is viewing.

Sudden changes in live data are of particular interest as they may represent trading opportunities or require action to reduce risks.

Although traders develop an ability to view and process vast amounts of information, systems which help them can enhance profitability and reduce errors. In designing such processes it is essential to know and understand how the trader operates. Then the machine can mimic the way the trader uses data.

Middle office: the middle office is charged with ensuring that trading processes run correctly. This encompasses the trades themselves and the market data feeding them. The middle office has to choose the most appropriate data source which is then, by definition, the official source. Middle office has to have operational procedures for dealing with bad data in the official source – this could include manual overrides, hence their use of user data.

Traders often have the best access to market data, as they are dealing with it continually. Middle office has to be wary before accepting data from traders for official use because:

- traders will naturally want to show their trades in a good light using data that maximises P&L;
- traders want to show they dealt trades at competitive prices. The trader will not want the embarrassment of official data contradicting his view of the market or showing his trade to be unnecessarily risky.

Back office: confirmations and settlements usually require small amounts of market data, but they must be very accurate and agreed with the counterparty. Often the data used is that quoted on a particular exchange at a particular time.

Market risk control: market risk control departments rely on market data. The approach they take to quantifying market risk will determine what type of market data they use. For analysis using historical data, they need to look back as far as possible. They will also need to deal with situations where current trades or markets did not exist historically and "invent" data using one of the techniques described below.

If they employ a stochastic model, they will use predicted data garnered from a small range of current and historical data; for simulations such as Monte Carlo they require random data.

As well as looking at the past, market risk needs a thorough understanding of current exposures and will generally use official data or possibly live data for this purpose.

Credit risk control: credit risk control staff are interested in measuring exposure to counterparties' default on payment. They are concerned with current and predicted market positions and will use data accordingly.

Finance: the finance department prepares and maintains the official books and records. It would normally use data approved by middle office.

Legal: the legal department is generally more concerned with the context and definition of data than the content. Staff there are more likely to use static data for definitions rather than market data. Some legal trading documents will use indicative or example data for illustration.

Audit: audit departments need to consider all use of data in the institution. They will be interested in seeing how the different types of data are used and what steps are taken to ensure the data is authentic.

General management: managers want to supervise the activities of all business functions. In order to be able to form strategy, deal with problems and report accurately, they will need official data. Live data might also be used for immediate issues.

20.7   BACK TESTING

This is a technique employed by several business functions to determine how a current real or potential trade would have performed with historical market data. This gives the tester some "feel" for the trade and allows the processes to be thought through to ensure that valuation, reporting, risk control and other activities would have enough data available to manage the trade. Back testing is instructive, but relies on the assumption that future data will be similar to past data, which may not be realistic.

20.8   HOW CAN DATA GO WRONG?

As trading processes are so reliant on data it is important to understand how data can go wrong. Here we present some of the common symptoms of bad data and some techniques for dealing with them.

Missing: any process that relies on a complete set of market data is going to fail when any data is missing. Missing data may not be due to any fault in the data supplier: genuinely missing data is an occupational hazard for the data user and arises because not all market data is published with the same frequency.

Extreme values: due to errors in data compilation or publication, sometimes data appears far too large or too small or negative when it should be positive or vice versa. It could also be a reasonable value, but not in the context of data on either side of it or in comparison with data the day before or day after from the same source. Detecting extremes can be very easy when the range of likely values is known and consistent. But on the other hand, it could require great experience and diligence. It is possible for machines to check for extremes if a test can be devised using logical rules.

Stale: if data arrives today exactly like yesterday's at one or many points this can cause problems. The lack of change could be genuine – the source not having altered – or it could be the symptom of a problem.

Incomplete: another data problem occurs when a source provides most data correctly, but some of the file or feed is missing from the start, middle or end. Although this manifests itself in the same way as missing data described above, it is usually for a completely different reason. In the case of incompleteness, the problem is nearly always due to an error on the side of the data provider and not because of inherent problems in the data itself.

Invalid: examples of invalid data are numbers that appear as text, columns in the wrong order, extra lines or characters appearing where they are not expected. If the format of data is different from what is expected, the reader process will either fail or use incorrect values.

20.8.1   Techniques for dealing with bad data

Reject: the process requiring data can be instructed to reject the data when it is bad. This would involve informing the user and probably also telling the data supplier. All subsequent processes would also have to be suspended if they were relying on outputs from this process. Of all the causes of bad data, the most likely to involve outright rejection would be invalid or incomplete data. If all data were stale that would also indicate a data supplier problem.

   Prompt user: if one or a number of data points were missing, stale or extreme the user could be alerted and prompted to input more reasonable data or accept that the data present is correct. This would involve the process waiting for the user response. If there were many problems it might be too time consuming or labour intensive for the user to fix them and a more systematic approach would be required.

   Warn user: another technique is for the processor of data to continue to work with bad data where possible and list all the errors and suspected errors as it goes, reporting the list to the user at the end. The user can then investigate the problems and decide what action to take. He could:

- disregard the results, fix the problems and re-run the process;
- proceed without fixing;
- fix the errors, but use the initial results in the interim until a run with the fixes has been completed.

   Interpolate across missing or bad point: a point is one data item usually existing in a set of data. Mathematical techniques can be used to estimate a point. This is most commonly used when data is missing, but can also be applied to extreme or stale data. Suppose we have data for futures data for EUR interest rates as follows:

6m	98.7675
9m	98.6175
15m	98.0125
18m	97.6775

   If the machine or user has detected that the 12m point is missing, we could apply some sort of interpolation (linear, cubic spline etc.). This interpolation could use the other future instruments shown here or an extrapolation from values of previous days for the missing instrument (12m).

   Data engineering: when interpolation is not appropriate, a wider means of correcting bad data is to look at the context of the existing good data and use trends to predict for the bad or missing points. Suppose we are missing an entire day's credit curve for HSBC which is in the UK banking sector. If we looked at the last month of credit data and found that five year credit spreads for HSBC were an average of 8 % lower than that of the UK banking sector, we could apply an 8 % reduction in today's UK banking sector values and use it for the missing five year spread. Similarly for the one year, two year, three year spreads etc. Alternatively, we could take the whole UK corporate credit market as our control set of data or we could take the international or European banking sector. The decision as to which control set is to be used is a subjective one, depending on experience of the market and the use to which the data is to be put.

   Data discovery: sometimes a financial entity is confronted with the problem of pricing a trade in a new business area or in an existing one where price data is or has been hard to come by. It might have to research new data sources to complement the existing ones or to make use of a one-off snapshot of data. An example might be when trading with a new, small counterparty and having to investigate its credit worthiness.

Using alternative sources of data can be expensive and requires a proper process of vetting to ensure the new source meets the required standard of validity and authenticity.

Data cleaning: data cleaning is a process automatically applied to data in anticipation of errors, rather than a reaction to errors once they are known. The cleaning is a two-stage process:

- detecting bad data – this could be bad in any of the ways described above;
- correcting bad data – again using one of the techniques above.

Time series analysis: periodic trends are commonplace in market data. Oil prices might be higher in November than July, share prices fall just after ex-dividend date and bid/offer spreads might be wider on the Friday afternoon before a public holiday. Mathematical models can analyse data for such trends and separate them from changes caused by market forces. This is particularly useful in fixing bad or missing data.

Some instruments have long-term trends that can be detected and measured if enough market data is present or if the fundamentals behind the instrument price are well-known. For example, the 30 year price of crude oil is mean-reverting so, irrespective of current ups and downs, the long-term price tends to converge on a fairly stable value.

20.8.2   When to fix bad data

Designing and building systems to fix bad data can be expensive and sometimes it is unnecessary. If the process using supplied data is of low importance or the data quality is generally very good, it may not be worth investing time in fixing bad data.

A judgement needs to be made taking into account the likelihood of bad data and the damage it may cause.

20.9   TYPICAL DATA SOURCES

Exchanges: trading exchanges publish market prices to the members of the exchange and sometimes to the public. These are generally very accurate and up to date.

Vendor data: there are many companies selling market data. They provide a range of services including live price tickers, on-demand queries and periodic data files. Most will also supply historical data. The data they quote consists of broker prices, bid and offer quotes and recent transaction prices. The daily price file might comprise an average set of prices throughout the day, through the last trading hour or the very last traded prices.

Many vendors apply data cleaning and engineering processes to the raw data. It is important for users of the data to be aware of exactly how the supplied data was derived. In making comparisons between different data suppliers or using multiple suppliers, the user might need to make adjustments to compensate for these differences.

Vendors often supply user interfaces or entire systems along with their data. Some incorporate trade booking and calculation functions. Many small institutions might be able to use the system for all their trade lifecycle processes. In such a case, care should be taken to understand the risks of complete dependency on a third-party vendor.

Often the challenge in accepting exchange or vendor data is incorporating the format into the finance house's existing processes and systems. Time and money should be budgeted for such conversion, which might also involve data transformation.

Internal data: a large organisation that has been trading for some time will have built up a considerable store of data. It is obviously in the firm's interests to use that data before paying for an external supply. Sometimes, however, there is a need for an independent source to check the integrity of the data already being held.

20.10   HOW TO COPE WITH CORRECTIONS TO DATA

It is useful and sometimes essential to record the source and exact time that data was received. If the source is a process, the username of the person running the process or the machine from which it is run could be recorded to ensure a full audit trail of data.

It is possible that daily reports were run using a set of data that was later corrected in time for a monthly report. So the monthly report is not going to give the same results as the daily reports from which it is comprised. Here we present two methods of indicating which data was used in a data process.

1. Record all the input data and log it against the process details so that at a later date, all of the data used in the process can be retrieved.
2. Record the timestamp from which the process drew its input data. Later data can be retrieved by searching for data that would have been present at that timestamp. Here is an illustration of how data might have changed and how the timestamp could be used.

Commodity X

Ref Date	Price	User	Timestamp	Reason
15 Jan 09	88.7	Amelia	15 Jan 17:06	Source
15 Jan 09	88.27	Billy	15 Jan 17:33	Correction
15 Jan 09	88.09	Charlie	21 Jan 12:03	Correction

Now, for the overnight process on 15 January the price used would be 88.27 (the last entered value on that day). However the end of month report for January would use 88.09 (as entered by Charlie later in the month).

An historical process running in July would return to using 88.27 in order to recreate the actual data run on that day.

When correcting data, some people like to maintain a record of the original value and add notes explaining how the corrected value was derived.

If data is not recorded carefully, it can be lost during the calculation process and deriving it from results is usually impossible. This means that the user can never repeat the original process and get the same results. When queries are raised about the results by management, auditors, shareholders or any other interested party, it will be hard to know if the cause was poor data or some other factor.

Exceptions and errors: a distinction can be made between when a process has failed because the data source is missing and when the data itself has errors. An exception is the term given by IT to when the process has not run properly; an error is when the process has run successfully but the data itself has faults.

Categories of error are described above. Exceptions could be caused by:

- power failure during process
- supplier not providing the data
- out of storage space
- expected input file misnamed or in the wrong place
- version of software not compatible with version of data.

To diagnose and fix problems it is helpful to make this distinction. The user will then know where to look for the cause of the problem.

20.11   DATA INTEGRITY

In order to be able to manage data effectively, it is helpful to maintain its integrity. This means making a distinction between the various stages input data goes through. It should also be clear where all data comes from.

Raw: raw data is that which is received directly from the data provider, warts and all. It is fed into the system and stored. It may be that more than one set of raw data is gathered each day, or that if one source fails another is used. Knowing the actual source of raw data then becomes more relevant.

Processed: raw data may suffer from some of the deficiencies described above, such as missing or unlikely values. Techniques to overcome these problems, also described above, will result in a modified set of input data which we can call processed input data.

Implied: many valuation and reporting processes require more than input data (be it raw or processed). For example, a CDO pricing function may require a hazard rate which is not a directly quoted instrument in the market place. The hazard rate can, however, be implied from the credit default swap instrument for which prices are available.

Therefore an intermediate process would be required to take the raw or processed data and convert it to an implied hazard rate curve. Although implied data can be recreated from source data, it is sometimes beneficial to store it:

- so that it can only be implied once and then can be reused many times saving processing time;
- to allow more thorough checking and understanding of the process. By breaking it down and storing the implied data, the user can see how implied is affected by raw and then how the final result is affected by the implied.

Sometimes implied data can be at a much simpler level. A mid price is the average of quoted bid and offer prices. It does not always exist in the market place in which case it would be implied data.

Although there is often a temptation to apply logic to raw input data and to store a modified value in the database, an assessment should be undertaken to balance the efficiency gained against the loss of integrity.

20.11.1   Importance of data integrity

Integrity is important when a query arises on a reported value. The report will be at the very final stage in the process, so the user will have to trace through all the input and intermediate processes to find if it was caused by incorrect data, incorrect processing or is indeed a valid result. If data has been automatically changed by the input process it makes this investigation harder. Proving the error was caused by the data provider is also more difficult if the client does not have the actual data supplied in his systems. Just as the police seek to secure and preserve a crime scene, so any auditor or investigator will want data to remain exactly as it was supplied.

Another advantage of preserving integrity is that historical data processes will always be working with the same data, even if adjustment processes have changed (see Figure 20.3).

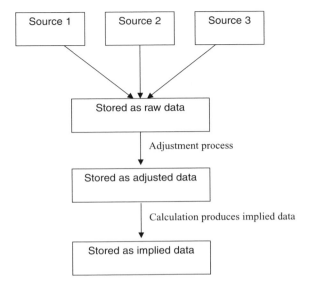

Figure 20.3 How data changes

20.12   THE BUSINESS RISKS OF DATA

20.12.1   Putting too much faith in data

Everybody involved in the trade lifecycle is using and working with the effects of input data. Key management strategies, day-to-day tasks and split second trading decisions are all based on input data – directly or through reports and calculations. It is easy to assume that data is correct – we have been receiving it for many years, the supplier is authentic and other people use the same data.

Due diligence would surely require the question to be raised of what happens if the data is wrong and perhaps more worryingly, what if it's wrong sometimes but not always? The success of the cake depends on the ingredients.

20.12.2   Not reacting to data

The other extreme is too little notice taken of input data. If the data is an accurate reflection of the state of the market, warning signs, such as larger than usual changes, should be detected quickly and reported to the people who can make decisions. It is of little use if a junior clerk in the back office spots an irregular pattern and by the time the news filters through to the management it is too late to react.

20.12.3   Coping when data not there

A good test of the resilience of an organisation is to switch off its market data supply for one day and see how it copes. Are there back-up procedures in place, can data be obtained or inferred from other sources? As data is so important, these scenarios should be taken into consideration.

20.12.4   Ensuring authentic data

Obviously data must be authentic to be a trusted source. This may be easy to verify in the case of a daily feed from a vendor's ftp^2 site or by a secure delivery mechanism, but other types of data can be potentially insecure. Live data arriving at users' machines or directly entering the database can be hazardous and difficult to monitor. The recipient of this data needs to balance the benefit of such data being available so easily with the security risk involved.

20.13   SUMMARY

Data is very important to the trade lifecycle. It comes in many forms and from many sources. Successful trading organisations rely upon good data. We have defined what makes good data and shown how it is used, processed and managed throughout the trade lifecycle and the various business functions.

---

^{2} File Transfer Protocol (FTP) is a standard network protocol used to exchange and manipulate files over a network, such as the Internet.

21

Reports

21.1 INTRODUCTION

A report is a mechanism for conveying information. A process works on data and produces results. These results are reported to interested parties. Examples of reports featured in the trade lifecycle are:

- opinion of the legal department on a proposed trade and issues requiring clarification;
- report on all new trades transacted today;
- current P&L per trader;
- combined asset holdings across all trading divisions;
- budget for forthcoming year;
- management explanation of sudden large losses;
- list of bonds paying coupon in the next seven days;
- research paper on the state of the lead mining industry.

Reporting is a fundamental part of the processing of a trade. In order for all business functions to perform their daily tasks, they need recent, relevant and accurate information about the trade. This information flows by way of reports.

Reports are generated from input data, other reports or both (see Figure 21.1).

They can consist of text, tables, graphs, pictures or any other media for conveying information.

21.2 WHAT MAKES A GOOD REPORT?

A good report is precise, concise, timely and relevant to its readership. It gives the appropriate level of detail and it communicates the information in a clear manner. Problems, errors and exceptions are clearly marked, as are differences from the norm. We shall now discuss factors influencing how a report should be planned and produced.

21.3 REPORTING REQUIREMENTS

21.3.1 Readership

The content and presentation of the report will depend upon the readership.

- An external audience will require more formal language and style.
- Management prefer brevity with information being summarised.
- Control functions may want a top down approach – where totals are on page one with details on subsequent pages should they want to drill down into the information.

When there is a mixed readership, combining the requirements of both may mean the information is not delivered in the best way. In this case it may be best to split the report in two.

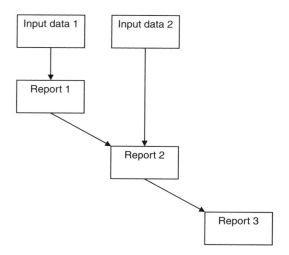

Figure 21.1   Inputs to reports

21.3.2   Content

Exactly what information is required? Is there additional information that, although not being absolutely necessary, will enhance the report? Too much information will overload the reader and he may miss something important; too little information and the report will fail to achieve its purpose. Is the content clear and unambiguous? Are abbreviations going to be understood? Where graphs and tables are not fully explained, will the reader know what they mean?

21.3.3   Presentation

The style and format of the report are as important as its contents. The human eye will be drawn to the unusual and the reader is more likely to take notice of something which is easy to read and understand – he does not want to plough through 10 pages of text to find the one number he needs from the report.

Careful use of colours can enhance a report, but will not show up on black and white hard copies. Font size can be used to distinguish between the essential, the useful and the nice to have. Similarly bold text and italics can convey extra meaning.

The old adage that a picture says a thousand words is applicable to reporting. A graph summarises a table of data and a table summarises a list of figures.

21.3.4   External readership

Producing any report sent outside the organisation may require a higher level of information such as legal disclaimers, copyright notices or regulatory wording. A written report may burden an institution with unwanted obligations and errors could be very costly, so external reports require a greater level of checking. People who may be required to check external reports include:

• legal counsel
• compliance

- press officers
- management
- staff responsible for corporate image.

21.3.5   Habit

Readers get accustomed to the layout of reports. If the layout is changed even slightly, it can cause confusion and frustration. When changes do have to be made the readership should at least be informed or, better still, consulted.

21.3.6   Distribution

Nowadays there are several means of distributing reports available:

- paper copies being transmitted by post or fax
- soft copy by manual email
- soft copy by automated email
- an application or system for report manipulation
- web-based dynamic reporting.

The means of distribution must suit the reporting requirements and are constrained by the reporting budget. Although more powerful than the alternatives, web-based reporting is not always the most cost effective solution. Automated emails are very good in principle, but if the report requires checking before distribution they can be dangerous. Where reports require a physical signature, paper hard copy is the only viable media of distribution. An application allowing the user to choose his own reports can be very useful but it may be expensive and too much for the user to cope with.

21.3.7   Timing

There are several constraints affecting the timing of reports.

- Input data must be present and correct.
- Any dependency reports must have been run.
- Machines must be available to run the report.
- The distribution mechanism must be ready to transmit the report – a report is not complete until it has reached its readers.

When scheduling reports, the generator must consider when they start and stop being useful to their readers. Some reports are for background information, while others form the basis of decisions and other processes. The timing of some reports is crucial – if they do not arrive on time, they might as well not arrive at all.

If constraints mean a report is not ready when it would be most useful to its readers, extra investment might be considered to bring forward its publication. Reporting priorities should be determined at the outset and then periodically reviewed as business needs change over time.

Table 21.1

Name	Time run	Duration	Accuracy
Flash	Evening	10 minutes	Approximate
Internal	Overnight	Several hours	Accurate but possibility of data errors etc.
External	End of month	Several hours	Accurate and errors removed

21.3.8   Accuracy

An appropriate level of accuracy should be applied to the report. Making it more accurate may be time consuming and unnecessary for certain reports – the user may prefer a faster, less accurate report than a slower, more accurate one. An example of this would be the P&L report which might be run to three different levels of accuracy (Table 21.1).

The risk of running a less than accurate report is that a reader may not realise the level of accuracy and make inappropriate decisions based upon it. This is particularly so if the report is read by people for whom it is not primarily intended. There is a human tendency to believe what one sees written down – to mitigate this risk the level of accuracy can be clearly printed on the report – for instance, "For guidance only".

21.3.9   Raw reporting

A report communicates information from the producer to the reader. As such, the needs of the reader should be taken into account. Very often the report is produced in a style and format dictated by the method of production. It may sometimes be appropriate to write an extra process that converts the raw report into something more readable. This is also useful when one report is going to be read by several different users. In general, production of the raw report takes more time than enhancing it, so several report enhancers could be written, all based upon the same raw report.

21.3.10   Configuration

Even if the user cannot change the actual report he receives dynamically, it may be very useful for him to be able to specify his own requirements and for the report to be produced with these in mind. This would not just be for the initial set-up but for ongoing changes as well.

If the data comprising the report is sufficiently granular then a layer of configuration can be applied to it to produce the required specification.

Consider the example report in Table 21.2 below.

1. The user might want to select his own fields: today he only wants lead, copper and total.
2. He may want to filter the report and only see items with P&L greater than USD 30 million or less than USD –30 million.
3. He may want to sort the traders by profitability, starting with the most profitable.

Selection of fields, filtering data and sorting are the most common examples of user configuration.

Configuration depends upon all the underlying data being available, a means by which the user can specify what he requires and a process that can take the user options and apply them to the data to produce the finished report.

Table 21.2 Precious metals P&L (USD millions) as of 6 Jan 2009 by trader

Alice	Tin	Steel	Lead	Aluminium	Copper	Total
Spot	45.63		99.40	74.50	−10.09	**209.44**
Future	−33.50					**−33.50**
Options						**0.00**
Total	**12.13**	**0.00**	**99.40**	**74.50**	**−10.09**	**175.94**

Barbara	Tin	Steel	Lead	Aluminium	Copper	Total
Spot		−30.00			4.44	**−25.56**
Future		−28.77		5.00	7.12	**−16.65**
Options		−303.33				**−303.33**
Total	**0.00**	**−362.10**	**0.00**	**5.00**	**11.56**	**−345.54**

Carmelle	Tin	Steel	Lead	Aluminium	Copper	Total
Spot						**0.00**
Future						**0.00**
Options	44.33	101.22	99.22	20.03	38.99	**303.79**
Total	**44.33**	**101.22**	**99.22**	**20.03**	**38.99**	**303.79**

All	Tin	Steel	Lead	Aluminium	Copper	Total
Spot	45.63	−30.00	99.40	74.50	−5.65	**183.88**
Future	−33.50	−28.77	0.00	5.00	7.12	**−50.15**
Options	44.33	−202.11	99.22	20.03	38.99	**0.46**
Total	**56.46**	**−260.88**	**198.62**	**99.53**	**40.46**	**134.19**

Configuration is a very powerful way of delivering an exact report to the reader – it can take one generated set of results and produce countless different reports.

Web-based reporting is a dynamic means by which the user can send his requirements to a remote machine controlled by the report supplier and quickly see the outputted report.

21.3.11   Dynamic

A dynamic report is one that allows the user to change it on the spot. He may add headings, change column widths, put in summary totals or change the content by adding filters and sorting criteria as described in the section above.

21.3.11.1   Advantages

- Dynamic reports reduce the need for a dialogue between the report producer and the user.
- Sophisticated reports can be produced tailor-made to user requirements with no extra work for the producer.

21.3.11.2   Disadvantages

- Some users do not have the time or the desire to learn how to produce dynamic reports.
- Very often documentation and guidance need to be provided.
- There may be the potential for a dynamically produced report to convey the wrong information or message. Dynamic reporting should allow changes in format but never changes in content.

21.3.12   Frame of reference

In general reports should state the date and time of their production. Thus if the user receives two similar reports he can immediately distinguish them. Auditors or others who are tracking historical reports will know the information available when the report was produced.

The report should also convey its terms of reference such as:

- timeframe of report – next six months, yesterday, past five years etc.;
- data sources;
- assumptions;
- input parameters;
- types of trade reported on – deleted, amended, open, matured, new etc.;
- a confidence interval should be applied to any statistical predictions, e.g. there is 95 % probability that the total risk will not exceed X dollars.

21.3.13   The problem of multiple dimensions

Most reports are constrained by only having two dimensions available to the reader. (Some graphs can be three-dimensional, as can computer-simulated graphics.) When results occur in multiple dimensions, the producer must decide how best to convey the information. He could break everything down into an array of two-dimensional outputs, he could let the user configure his own results (see the configuration section above) or data could be combined to reduce it to two dimensions. This solution will depend upon the level of detail or brevity of report required.

21.4   WHEN THINGS GO WRONG

There are three main areas in which a report can go wrong:

- Results are wrong.
- Results are correct but incomplete.
- The report is not generated at all.

Depending upon the importance of the material, it may be worth having a report testing process (human or systematic), which can look for any of these problems and take action if it finds one.

Other useful additions to the reporting process are:

- Putting a status on the report such as number of records processed or time taken to run. Then the user can see if the number or time is different from usual.

- The reporting process may generate warnings and errors as it goes – these could be reported to the user. (It may be that the user is not interested in the specifics, but just needs to know the number and type of errors.)
- When no report is produced a blank report could be sent explaining the absence. This is often preferable to nothing being sent and the user just assuming it is late or that it was received but he mislaid it. People like to know as early as possible when a problem arises, even if it has not been resolved.
- Provide a mechanism for the user to report suspected problems. The readers of reports are often the best people to detect faults – if they can report them and know their report will be acted upon, everybody gains.
- Important reports can be sent in two or more stages. First to friendly users who can provide constructive feedback and then to more remote or demanding users, who expect a higher degree of quality. Blitzing the whole readership in one go can be dangerous for one-off or unusual reports that are not tried and tested.

21.5 REDUNDANCY

Over the course of time, there is a tendency for a report's distribution list to grow. Generally people are quick to ask for a report they need but less inclined to inform the distributor when they no longer need it. This can lead to problems.

- For sensitive information it may be important to know who is reading the report.
- When contemplating switching off a report, it is necessary to know who may still be reading it.
- The size of the readership may determine the resources invested in maintaining or enhancing a report – if this size is inaccurate, perhaps the resources are being misused.

Several years ago an investment bank discovered an old mainframe system was producing 532 different reports for 212 users across the organisation with each receiving between one and 10 different reports. The system was going to be replaced and an audit was undertaken to decide which reports were still required. After a three month process it was discovered that only five different reports were being used and that 80 % of the mainframe readership had either left the company altogether or had moved to a job no longer requiring the reports.

Many reporting systems have an easy way of adding and deleting from the readership. They may also have built in diagnostics to show if a user no longer exists or is no longer reading the report. Some report producers carry out regular surveys to ensure their distribution list is current and appropriate.

21.6 CONTROL

A key decision in the operation of any report is who is going to control the production and distribution. Sometimes the generation of the report is separate from the distribution mechanism. There are usually three choices:

- operator: a person independent from the readership;
- automated: such as via a computer system;
- user: a member of the readership produces the report for himself. He may also be responsible for distribution to other people.

21.7   ENHANCEMENT

The basis of a report is the production of results from a set of input data and parameters. Some reports take this basic level of results and enhance it by means of opinions, summaries, conclusions, trend lines or by any other narrative. It is often this "value added" report that contains the real benefit to the readership. However it is a good idea to try to separate facts (or basic results) from opinion (or enhancements). Any enhancement should also state the author in case of query or the need for further information.

21.8   SECURITY

The transmission of any report requires an appropriate level of security to ensure it does not fall into the wrong hands. This might involve:

- secure transmission
- encoding
- password protection
- request-only distribution
- monitoring
- limited copies being produced.

21.9   RISKS

We have mentioned two reporting risks above: security lapses and the acceptance of inaccuracies because they are written in the report. But there are other risks associated with reports.

Even correctly produced reports are subject to misinterpretation, if the readership is not fully educated about their limitations and scope.

If a report is the basis for decision-making there must be somebody receiving the report who is in a position to make the decisions. Moreover, if two or more people attempt to act upon a report, it is important they are acting in concert and not duplicating or contradicting each other.

Once a report has been distributed there is a risk that nobody can interpret the results or explain how they were derived. The production team might have gone home, it may be another time zone or the producers themselves are not able to answer the queries. An unexpected result might indicate a major problem requiring urgent action or it may be a false alarm. Either way prompt dialogue can avert many problems and requires people of sufficient knowledge being available.

Lack of coordination in report production or distribution might lead to mixed signals being transmitted, confusing or misleading the readership. Inaccurate translation can also carry risks in multiple language environments.

If a report requires retraction or correction, it is important to act fast. Generally, once something is in writing, it is hard to erase its effects whether they are benign or malign – and a written or electronic report always has a potential to be quoted or reused.

21.10   SUMMARY

Here we have discussed what makes a good report, how reports are used within a financial entity and how reporting requires careful management and awareness of inherent risks.

22

Calculation

Between the input data and the output reports sits the calculation process. The calculation could be anything from a "back of an envelope" approximation taking milliseconds to a precise multi-factor mathematical model taking days to run.

The degree of expenditure in the calculation process depends upon many factors including:

- Are trusted mark-to-market valuations available in the market place?
- Is there an accepted calculation model?
- Are other valuation processes available and accessible?
- What is the required level of accuracy?
- How sophisticated are the products to be valued?
- Is scenario analysis desirable?
- What are the range and type of output reports required?
- What is the extent of risk calculations?

22.1 WHAT DOES THE CALCULATION PROCESS ACTUALLY DO?

22.1.1 Example from outside the financial world

In order to illustrate how to calculate the value of a trade let us consider an example of a second hand motor vehicle (see Table 22.1).

I own a five-year-old Ford Galaxy diesel, manual transmission car. If cars with the same specification are available in the second hand car market, I can mark-to-market my car and gauge its current value. Let us suppose it is worth £8500.

Now my car has extras which are not part of the quoted market prices, so I need to make an estimate of their worth and add it to the price.

Hence I might mark my car as $8500 + 790 = £9390$.

A similar example would be valuing a house. Unless identical houses are for sale in virtually the same location then it is necessary to obtain data on house prices in the area, their sizes, ages, plot areas, condition, frontage and other relevant factors and use this data to gauge the price of the particular house. Where sufficient data is available we may use an "interpolation" model – some means of combining the known data and prices, and the known data about the particular house in order to calculate a price for the house.

In the following "value" means the net value of the trade taking into account the current market price of the underlying instrument. Where there is no market price (such as a structured product or an illiquid asset) instead of market price we use "model price" – the model being a means of interpolation using known data – which in turn is calculated from known asset prices and a mark-to-model pricing model.

The calculation process values each live trade in the system. It may report results per trade or aggregate them and report in predefined combinations or do both.

Table 22.1

Feature	Estimated additional worth (£)
Alloy wheels	400
Sports suspension	150
Rear bumper skirt	175
Colour: Green	0
Customised registration	65
Total extra value	790

Table 22.2   Calculation reporting summary

	NPV	Risk
Single trade	Single value	By each risk type
Multiple trades	Aggregation by any of • Product type • Currency • Asset class • Maturity • Etc.	Aggregated by any of • Product type • Risk type • Currency • Time bucket • Etc.

The valuation of a trade generally involves the calculation of net present value and risks (see Table 22.2).

22.1.2   Valuation of one trade

Net present value (NPV or simply PV): this is the present value of the trade given the input market data and trade data at the time of valuation. It is the trade's predicted current worth. The NPV can be ascertained from a calculated value or from the mark-to-market value.

   Calculated value: this is the NPV derived from the calculation process.

   Mark-to-market value: this is the market's view of the current value of the trade. It is the price that one would be charged for purchasing the trade right now. To value a held trade using mark-to-market, the trade has to be relatively standard and liquid.

   For simple trades using standard pricing algorithms the NPV and mark-to-market should be very similar. There will be some differences caused by:

• the market maker taking profit in providing the trade in the form of the bid/offer spread;
• a special desire on the part of the buyers or sellers to make the trade which will distort the market price being offered;
• liquidity and other factors affecting price.

22.1.3   Why not use mark-to-market?

The reader should remember that "valuation" may be performed (as discussed later in this chapter) to estimate a market price – as is often required by regulators of banks and other institutions. Alternatively "valuation" may be performed in order to estimate the value of "anticipated" receipts – what the investor thinks will actually happen during the life of the trade.

In many trades it is appropriate to use mark-to-market valuations but in the following situations it may not be desirable or possible.

Illiquid: some trades are illiquid meaning that prices are only quoted infrequently and therefore comparison with the market will usually not be valid. Alternatively there may be prices quoted every day, but they are unrealistic because they are based on very few actual trades transacted.

For example, if one thousand exchange-traded futures on 12 month USD were transacted in the last hour of the day, the quoted market price (some sort of average of the one thousand) will be a good reflection of market value. If only one or two futures on Bangladeshi Taka were transacted in the course of an entire day, the market price would not give a very good indication.

Another example is a call option on BT at a strike of 140p and maturing in three months and 20 days. Such options may trade regularly with a three and six month maturity, but not the exact maturity of the trade. The basic product (call options on BT) is liquid, but the specific trade is not.

No prices available: for complicated or illiquid trades there may be no equivalent trade available in the market place and so mark-to-market is impossible. To take the car example, if I owned a car which I customised in some way so that very few cars like it were available in the market place, I would not be able to get a direct valuation. I would have to estimate how much difference my modification had made to the price of the standard model and add that to the standard model price.

Market sentiment: it is rare that one would not use market prices if they are available: to ignore such data is to say that we believe the market price is unreliable.

Common trades may undergo temporary market price changes because of current market sentiment. This sentiment might be applicable only for a short time and so to value the trade fairly and consistently day on day from before the sentiment took hold, through the current period and into the future it may be better to use an unsentimental mathematical model. Examples of factors affecting market sentiment are:

- panic caused by natural disasters, wars and terrorism;
- proximity to major announcements;
- uncertainty – lack of information or conflicting information.

It should be noted that this type of market sentiment is different from an overall market view on the direction of a particular security or instrument. For instance, the NPV of an option on gold is driven by the spot and futures prices of gold (among other things). If a war is possible and market sentiment sends the spot price of gold up but leaves futures relatively unchanged, there will be a mismatch between the mark-to-market and calculated value of the option. Should the threat of war disappear the spot price will come down. If the war actually starts the futures prices will also rise – either way the mismatch between market and calculated value will reduce. Market sentiment may cause arbitrages to open up which makes valuation difficult – such times often being associated with wide bid/offer spreads – and it becomes unclear what "market value" might mean in such circumstances.

Complicated trades: when trades are complicated even if they are liquid, the trader may take the view that his model is better than the one being used by the market to derive the market prices. An example might be certain types of interest rate options where broker or market maker quotes are readily available but vary according to source.

Of course there is no one entity called the market, each contributor to the market price will have his own models and so the market price is a sort of average of all the models.

This is of particular relevance when the decision for entering into the trade was based on the belief that the true value (as predicted by the calculation) was different from that being quoted in the market. To switch to a mark-to-market valuation would now be inconsistent.

22.1.4   Other reasons why having a calculation engine is useful

Valuation is necessary where a reliable market price is not available. A trade value is required by banking institutions to mark their books to market every day. There are a variety of additional calculation engine uses as follows.

Risk: for mature products the market data may provide some basic risk results, such as delta together with the spot prices. This may be sufficient for simple risk analysis but most traders and risk managers would like to have the ability to do more extensive calculations. For nonmature products there will not be any risk measures available from the market (see Chapter 10 for full explanation of risk management).

Scenario analysis: in order to get a feel for how trades may change in value over time, many traders and risk control functions like to play with market data. Once a calculation engine has been built and tested, it is easy to apply any set of market data and get results. This lends itself to scenario analysis which, in essence, is a process of generating the market data you want to use, valuing with that market data and comparing the results. Some typical scenarios:

- Bump all market data up by 5 %.
- Set all market data to be at its lowest value for the past month.
- Set volatility of spot prices to 15 %.
- Assume all credit recovery rates fall to 5 %.

Value at Risk (VaR): VaR is a type of worst case valuation – over the next day (week, month ...) with an unchanged portfolio asking how bad could the valuation get? Typically this is done on a portfolio basis and requires, in addition to a valuation model, a model of the variability (volatility) of the driving variables (interest and exchange rates, equity prices, etc.) and their relationship (correlation). (See Chapter 11.)

Parameter variation: designers of washing machines put switches on the machine to allow the same basic washing process to be run in different ways according to the user's personal requirements, such as temperature, duration, economy and amount of spinning. This is analogous to the parameters on a mathematical model. Examples of model parameters are:

- ability to control speed versus accuracy
- tolerance to bad data
- acceptable levels of calculation error
- assumptions to be used or ignored.

Any model involving parameters may require these parameters to be varied according to the circumstances of the valuation.

Aggregation and reporting flexibility: although mark-to-market calculations can be aggregated after they are read, some forms of aggregation are quicker or more accurate when performed from within the calculation engine itself. This is because mathematical techniques can be applied to take known short cuts.

If one controls the calculation engine and knows the reporting requirements, the results can be generated with reporting in mind, making the process more seamless, accurate and efficient. This is often preferable to taking market supplied results and bolting them into a report generation process.

Adaptability: relying on mark-to-market prices can be restrictive. The way a trader wants to trade may change to take advantage of new possibilities and he may be unduly handicapped if he has to rely solely on mark-to-market prices for his valuations.

Also, it is possible that market prices may be temporarily unavailable, for instance, due to an exchange losing its systems and not reporting prices or the market data supplier having a transmission problem. In such cases the organisation will not be able to see its current valuation unless it has a calculation engine to provide it.

22.1.5   Why not rely solely on calculation engines?

The following discussion concerns trades for which mark-to-market valuations are available. As we have said there are many trades that are too complicated or nonstandard for mark-to-market. Then, of course, there is no alternative to bespoke calculation of NPV. It should also be noted that for any realistic NPV calculation the engine must use input data which is related to the market prices. These prices are the mark-to-market prices of underlying instruments and so a calculation is always in some measure dependent on the market.

Aside from this, regulators, auditors and managers are wary of calculated values if they are very different from market prices. However reliable the model, the trading environment is in the market place and so reporting needs to take into account market prices. Should a trade need to be reversed, it is the market price that will determine how much the reversal will cost not the predicted current worth coming from the model. Additionally it would take a very brave manager to be able to stand up in front of his investors or regulators and claim that because of the model he is using he need not take into account the mark-to-market.

NPV calculations are not exact measures of reality. For all but the simplest products they rely on a model of the world (see below) and hence, at best, they are likely predictions. It is therefore possible that the model is wrong: either at certain underlying prices or in certain market conditions it is not a true reflection of current value. Different models may provide different results. In many cases a calculation built around a model may be too complex and take more time to evaluate than is available. Therefore assumptions have to be introduced to speed the calculation – the assumptions could be unfounded in certain circumstances again making the results less than reliable.

Models of complex structures – and the traders trading them! – may not be completely trustworthy. It is common in such cases to override the model value with offsetting reserves reducing the model profit and only allowing profit to emerge over the life of the trade or until such time that the model proves its validity.

22.1.6   Compromise

Many financial entities have arrived at a compromise whereby results are reported based on mark-to-market valuations but calculated values are used for scenario analysis, risk predictions and trading strategies. In this way, the mathematical innovations of the model are balanced by the discipline of market forces.

22.1.7   The model

A mathematical model is an attempt to mimic what happens in the real world. It is similar to the way a map is used to condense and represent the geography of a region.

Models may arise in many ways; here we illustrate a common progression which is loosely based on the case history of a real model.

1. Someone observing stock prices thought they behaved according to a special pattern in which the logarithm of the random jump in prices followed a process known as Brownian Motion (or a Wiener process). (Brownian motion is the mathematical model for the apparently random movement of particles suspended in a fluid.)
2. A crude formula was developed to encapsulate this distribution.
3. The formula was tested and refined using empirical prices and found to be a good approximation to reality.
4. Trading processes could use the model to assess the value of the products. At first few people had implemented the model and those who had produced very different results so there was a wide discrepancy in prices being traded.
5. The market for the product developed and became more mature. The implementation of the model became more standard and was widely available.
6. Offshoots (or exotic derivatives) of the original product started to be traded which required adaptations of the basic model. Again, at first only a few trading houses had developed these and so held a market advantage. Later others caught up and the exotic derivatives became more standard.

22.2   THE CALCULATION ITSELF

The NPV of a trade is the sum of the current value of all future cashflows in the trade. If the cashflows are known we can add them and produce the NPV without resort to anything beyond interest rate models.

There are two basic components to most NPV calculations – discounting and conversion to reporting currency. We shall illustrate the principle of discounting by the following example:

Suppose we have an annual fixed coupon bond of 5 % on a notional of 10 million dollars with one and half years left to maturity. There are two future cashflows

In 6 months	5 % of 10 million
In 18 months	5 % of 10 million plus the 10 million redemption

Now what are those cashflows worth today? Money now is preferable to money at a future date (a property known as "the time value of money"). One dollar in six months will be worth less than one dollar today. We apply a principle known as discounting to calculate how much a future cash amount is worth today. Using an interest rate curve, we derive discount factors for any given future date (see bootstrapping section below).

Table 22.3

Date	Discount Factor
Today	1
1 week	0.99900
2 weeks	0.99823
1 month	0.99623
3 months	0.98976
6 months	0.97951
9 months	0.97023
12 months	0.96720
18 months	0.95983
24 months	0.95427

Suppose the discount factors for the next two years are as shown in Table 22.3. Then the sum of the future cashflows for the bond discounted to today is

$$0.97951^1 \times 0.05 \times 10\,000\,000 + 0.95983^2 \times 1.05 \times 10\,000\,000 = \text{USD } 10\,567\,970$$

22.2.1   Conversion to reporting currency

It is necessary to convert all the flows to the reporting currency for any trade that has cash-flows in a currency other than the reporting currency or for trades involving an exchange of commodities. Typically, valuations are carried out in the local currency, then converted at the current spot rate to the reporting currency. This is equivalent to converting cashflows using forward FX rates and then valuing using the reporting currency discount factors as will be shown.

Suppose in the example above our reporting currency was EUR and the trade is in USD. We need to calculate the two cashflows and convert them into EUR before adding them together. This is because the exchange rate will be different for each flow.

The exchange rate applied will be the forward exchange rate at the time of the flow. This can be derived in two ways:

1. Take the forward curve for the currency pair (in our case EUR/USD).
2. Use the forward (discounting curve) for EUR and USD and the spot rate for EUR/USD.

Today	buy USD 125 for EUR 100 (FX is 0.8 EUR per USD)
In six months	USD 125 is worth USD 128.125 (2.5 % interest in 6 months)
	EUR 100 is worth EUR 103.600 (3.6 % interest in 6 months)
	Sell USD 128.125 for EUR 103.600 (implied FX is 0.8086)

Because the spot and forward market for interest rates and foreign exchange is very efficient these two methods will be equivalent – otherwise an arbitrage would exist which the market would soon close out.

So the six months FX rate is 0.8086 and let us suppose the 18 month FX rate is 0.7904.

---

[1] The 6 months discount factor.
[2] The 18 months discount factor.

Then in our fixed bond we have the EUR cashflows as:

$0.97951 \times 0.05 \times 10\,000\,000 \times 0.8086 = 396\,015.9$ and

$0.95983 \times 1.05 \times 10\,000\,000 \times 0.7904 = 7\,965\,821$

giving an NPV of EUR 8 361 837.

22.2.2   Unknown cashflows

In many cases cashflows are not known with certainty. An option is an example of a product that has an unknown cashflow. To value the option we have to use some sort of statistical model that predicts the likely price of the underlying instrument on the exercise date and from there we can calculate the value of the option.

Let's examine a simple case where the underlying price could only be one of a discrete set of possibilities.

Suppose an option is struck at 0.9 and the probability of certain prices is:

Price	Probability	Payoff at exercise
0.7	0.2	0
0.8	0.2	0
0.9	0.2	0
1.0	0.2	100
2.0	0.1	1100
3.0	0.1	2100

Then the future payoff (for a call) is estimated at:

$0.2 \times 100 + 0.1 \times 1100 + 0.2 \times 2100 = 340.$

We would discount the 340 using discount factors to arrive at the value of the option.

Notice that the mathematics does not care what the underlying asset actually is and so option modelling is applicable across asset classes.

A more likely distribution of underlying prices is to assume that they are log normal. Then we can use the industry standard Black-Scholes formula to calculate the option NPV.

22.2.3   Other dependencies

An exotics trade such as the knock out single barrier option pays a return conditional on two events:

- The underlying price did not reach the barrier at any point in the life of the trade.
- The option was exercised meaning the spot price was greater than the strike at maturity (for European style options).

To calculate the NPV the probability of both events must be calculated. Since both are dependent upon the underlying price, we could still use the log normal price distribution and a variant of the Black-Scholes formula.

22.2.4   Monte Carlo

The Black-Scholes option pricing formula is an example of a closed form solution – that is the result can be expressed in some formulaic combination of the input parameters. Many trade pricing functions are closed form or semi-closed form and they work like a black-box: input data is fed in, the parameters are set, the button is pushed and results come out. In some cases a "closed form" solution may not be available and numerical techniques may have to be used. One such is Monte Carlo,[3] which uses random numbers and "simulation" to generate the outcome, and a large number of calculations are repeated to calculate the average value and thereby estimate the value of the trade. For option pricing it could work like this:

1. Generate a set of random numbers (many programming languages have a means of pseudo random number generation in a uniform distribution between 0 and 1).
2. Using standard mathematical techniques convert these uniform distribution random numbers into a number with log normal distribution of required mean and standard deviation and call it X (could use forward price at maturity date for mean and volatility for standard distribution).
3. Calculate the payoff given price of X at maturity (or 0 if strike is greater than or equal to X) and call the result V.
4. Repeat 1–3 so that there is a total of one million runs.
5. Find the average of the one million Vs.

22.3   SENSITIVITY ANALYSIS

As mentioned, NPV is a snapshot based on the market data at time of calculation. It gives no indication of the likely direction of the NPV or what might happen if the market data changes. Traders and other people concerned with market risk (that is exposure to change caused by market forces) often like to measure the sensitivity of a trade to a change in market data.

The various risk measures are explained in the chapter on risk management. Here we will explain the means by which this exposure can be calculated.

If we want to examine the sensitivity of the NPV to one particular instrument used in the calculation of the NPV we perturb the price of that instrument and recalculate the NPV. The sensitivity is then the difference in NPV caused by that price change.

Suppose the NPV of an option on aluminium NPV was USD 15 600 722.

The overnight spot rate for USD was 0.8375 %. To find the option sensitivity to this spot rate instrument we bump it by one basis point to be 0.8475 % and revalue the option giving us a value of say USD 15 600 798. We then define the sensitivity to spot rate as 15 600 798 – 15 600 722 = USD 76.

We can calculate sensitivity to any instrument used in the trade calculation. Since the sensitivity comes out as a currency amount, we can aggregate sensitivities across many trades. If the trader had a portfolio of two barrier options, five vanilla options, four forwards and a spot trade we could calculate the sensitivities of each trade to one instrument and show the aggregated portfolio sensitivity to that instrument.

---

[3] See Peter Jäckel, *Monte Carlo Methods in Finance*, Wiley Finance, 2002.

The sensitivity to the underlying spot instrument is known as delta.[4] If we want to know the sensitivity to a change in delta (known as gamma) we could employ a second order sensitivity calculation such as:

Calculate the basis NPV (call it V_0)
Bump the underlying spot up by one basis point and revalue (V_1)
Then delta is $V_1 - V_0$ and call it Δ_u
Bump the underlying spot down by one basis point and revalue (V_2)
Then delta is $V_2 - V_0$ and call it Δ_d
Gamma is then Δ_u - Δ_d

An equivalent method of calculating the sensitivity to a particular instrument can be used when the NPV can be expressed as a continuous function of that instrument. Then the delta sensitivity is the first order derivative to the instrument at the market price and gamma is the second order derivative.

It is often the case that calculation of sensitivities can be done at the same time as calculation of the NPV within the same run. This is faster than bumping the market data and rerunning the calculation.

Note that the above sensitivity measures assume that underlying variables (driving the market price) change continuously over time. Such measures are often incorrectly applied to markets which do not have this property and where market prices undergo "jumps" rather than smooth changes. Such behaviour makes hedging difficult and should in principle be analysed with different risk measures – for example sensitivity to a 20 % change in the underlying driving variable.

Where the pricing model is implemented by Monte Carlo simulation the calculation of sensitivities can present problems. Differences between calculations generated by random numbers may reflect more of the randomness than the underlying change so special techniques have to be used, or simpler sensitivity analysis performed.

22.4 BOOTSTRAPPING

Above we alluded to the calculation of an interest rate curve using a process known as bootstrapping. This is a generic process and the name comes from pulling oneself up by one's own bootstraps. Here is a simple explanation.

Suppose we know that the interest rate for borrowing money for 12 months is 2.3 % and for 24 months is 3.7 %. This means if I borrowed 100 units today I would pay back 102.3 in 12 months or 103.7 in 24 months. I would like to know what the 12 month interest rate will be in 12 months' time.

Borrowing for 24 months is the same as borrowing for 12 months and then taking out a new loan for another 12 months. Let's suppose this second loan which is a 12 months' loan forward 12 months attracts r % interest.

Then we have two calculations which must be equivalent:

Borrow for 24 months $= 103.7$
Borrow for 12 months $+$ Borrow again at 12 months forward 12 months
$103.7 = 102.3 \times (100 + r) / 100$

---

[4] This is the interest rate delta. For this instrument there would also be an aluminium price delta.

r = (103.7 / 102.3) x 100 – 100
r = 1.368524 %

Thus I have used information I know to calculate a new instrument via bootstrapping.

Note that in practice such calculations are made more complicated by the presence of different means of calculation time periods (known as day-count conventions) (see below) and different ways of quoting interest rates (annual, semi-annual etc.).

22.5 CALCULATION OF DATES

Accrual convention: a very important component of all cashflow calculations is the actual dates to be used. In our experience, problems with dates account for many pricing errors. For trades with regular cashflows such as bonds and swaps there are four properties of the trade that determine the dates to be used.

1. Frequency – how often does the cashflow occur?
2. Day-count convention – how to split an annually agreed rate across the cashflow dates?
3. Business day convention – what to do when a payment is due on a non business day?
4. Holiday calendar – what constitutes non business days?

It is possible that an OTC trade may have exact dates for payments recorded as part of the trade agreement and therefore no date calculations are required. But for all exchange traded and for most OTCs the four properties will be stipulated and then the dates will be derived by the calculation process.

To see how these factors are used let us consider a fixed bond trade paying an annual coupon of 400 000 quarterly and let's consider the next four payments, the first being on 8 March 2007. Without any modifications the payments should be:

Thu 8 March 2007	100 000
Fri 8 June 2007	100 000
Sat 8 September 2007	100 000
Sat 8 December 2007	100 000

Now suppose the holiday calendar tells us that nontrading days are Saturdays, Sundays and a list of holidays including Monday 10 December 2007.

Our day-count convention is "Following", this means take the first business day when the payment is due on a non-business day.

Our revised dates become:

Thu 8 March 2007
Fri 8 June 2007
Mon 10 September 2007
Tue 11 December 2007.

We now employ the day-count convention (sometimes known as the accrual convention) to calculate the size of the payments. Here are some common conventions:

Actual/Actual: this means calculate the actual number of days between payments and divide it by the actual number of days in a year.

Actual/360: this means calculate the actual number of days between payments and divide it by 360 regardless of the length of the year.

Table 22.4

Raw date	Adjusted date	Days since last payment	Factor	Amount
8 Mar 07	8 Mar 07	90	0.25	100 000
8 Jun 07	8 Jun 07	92	0.25556	102 222.22
8 Sep 07	10 Sep 07	94	0.26111	104 444.44
8 Dec 07	11 Dec 07	91	0.25278	101 111.11

Actual/365: this means calculate the actual number of days between payments and divide it by 365 regardless of the length of the year.

30/360: this is a little complicated but involves considering months as always being of 30 days and years being of 360 days. There are some variations such as 30E/360 and 30E+/360 which handle months of 31 days in different ways.

For our example let us take Actual/360.

Then to calculate our second payment amount we take the number of days between 8 March and 8 June and divide by 360. This is 92/360 and so the payment is:

$$400\,000 \times 92/360 = 102\,222.22.$$

Assuming the payment date prior to the first date is Friday 8 December 2006.

Table 22.4 shows the full payment schedule.

This market convention pays a total of 367 days assuming a year of 360 days. The setting of the coupon or swap rate will take this into account and be slightly lower than for the equivalent using, say, an actual/actual convention.

22.6   CALIBRATION TO MARKET

A scientist wishing to perform an experiment where local conditions affect the results will first calibrate his equipment. This means he will take readings locally and derive some simple calculations from them. Comparing these results to standard results from other places, he will see how much adjustment need be made to take into account those local conditions.

It is sometimes necessary for valuation algorithms to perform a similar process. This involves taking market data to produce curves which are then used later in the calculation. This is known as calibrating to market and a typical example is in the pricing of collateralised debt obligations. Here the default (or survival) curves are generated from the market credit default swap prices. These curves are then stored and used in future valuations.

22.7   TESTING

There are various tests required for valuations. The valuation is a precise mechanism, the results of which have serious consequences. So rigorous and thorough testing is very important. Chapter 19 discusses testing at greater length and Chapter 23 discusses mathematical model validation. Here we briefly note some of the tests relevant to calculations.

Sanity check: do the results look reasonable? If they are very different from mark-to-market, can these differences be accounted for?

Regular testing: does the model give the expected results when regular input data is applied to it?

Boundary testing: at the boundaries, model effects are often more pronounced, so testing here is essential. By boundaries we mean scenarios, such as just before and just after at-the-money conditions for a vanilla option or just before a barrier is reached for a barrier option.

Unusual values: this involves testing the valuation with especially high, low or otherwise unusual input values and calculation parameters.

22.8   INTEGRATING A MODEL WITHIN A FULL SYSTEM

The model rarely stands on its own. It is generally integrated into a whole pricing and risk management system. After the quant has tested the model in isolation, it must also be tested from within the full system to ensure the results remain unaltered.

22.9   RISKS ASSOCIATED WITH THE VALUATION PROCESS

Most of the risks connected to the valuation process arise through insufficient testing and documentation. By documentation we also mean communication of how and when to use the valuation.

In addition, the valuation must only be used within the parameters for which it was designed and built. There is often a temptation to take a model designed for one class of trades and apply it to other trades that appear similar. Insufficient appreciation of the subtlety and limitations of the model can lead to erroneous results in this situation. The model should really come with clear guidelines as to when it should and should not be used.

Model approval is usually only given to a model when used with a defined set of trades and a defined set or range of market conditions.

Another common practice is to start using a prototype model in real situations before it has been fully tested. This is due to the pressures of the fast-changing business environment, the length of time required for testing and the lack of alternatives.

All settings and input requirements to a model must meet the quality and completeness expected by the model otherwise inaccurate results may be produced.

22.10   SUMMARY

Successful trading depends on accurate and available valuation of trades and risks arising from changes in market prices. In this chapter we have discussed mathematical models, shown some valuation techniques and outlined the inherent risks.

23

Mathematical Model and Systems Validation

Dr Geoff Chaplin, *Reoch Credit Partners LLP*

This chapter discusses the implementation of a credit derivatives system. Much of what is covered here is relevant to other systems and is written in as general a form as possible. On the other hand some aspects are less relevant for some applications – for example the implementation of market-accepted models for single name CDS valuation requires little emphasis on the testing of the mathematical model

23.1 TESTING PROCEDURES

The following describes current practice within risk-control departments of banks and large hedge funds and is commonly used with regard to internal (self-written) and external (off-the-shelf or bespoke) systems and models used for valuation and risk reporting. Without approval at this level trading desks for example, are generally not allowed to trade using the trading desk's systems and models. An exception applies at start-up of a new desk – generally a limited trading approval is given which may restrict the number of deals, their size, duration of trading period, and other aspects of the transactions. This limited trading approval gives the desk and other departments within the bank time and experience to set up management procedures and ensure transactions are properly booked, reported and controlled throughout all aspects of the deal. It should also be borne in mind that the testing process is not an attempt to annoy traders and stand in the way of product development – although it may seem so from the point of view of the trading desk. It is a requirement imposed by regulators and a responsibility to shareholders and investors.

The testing process typically takes 1–6 months for a new "product" of some complexity (such as a bank starting in CDS or CDO products). This process is usually (but not necessarily) undertaken by someone remote from the trading desk – such as risk control or a "quant" group – and follows certain formal steps which help separate the analysis from the pressure of the business. The process would include the following major steps.

1. Write a description of the product – in this case the underlying business and contracts; how the products work, what the cashflows are and what triggers the cashflows.
2. Write a verbal description of the mathematical model to be used to value and hedge mature deals (this may simply be references to standard works or papers).
3. Write a mathematical description of the model (formulae).
4. Write a description of input data required for the model and any data assumptions.
5. Write a summary of the key elements of the model and its shortcomings, and key data items and assumptions.

6. Develop (or purchase) a software implementation of the mathematical model.
7. Perform a series of tests on the software which would include the following (the list is not exclusive and in practice expands as testing is undertaken and further reasonable test ideas present themselves):
   (a) Perform tests on independent components of the system where possible – for example tests of the discounting (interest rate) functionality and tests on the survival curve.
   (b) Perform simplified case tests – for example reducing the portfolio of contracts to a single contract and comparing the system results against manual calculation.
   (c) Build an independent pricing system (typically in Excel or a "4th generation language"). Typically this would be a simplified implementation and in this case might include key contract types. The independent model is then used to value a deal and is compared against the software supplied. Any significant differences would have to be resolved before the independent software could be regarded as acceptable.
   (d) Perform stress tests. Extreme data values would be input (such as high/low interest rates, high/low default rates, etc.) to see if the software continued to function and that the results produced were in line with expectations.
8. In addition if valuation uses historical rather than market implied data (typically the case for structured asset-backed deals) then this data should be subject to additional testing and analysis. In particular:
   (a) Spot checks on the consistency of data supplied – e.g. if summary values such as means and standard deviations are supplied these should be spot checked.
   (b) Bearing in mind the underlying contracts and business some analysis of trends (for example of default or termination rates) over time might be appropriate.
   (c) Specific questions on data supplied are likely to arise out of this analysis, in particular, how applicable is the past data to the future?

In addition to the mathematical and software review described above a "business systems" review would need to be implemented. In particular this should cover the following (in considerably more detail):

9. What are the interactions between the desk and its transactions and other departments of the institution (internal interaction) and other bodies (external interaction).
10. What data flows/reports are needed to support these interactions.
11. How best to implement the required reporting and control procedures.

Items 1 to 5 above may constitute a substantial and complex document – similar to this book in the case of complex new products – and would require considerable effort and dedication on the part of both the trading desk and the risk control department. The business review would additionally require the cooperation of many departments in the institution and would be likely to be managed by a business systems specialist rather than (but not remote from) the risk control function.

The process should begin with an open-ended section covering:

- key elements of the model
- shortcomings of the model
- key data items and assumptions.

For example, what business risks does the introduction of this product bring – both for the institution and for the financial market place as a whole? Once a business had started what risks are there to the continuation of the business (e.g. market data, liquidity, staff risks)?

23.2   IMPLEMENTATION AND DOCUMENTATION

A live implementation is likely to be integrated into the institution's systems. Two key aspects need to be considered initially and on an ongoing basis:

1. Documentation
2. Implementation testing.

Documentation on the models and implementation needs to cover aspects discussed in the section above and in addition:

(a) A user manual – how to operate the system
(b) Systems/programming documentation.

The former is needed for new staff; the latter – often forgotten – is needed to enable the system software to be maintained.

Continued implementation testing is needed if – as is usually the case – there are fixed assumptions incorporated into the software which may have a bearing on the results. For example it is often the case that certain calculations are performed by numerical integration. This may be done in such a way that it is self checking – several calculations being performed until the result converges to the required accuracy – or a fixed number of integration steps may have been decided at the outset (which has the advantage of implementation speed). In the latter case regular checks need to be performed on such system parameters to establish that they continue to be sufficiently accurate. In particular if spreads widen significantly it may be that such fixed parameters cease to give sufficiently accurate results. Of course the model and system documentation should have identified the presence of any such parameters. More problematic assumptions are often hidden ones. For example on large pools of data a zero correlation model may have been used. Such assumptions can and do fail with catastrophic results – for example prepayment of fixed rate mortgages or underlying asset values are highly correlated phenomena but often not explicitly incorporated in MBS models.

23.3   SUMMARY

In this chapter we have shown some of the factors to be considered when models are used and require validation.

24

Regulatory, Legal and Compliance

24.1 REGULATORY REQUIREMENTS

In order to regulate the financial services industry, most governments have set up regulatory bodies which have legal powers and responsibilities. For example, in Britain there is the Financial Services Authority (FSA), in the US there are at least five different regulators including the Federal Deposit Insurance Corporation (FDIC) and the Securities and Exchange Commission (SEC) and in Brazil the Comissao de Valores Mobiliarios.

The regulators have several aims including:

- to enforce applicable laws;
- to prosecute cases of market misconduct, such as insider trading;
- to license providers of financial services;
- to protect clients and investigate complaints;
- to maintain confidence in the financial system.

A regulated entity has several responsibilites to the regulator in its operating jurisdiction.

24.1.1 Registration

The entity must register with the regulator. Registration involves stating:

- scope of trading activity
- capital provision
- personnel
- demonstrable expertise in the chosen area of business
- internal controls and procedures to manage trading.

The regulator will inspect the entity and if everything is in order grant permission for certain activities. Each activity will have a list of trading types permitted. For example a hedge fund might be allowed to arrange (bring about) deals in investments for the following set of instruments:[1]

- certificates representing certain security
- commodity future
- commodity option and option on commodity future
- contract for differences (excluding a spread bet and a rolling spot forex contract)
- debenture
- future (excluding a commodity future and a rolling spot forex contract)
- government and public security
- option (excluding a commodity option and an option on a commodity future)
- rights to or interests in investments (Contractually Based Investments)

---

[1] Example permissions taken from Financial Services Authority register.

- rights to or interests in investments (Security)
- rolling spot forex contract
- share
- unit
- warrant.

The activity will generally be limited to a set of customer types such as financial counter-parties, sophisticated investors or retail customers.

The scope of the activities also reflects the nature of the organisation. A hedge fund typically will be limited to advisory and trading activities while a bank may be granted registration to "hold client monies" or take custody of securities.

24.1.2   Reporting

The entity is obliged to file periodic reports with the regulator. These reports show, amongst other things, the scale of trading undertaken, the amount of capital committed and the current leverage. They allow the regulator to keep track of the status of the entity.

24.1.3   Inspections

The entity has to be available for inspection and spot checks upon its activities by the regulator who may want to verify that the registration and reporting is accurate and up to date. These checks also serve as a deterrent to engaging in unlawful or nonpermitted activities.

24.1.4   Personal registration

Apart from the financial entity requiring registration with a regulator, individual employees also require registration in order to engage in certain activities such as trading and advising clients. Individuals must demonstrate competence by reference to past experience or through passing examinations and can have their registration revoked if they breach regulatory requirements. They are typically registered by name and by reference to the company for whom they work. It is a responsibility of the company employing them to ensure that staff are properly registered before they can conduct duties requiring registration.

24.2   LEGAL

As a trade is a legally binding contract, the terms of the trade should be reflected in documentation that has been approved by both counterparties. This documentation process is simplified where trade documentation has been standardised for the relevant market. The legal representative or department for each financial entity typically has the task of agreeing documentation for each type of trade and with each counterparty. For exchange-traded transactions, this is a simple process as the products are standard and well-established. For over-the-counter trades, the documentation can be anything agreed by the parties, with documentation varying in degrees of complexity depending upon the nature of the trade and the status and requirements of the relevant counterparties.

To standardise the market place in derivatives, ISDA (International Swaps and Derivatives Association) has formulated standard documentation, including the Master Agreement (a form of master agreement that sets out principal terms) and a form of Master Agreement Schedule (pursuant to which parties can vary or supplement those principal terms). The initial version of the ISDA Master Agreement was published in 1992 and was updated in 2002. This standardised ISDA documentation is used for the OTC trading of many products.

The process for arriving at suitable documentation is now simplified into these three steps:

1. Execution of Master Agreement, setting out names of the two counterparties.
2. Schedule: decide which parts of the master agreement should apply. This will involve negotiation on particular details such as early termination events, threshold requirements and any counterparty specific clauses.
3. Confirmation: every time a trade is transacted, it will be evidenced by a confirmation which, together with the master agreement and schedule, form the contract documentation for the trade. The confirmation contains trade specific details and is discussed in Section 8.3.

The first two stages of documentation will be established before any trading with the counterparty begins, the third will arise as trades are transacted. Once the first two stages have been settled, it is rare for the legal department to be involved in confirmation unless there is a dispute or something unusual pertaining to an individual trade.

24.3 COMPLIANCE

The financial entity has a legal obligation to ensure that both the firm and its staff comply with all relevant legislation. It is usually a requirement that the entity appoint a named compliance officer or officers to carry out these duties.

The two areas of legislation most connected to the trading process are money laundering and insider trading.

24.3.1 Money laundering

This is the process by which criminals seek to legitimise money that was illegally obtained. The financial sector is prone to money laundering because it offers the criminal the opportunity to buy legitimate financial instruments that can be used to mask the illegal source of the purchase. Compliance officers have a duty to train staff to report suspicious behaviour. This behaviour might include:

- suspicious counterparty details, such as a post office box instead of a fixed address;
- suspicious dealings, such as seeking to pay for purchases in cash;
- counterparty being prepared to pay more than is necessary for the deal or investing in deals certain to lose money;
- intermediaries masking the true identity of a counterparty.

All staff who engage in a client facing role must be aware of their responsibilities to be vigilant and to report suspected money laundering.

Occasionally a financial entity unwittingly has an employee directly engaged by criminal elements to launder money through the entity. Compliance officers must therefore scrutinise employee activities and investigate anything suspicious from within the organisation as well as from outside.

24.3.2   Insider trading

In order to ensure that all trading is fair, the process by which a person uses his position to gain knowledge that is not generally available and trades personally at an advantage caused by that knowledge has been criminalised. This illegal activity is known as insider trading. Examples include:

- making a personal trade in the same instrument that is about to be transacted by the financial entity in order to take advantage of the price movement caused;
- personal trading in the shares of a company that a member of staff knows from his professional role is about to be taken over (and where shares are therefore likely to increase in price) where the information has not been made public.

Insider trading is not limited to traders. Anyone having access to trading processes and systems may gain knowledge that is not yet in the public domain and attempt to take advantage of such knowledge. As such, all employees of a financial entity must register their personal trading activities so that these can be monitored for insider trading. It is up to the individual institution to devise rules for what is acceptable personal trading. For example, a company that trades commodities but not equities may allow personal share dealing but may require an employee to get the approval of his manager or the compliance officer before trading in commodities.

The responsibility of the compliance officer is to educate staff on what is considered insider trading and to monitor personal dealing activities for potential insider trading.

24.4   RISKS

24.4.1   Closure

If a firm fails to fulfil its regulatory responsibilities it could have part or all of its activities closed down.

24.4.2   Penalties and prosecution

Depending on the nature of the breach, companies or individuals who have breached the laws or regulations governing their conduct may be subject to significant fines, criminal prosecution or both.

24.4.3   Litigation

A company that breaches its legal and regulatory obligations may also be liable to civil litigation brought by any party that has suffered as a result. If the entity fails to perform its activities with sufficient care, it could be liable to a claim of negligence. While the standard of care owed by the entity will depend on the sophistication of the particular investor (with professional institutions viewed as requiring less protection than members of the public), courts will look to standards mandated by regulation and applied by other firms in determining whether the requisite standard has been met.

24.4.4   Costs

The resolution of proceedings initiated by a regulator or the defence of a lawsuit can be very costly. They will typically require significant management time in addition to legal costs.

24.4.5   Reputational risk

In any case of personal or corporate malpractice, the company may suffer reputational risk. Potential clients may steer clear of companies that have breached legal or regulatory requirements. Counterparties may also be wary of trading with a company that does not play by the rules.

24.4.6   Advisory risk

Legal risk does not rest solely on actual trading activities. There is also a considerable legal responsibility when advising clients on financial services. Thus advisory activities must be policed to the same degree as those of trading.

24.5   SUMMARY

A trading entity must be cognisant of all its legal and regulatory obligations. It must put in place processes to ensure compliance and minimise legal and reputational risk.

25

Business Continuity Planning

25.1 WHAT IS BUSINESS CONTINUITY PLANNING?

Should a major event occur that seriously disrupts the business of a financial entity, procedures need to be activated to manage the situation and reduce the damage caused. These procedures are known as business continuity planning (BCP) and sometimes disaster recovery, although the latter term generally refers to the IT aspects of business continuity.

Obviously, it is too late to wait for the event to actually happen, so organisations have a person or team responsible for drawing up plans and testing them. In fact it has now become a regulatory requirement that investment banks and other finance houses have in place a plan for business continuity, which can be inspected and approved. This is to prevent damage to one institution spreading to others and destroying confidence in the financial system as a whole.

25.2 WHY IS IT IMPORTANT?

There is a joke in many financial entities about disaster recovery, that they are good at the disaster, but not so good at the recovery – unfortunately it is not always just a joke. BCP requires a deep level of planning and extensive knowledge of the trade processes at the heart of most financial businesses. If disaster strikes, the trades and asset holdings of the institution are still extant and require all the standard processes to continue as close to normally as possible.

If there is no business continuity then:

- the trades themselves may start losing money;
- risks arising from the trades, such as market and counterparty risk, may grow to an unacceptable size;
- the organisation may be opening itself to the legal risk of being sued;
- regulators may step in to close or take over some or all of the business;
- management may be liable to criminal prosecution for negligence.

25.3 TYPES OF DISASTER

Listing the potential causes of disaster enables an assessment to be made of the best way to deal with each event. Here we divide the types into two major groups:

1. No staff available due to:
   - illness likely to affect many people (e.g. influenza, swine flu, stomach bug)
   - industrial dispute
   - no access to the building (bomb scare, gas leak, building unsafe, action by demonstrators etc.)
   - terrorism
   - transport problems

- earthquake or other natural disaster
- fire or flood.
2. No computer systems available due to:
   - power cut
   - network failure
   - server failure
   - bug in common software
   - virus or sabotage
   - fire or flood.

25.4   HOW DOES IT WORK?

If somebody was considering home safety and evacuation procedures, he would start with the occupants of the house (hopefully!) and then draw up a list of the most important items to save, according to their worth or cost of replacement.

BCP is partly about rescuing the physical assets of the company (similar to those of the house) and partly about replicating the business of the company. To do the latter, one must fully understand the essential business processes. These will involve people, data, computers and computer programs.

BCP involves finding a suitable alternative site for the plans to be activated while the original site is out of action. Then there must be sufficient data sources, hardware and software available and staff with enough knowledge to carry out the required activities.

Sometimes it is possible to resume operations at another branch or office of the same company. For example, the middle office might be divided between New York and Tokyo. If disaster hits Tokyo, it may be that staff in New York have enough resources and knowledge to take over the Tokyo processes.

Each area at risk must be given a backup plan of action. This has to be thoroughly tested with run-throughs as close as possible to reality.

BCP will:

- define when an emergency has occurred;
- empower a senior member of staff to "push the red button" to activate the procedures;
- draw up and test a notification procedure to inform all staff of the emergency;
- stop staff travelling to their normal place of work – those involved in replicating processes will be told to travel to the alternative site; others will be placed on standby in case they are needed;
- educate the staff as to their responsibilities in the event of emergency.

Of course, prevention is better than cure so BCP might instigate:

- computer health checks and anti-virus software
- fire prevention
- special protection for senior staff, such as not travelling in the same aircraft
- investment in backup hardware
- regular backups and safe storage of company data
- telecommunication backups.

25.5   RISKS ASSOCIATED WITH BCP

The BCP is a plan of action. Unless it is thoroughly tested, it has achieved nothing and, in fact, it could make things worse by creating a false sense of confidence. If everybody trusts the dam to hold back the water, then a whole city might be built next to it. But if the dam is not up to the job, it would be better not to build the city there and for people to be aware of the risk.

Linked to this risk is the tendency of many people to undervalue the purpose of BCP. The BCP staff are dependent upon IT and business professionals to tell them what is required – if the exercise is not taken seriously, key components or activities might be missed. No one checks their insurance policy until the day after the fire.

BCP is not just a one-off exercise. A business is fluid and dynamic and the BCP must reflect changes in business practices, data inputs and processes.

Another risk is that the BCP is thorough, but cannot cope with an extensive disaster or more than one happening at once. For example, a company operating in the City of London might have located its disaster recovery 10 miles away on the outskirts of London. If there is a terrorist attack, disruption to the transport network serving the main site will also affect the recovery site.

When major things happen, major decisions are often required. The BCP must have staff with sufficient seniority on hand to make those decisions. Damage limitation is very much dependent on seeing the important issues among a whole bunch of distractions. In order to make those decisions, the manager will require reports on the current status of the business and the nature and extent of the disaster. Above all, he will need good communication.

25.6   SUMMARY

A financial entity must devote time and effort to planning for the unknown and unexpected. Business continuity planning is a structured process for reducing risks caused by a major event.

Part IV

What Can Go Wrong, the Credit Crisis

Credit Derivatives and the Crisis of 2007

Robert Reoch, *Founding Partner, Reoch Credit Partners LLP*

The following chapter discusses many types of risk and explains how a recent and well-known financial crisis was linked to issues connected to the trade lifecycle.

26.1 BACKGROUND

26.1.1 SIVs

The use of Conduit Financing Vehicles ("CFVs") or Structured Investment Vehicles ("SIVs") was extensive and was established in the late 1980s. The structures disintermediate banks by enabling a range of long dated debt instruments to be financed by short-term debt. To the extent that short-term financing becomes unavailable, the structures use a back-stop facility provided by a bank. This secondary source of financing is designed to plug any financing gaps and generally will only be used when liquidity is in short supply. As a result of the back-stop, the ratings agencies are prepared to give the short-term debt a high credit rating.

An SIV[1] is structured as an SPV that buys long dated assets such as debt instruments and finances the purchase by issuing short-term debt such as commercial paper. The debt instruments that the SIV buys can be corporate debt – bonds and loans, or retail debt – pools of mortgages, credit card receivables, car loans etc. The SIV normally enjoys a healthy profit due to the fact that short-term borrowing rates (what the SIV pays) are normally less that the return on the longer dated assets. SIVs can be very profitable because they are highly leveraged and the returns on the small amount of equity may therefore be very high.

Originally SIVs were set up to allow banks to put capital-expensive assets off balance sheet. Basel 1 (introduced in 1998) applied the same capital charge to AAA rated bonds as to CCC rated bonds. The former yields very little so the return on regulatory capital was not attractive. SIVs only worked (initially) because their assets were top quality and very liquid: without these characteristics the providers of SIV financing would not have been so willing. The owners were often the banks but soon spread very wide: the economics were compelling. A portfolio of AAA bonds was financed 95 % with 3–9 month commercial paper and 5 % with equity. The positive carry in the bonds portfolio delivered more than 20 % annual returns to the equity investors.

---

[1] A special purpose vehicle (SPV) or special purpose company (SPC) is a company that is created solely for a particular financial transaction or series of transactions. It may sometimes be structured as a trust. SPVs are often used to make a transaction tax efficient by choosing the most favourable tax residence for the vehicle. They can also remove assets or liabilities from a bank's or corporate's balance sheet, transfer risk and (in securitisations) allow the effective sale of future cashflows. The management of an SPV is structured according to accounting standards that require a company controlled by another to be consolidated as a subsidiary; normally the objective is for the SPV not to consolidate and is easy to achieve as SPVs require very little in the way of management.

SIVs are also called conduits because they create a channel through which the long-term debt they invest in can be funded by short-term debt. The business model (borrow short term, lend long term) is very similar to that of a bank, but by conducting its business through capital markets (rather than taking deposits) and by being an offshore entity it escapes the regulation that banks are subject to. Their risk can be summarised as follows:

Credit Risk: the assets in the SIV are risky in that they are exposed to issuer default risk. Where the asset is synthetic (for example a CDS) then in addition to issuer risk there is also counterparty risk. Although the assets in an SIV are generally of high quality, the SIV will need (i) processes for credit decisions and portfolio monitoring, and (ii) limits to control exposure by company, sector, country and rating. Minimum standards for the latter are normally set by the Rating Agencies to give the SIV debt the best possible rating.

Liquidity Risk: the SIV has a continual refinancing need as the maturity of the assets is often significantly longer than the tenor of the SIV's debt. A number of safeguards are employed: the highest credit rating is maintained to ensure access to a wide range of investors; diversity of investor is achieved by using multiple debt programs throughout the global capital markets; controls ensure that the funding requirement at any point in time does not exceed a set limit; a back-stop facility is in place to fill any funding gaps; and, normally, the SIV would expect to be able to quickly liquidate the highest quality assets to raise additional funds.

Market Risk: to the extent that the SIV is exposed to interest rate or exchange rate risk, limits are put in place and active hedging ensures that these risks are minimised. The objective is to make the SIV insensitive to market risks.

Operational Risk: an SIV would normally have procedures, control and necessary reporting to address operational risk: the possibility of losses resulting from substandard or failed internal processes. The combination of rating agency and auditor reviews and reporting is considered adequate to mitigate these risks. A key success factor is the SIV's platform that needs to both book a variety of assets and monitor the portfolio and the liabilities. As important however are its independent control functions that ensure the maintenance of its strong credit rating.

Pre crisis the use of SIVs was extensive and they were a large component of bank disintermediation. Following their catastrophic performance during the early days of the crisis most structures were unwound and renewed usage seems unlikely in the near term.

26.1.2   Market liquidity

Contrary to common belief, the liquidity of a market rests not so much on its size (as measured by market capitalisation or turnover) but in the diversity of its participants. It is easier for observers to see this distinction in the midst of a crisis than during the quiet time before a crisis when liquidity appears high and capitalisation is galloping ahead.

In many markets there are many different types of market participants like hedge funds or pension funds and within each type there are many different investment strategies. But diversity is often richer in appearance than in the reality of behaviour. A key measure of the critical degree of diversity required for liquid markets is how differently market participants respond at times of stress to short-term price declines. A market where, for whatever reason, falling prices trigger selling by most players and generate few buyers, is one that may be large and appear liquid in quiet times, but will be fragile and illiquid in stressful times. This is a stylised description of what has occurred in the global credit markets.

Many investors have long-term liabilities that do not require sensitivity to daily market moves. Examples would be pension funds, insurance companies, Sovereign Wealth Funds

(SWFs) or any other investor where funding or liabilities are long-term. These investors can earn a liquidity premium versus other investors who require short-term liquidity. From a systemic point of view these investors act as a liquidity absorber during times of stress.

Investors who have short-term funding, or are forced to follow short-term solvency or stop-loss rules, or who intended to trade an asset and so are not incentivised to understand it sufficiently to hold on to losing positions – will be forced to sell assets when they fall sharply in price. Indeed, they are incentivised to try to be the first to sell assets before other investors do. Liquidity disappears in this rush for the exit. These liquidity-hungry investors act not as risk absorbers, but risk amplifiers.

Many regulators used to argue that the transfer of risk from one bank's balance sheet to several investors was a desirable spreading of risk. But what matters is not the number or name of those that risk is transferred to, but their behaviour. The transfer of risk from banks was a transfer from a risk absorber to entities that acted as risk traders or amplifiers. This did not spread risk, it concentrated it. Supervisors ignored or misunderstood the distinction between risk traders and risk absorbers, and the need for heterogeneity.

26.2   THE EVENTS OF MID-2007

The events leading up to and during the credit crisis were a complicated combination of real losses and distressed valuations causing and being caused by liquidity problems for hedge funds, SIVs and banks. To understand the full sequence of events we need to start where the real losses started – the subprime mortgage market.

26.2.1   Subprime mortgages

The process of originating and securitising mortgages is well-established, especially in the US market where it has long been accepted that mortgages could be bundled together and sold to specialist mortgage companies. These companies raised the necessary funding from an array of investors who were given the choice of participating in the risk of the mortgage pool at a junior, mezzanine or senior level. There are a number of classifications, credit scores and other underwriting tests which provided the investors with some comfort as to the risk of the pool that they were exposed to. It is beyond the scope of this book to describe the securitisation of mortgages in detail. There are however two important features that help explain the extensive confusion surrounding the size and extent of losses in the subprime sector.

Recovery of losses by the mortgage servicer: although mortgages may be moved into specialist financing companies (MBS) to allow the risk to be spread far and wide, the actual management of the mortgage relationship with the borrower is through mortgage servicing companies. They are required to make payments to the MBS which would normally be covered by back-to-back payments from the borrower. If the borrower misses a payment then the servicer pursues payment culminating, in the worst case, in a foreclosure on the mortgage and taking possession of the house to sell it and repay the loan. Normally the servicer can only reclaim losses from the MBS when they have reached the last legal remedy of foreclosure. If for some reason foreclosure cannot happen, due perhaps to government intervention that prohibits foreclosure to prevent a social crisis, then the servicer will be making cash payments to the MBS which are not to be covered by the borrower.

The underwriting process: the second problem related to the actual underwriting process. A number of the tests that allow a mortgage to be placed in an MBS were enforced by the local lender. Checking the credit scores of the borrowers, checking that the borrowers actually live in the house that is to be mortgaged and ensuring that the borrower makes the first few mortgage payments are all open to abuse. Feedback from those close to the industry suggests that there had been fraudulent activity in this process: the credit score of one borrower might be represented as being the average credit score of a borrowing couple (when in fact the other borrower has a poor score); checks on whether a property is the borrower's primary residence were poor or nonexistent; and it was not unusual for the mortgage arranger to offer to make the first mortgage payment as a "sweetener" for the deal. Whether this actually happened may be revealed as investigations proceed but there is some certainty that many mortgages would never have been transferred into MBSs if the underwriting rules had been rigidly enforced.

By the time these pools of subprime mortgages had been financed by different risk tranches and some of these tranches had been placed in CDOs to be further tranched, it should come as no surprise to discover that the CDO investors had little clue as to the risk and therefore value of their positions. Cashflows are vague due to uncertainties at the servicer level and the average risk of the portfolio is uncertain due to possible flaws in the underwriting process.

The credit modelling tools used by the mortgage markets may have been adequate for valuing individual mortgage-backed tranches in normal market conditions but proved ineffective (if used at all) to revalue CDO tranches that were exposed to mortgage-backed tranches in distressed market conditions. To add to the confusion it is likely that many CDO investors (i) didn't know whether they were exposed to the MBS sector and (ii) even if they knew of MBS positions in the portfolio didn't know the quality of such positions.

It is easy to blame those who originated the mortgages for being sloppy and maybe fraudulent in the underwriting process, those who packaged and rated the pools of mortgages for not performing better due diligence, and those who distributed the securities for being irresponsible in their assessment of this risk. However, it is impossible to point the finger of blame at anybody other than all of those involved in the process. Everybody was motivated by the rewards: from the commission for originating a mortgage right through to the higher yields paid to end investors. Those involved early in the chain were never going to bear the risk, those later in the chain didn't know what the risk was. The former were maybe negligent in their regard for the latter, the latter were maybe negligent in not questioning the seemingly endless supply of high yielding low-risk product from the former.

26.2.2   Investor impact

The impact of the uncertainty described in the previous section was a significant downward revaluation of all CDO tranches with little distinction between underlying portfolio asset mix. Even those deals with no subprime risk were marked down. This had the following impact on different types of investors:

Hedge funds: for the funds that were long CDO tranches the revaluation resulted in margin calls. For some funds the margin calls exceeded available collateral and the hedge funds were forced to de-leverage. This could only be achieved by actually selling or terminating the CDO positions that the market was struggling to value. Not surprisingly the termination values were poor reflecting the market's reluctance to take on tranched credit risk.

SIVs: it was well-known that SIVs invested in the AAA tranches of CDOs and hence when such tranches started being revalued at lower levels there was an increased degree of nervousness in the asset-backed commercial paper market. Supplies of liquidity slowed, forcing some SIVs to liquidate parts of their holdings. This added to the downward pressure on asset prices and was compounded by the problems being faced by the hedge fund industry.

Mark-to-market investor: most financial institutions that held CDO investments were required to mark their positions to market. The significant revaluations that started to appear as the liquidations in the hedge fund and SIV markets gained momentum, causing material MTM losses for many investors. In some cases the losses triggered an informal decision or a formal requirement to sell. This was particularly frustrating where the investment was taken on with a hold-to-maturity mentality and the underlying position was probably no riskier than pre crisis.

Nervous investor: for most of 2007 the financial press covered the structured credit market with a level of detail never seen in the market's 13 years of history. The coverage during the crisis was very detailed but frequently misleading. For example, the highest rated CDO tranches – the "AAA" tranches – were often referred to as one group with little attempt to distinguish between the different underlying pools of risk. This may have contributed to all AAA tranches being revalued at much lower prices even where the underlying portfolio was 100 % investment grade corporate risk.

Hold-to-maturity investor: the group of investors who provided much needed stability during the period of CDO revaluation and liquidation were the investors who were not affected by liquidity needs, either did not mark their positions to market or were able to absorb significant MTM movements, and who were sophisticated enough to assess the true meaning of the market's revaluations.

26.2.3   Bank impact

The impact on banks was more complicated given their involvement in so many areas of the origination and distribution process. Assets due to be securitised unexpectedly stayed on balance sheet, unsold CDO risk positions fell in value, some collateralised credit lines failed, SIV back-stops were called and some SIV and CDO deals had to be brought back on balance sheet. These are discussed in more detail below.

Warehousing of assets for CDOs: by mid-2007 the CDO machine was in full swing with a broad range of asset classes being securitised. In order to speed up the process it was common for banks to "warehouse" assets that were destined for a CDO. Since there was a reasonable certainty that any debt held in this way was only going to be on balance sheet for a short period of time, it was possible that the attention paid to hold limits or underwriting standards was less than it would have been if the debt was destined to be held for a longer period of time.

A fall in value for unsold positions: the credit crisis left banks holding two sorts of CDO positions: those that it had always planned to hold – mainly senior positions – and those that it was unable to sell. Both had to be written down in value and it is likely that the former created the largest problem because of the sheer size of senior positions held by banks.

26.2.4   The failure of Lehman Brothers and the bailout of AIG

In 2004 the US Securities and Investment Commission relaxed a rule limiting the amount of leverage that Lehman and other investment banks could take. Lehman Brothers proceeded to take on substantial exposure to low-quality mortgages by way of asset-backed securities and credit derivatives. As a result of the fall in the market for subprime mortgages and securitised mortgages, Lehman faced massive losses and was forced to raise US$6 billion through a share issue. After further losses the US government decided not to bail out the bank, no buyer could be found, so on 15 September 2008 the company filed for insolvency in the US and soon after in the UK.

By contrast with its traditional, relatively low-risk business of life insurance and retirement services, from 1998 AIG diversified into more risky investments, taking massive exposures across mortgage-backed securities, CDS contracts and particularly CDOs on asset-backed securities (ABSs), many based on bad asset classes such as subprime debt. In spite of its huge exposures to these products, its financial models only estimated the risk of default of the underlying obligations. It was only in the second half of 2007 that AIG began to model the risk of the value of underlying obligations falling (as distinct from their default) and so started having to post collateral to counterparties and make writedowns on its balance sheet. However by this time it was too late, with major counterparties demanding billions of dollars of collateral as a result of worsening credit markets. Needless to say, AIG did not have access to the liquidity to finance these payments.

To exacerbate the problem, on 17 September 2008 AIG's long-term credit ratings were downgraded by S&P from AAA to A and by Moody's from AAA to A2. AIG was suddenly obliged to post more than US$13 billion in collateral as a result of that downgrade. On 17 September 2008, with Lehman having gone into insolvency two days before and credit markets freezing, the US Treasury decided it could not let AIG take the same route, and offered a bail-out in the form of a US$85 billion credit facility, later extended to $153 billion, in return for a 79.9 % stake in the group.

It is worth noting that the majority of AIG's actual losses occurred on CDOs of ABS. While its CDS book had a notional value of US$270 billion its actual losses were only US$3 billion, whereas its CDOs of ABS had a notional value of US$300 billion and an actual loss of US$46 billion.

All market observers have consistently exhibited great surprise at AIG's involvement in the structured credit markets. However, as the extracts from a Fitch 2006 survey show, in September 2006 it was well-known that AIG's activity in this sector dwarfed its peers and many of the banks.

26.3   ISSUES TO BE ADDRESSED

26.3.1   A different rating agency process

Credit rating agencies were critical of the growth of securitisation, CDOs and SIVs. Banks would have found it hard to profitably sell on individual loans of borrowers that generally were denied direct access to the capital markets. Packaging and structuring slices of the loans together into a CDO or SIV created a focus on credit risk and a diversification of credit risks that were attractive to a wider group of investors, but it also made the instruments more obtuse and so, for the market to work, investors required a credit rating.

Increasing attention has been placed on the inherent conflicts of interest in the relationship between banks, credit ratings and investors. The credit ratings were for the use of investors, but were paid for by the arrangers – the banks. The arrangers made more profit the more they could convince the rating agencies to give packages made up of risky instruments a higher credit rating. The rating agencies made more profit the more banks gave them packages to rate. The more discerning the rating agency was over what it rated and the less generous its ratings, the less business the rating agencies would do. Were the rating agencies overly influenced by the banks which were paying them to give the packages a higher rating than they deserved, at the eventual cost of investors? An analogy is with the bank analysts during the dotcom bubble, who, it is alleged, were encouraged to give generous ratings to companies in order to help them win lucrative corporate finance mandates.

It is clear that investors have, yet again, paid a price. It is also clear that the ratings appeared generous and that these credit ratings have become so mistrusted that the assets did not have the liquidity expected of instruments with good ratings. Proving that credit rating agencies connived with banks to push up ratings is less clear.

It has been argued that one of the problems was that investors did not understand what the ratings meant. It is possible that they were confused between credit risk – the risk of default or some credit event, which is what the ratings were for – and liquidity risk – the risk that the assets could not be sold on to someone else. Some have suggested that the rating agencies should have provided a liquidity rating as well. Liquidity and credit analysis are very different. A credit view can be taken by an analyst working at home with publicly available data on an entity's liabilities. Once established, it is a view that is likely to change only slowly, especially for the highest rated entities. Liquidity conditions can change rapidly and require an appreciation of market liquidity not easily gained outside the market places. Liquidity judgements are best left to market participants.

But the degree of confusion over what ratings mean is worrying. It is not clear that this confusion was deliberate but there were commercial forces that made it likely to happen. Rating agencies were trying to extend their "brand" from corporate bond ratings, where they have an established presence, to structured credit. To support the brand they wanted to use rating labels that had a resonance with their existing ratings.

At first sight it would appear that the principal solution to the concern over the veracity of ratings is to ban arrangers and issuers from paying for ratings as a result of the conflict of interest and lack of independence. The problem is that this neglects the fact that ratings are a "public good" in that they only have value to issuer, investor and market if all investors are aware of them, and if all investors are aware of them, it is hard to get any individual investor to pay for them. Rating agencies have tried. If investors will not pay, the only alternative is issuers or government. But the public sector should steer clear of impinging on how ratings are derived. At best this would lead to a perception that the government was morally obliged to protect investors from losses that were the result of following government funded or approved ratings. At worst, there could be a loss of confidence in ratings if what little scope for innovation and competition there was left in the industry's oligopoly structure was eroded by prescriptive and burdensome regulation.

26.3.2 Standardised nomenclature for credit ratings

The three main credit rating agencies each have their own similar, but different rating nomenclature, which they augmented in similar but different ways to extend ratings to credit derivatives and structured finance instruments. In quiet times these differences appeared insignificant and were easily ignored by investors. In stressful times these differences and confusion around them became important.

The rating agencies should be invited to consult with each other, with no fear of being accused of anti-competitive behaviour, to develop standard definitions and nomenclature. How rating judgements are arrived at and the basis for applying them to specific entities will remain the preserve of the individual rating agency. Public coordination around the definition of ratings should not lead to any implicit public approval or guarantee of ratings.

26.3.3   Keeping a percentage of originated risk on balance sheet

One of the compelling features of balance sheet CDO is the market's requirement for the arranger to keep some or all of the first loss tranche. This is based on the belief that there needs to be a financial incentive to ensure that a bank continues to monitor lenders whose debt has been transferred into the CDO. To the extent that bank originated debt is transferred into a CDO, this first loss ownership also ensures that underwriting standards remain robust.

The bulk of deals done in the last few years have been arbitrage CDOs and in the deals where recently originated debt (e.g. leveraged loans) is transferred into CDOs, there is no requirement for the arranger to keep a first loss position. The only mechanisms for ensuring the quality of deals sold to investors are compliance and reputation risk. The former is meant to ensure that the investor is sufficiently sophisticated and has all of the risks explained; the latter puts the arranger on notice that bad deals will come back to haunt you.

26.3.4   Undrawn credit facility capital charge

One of the great unknowns of the credit crisis was the size of the back-stop facilities granted by banks to facilitate the financing of SIVs. In order to secure a high rating for the commercial paper that is financing the bulk of an SIV's balance sheet, there is normally a bank back-stop in place to act as lender of last resort. Should short-term financing ever be unavailable then the SIV may liquidate some of its assets (hence reducing its need for financing) or may call on its back-stop facility and fill any financing gap.

26.3.5   The future of CDOs

The development of credit derivatives and the CDO market has had a significantly positive impact on risk bearing and risk management in financial markets. It has also produced a systemic crisis of massive proportions. The problem is clearly to develop a market structure that enjoys the benefits of credit risk transfer, and at the same time mitigates the downside risks.

A major difficulty is the lack of comprehensive information on the transfer of risk. If the location of risk could be clearly mapped by the regulatory authorities, then measures could be taken, for example by means of capital charges, to disincentivise the accumulation of risk holdings that pose systemic risk.

As mentioned above, one of the compelling features of balance sheet CDO is the market's requirement for the arranger to keep some or all of the first loss tranche. To extend this discipline into the structured credit market might ensure better quality product but it would be hard to achieve in practice. The implications of holding a prescribed or recommended amount of every deal would be an operational challenge. It would also transform a bank's structuring function into a risk-taking group with necessary allocations of capital etc. And unfortunately, even if some of the risk was retained by a visible holding of a bond, the actual risk could be subtly removed by an appropriate hedging strategy.

26.3.6   Mitigating the negative impact of mark-to-market

The spread of mark-to-market requirements (whether internally developed within firms or required by regulators) has been a major stimulus to the development of risk trading at the expense of risk absorption. This is another area in which there is a need to balance the positive benefits with negative systemic effects. Without the requirement of mark-to-market the serious deficits in many pension funds would not have been revealed, and the funding of pensions today would be far weaker and less secure. Perhaps there should be a better balance between providing more detailed information about liabilities and risks, but doing so less frequently.

But going beyond these market developments there is a need for regulators to assess the systemic impact of their mark-to-market requirements and to manage them in such a way as to reduce the likelihood of disruptive forced sales. This will require regulators to take a wider view of macroeconomic conditions than they have previously done.

26.4   SUMMARY

It is overly simplistic to point blame for market turmoil at an individual financial product. To the extent credit derivatives and particularly CDSs were implicated in the current crisis, it was largely to the extent that they wrapped underlying exposures that were simply not sustainable.

Centralised clearing may improve transparency and may be appropriate for certain standardised CDS contracts that are traded in high volumes. However, it would be not be appropriate for those transactions where parties are seeking to hedge risks in ways that are tailored to their specific needs.

Reform proposals have clearly been driven by market turmoil. To the extent that some types of credit default swaps were implicated in the financial crisis and the collapse of the likes of Lehman and AIG, it is important to distinguish them from other credit derivatives and OTC derivatives in general. Interest, foreign exchange and equity derivatives were not involved, yet are often caught up in proposals for centralised clearing. Amongst credit derivatives, CDOs on ABSs, particularly those backed by subprime mortgage, caused huge liabilities when the market for their underlying obligations collapsed. However, exposures under single-name CDS contracts fared well, as indicated by the successful close-out and settlement of the CDS transactions on Lehman's books.

Appendix
Summary of Risks

The following brings together all the risks described elsewhere in the book. For convenience they are grouped by general categories. Some risks not previously mentioned are included for completeness.

GENERAL COMMENT – UNFORESEEN RISK

No stakeholders in a business – investors, managers, employees or customers – want unforeseen risk. Due to its sudden effect, the organisation is ill-equipped to deal with it and its consequences are unknown. One of the major causes of the recent credit crunch was the failure of many organisations to take into account a particular risk: that so many American subprime mortgage borrowers would be unable to repay their debt. Unforeseen risk points to poor management and supervision and reduces confidence in the financial entity. If risk is present, it should be known about and then sensible decisions can be taken about how to manage it.

OPERATIONAL RISK (IN THE TRADE LIFECYCLE)

The longer mistakes remain in the trade lifecycle, the more costly they are to correct. Here we list some of the common risks associated with the lifecycle.

Confirmation: a poor confirmation causes delays in the processing and settlement of a trade. This increases the probability of settlement risk occurring. Moreover, since confirmation is a two way process, other organisations will quickly see mistakes and sloppy practices, and these damage the reputation of the firm.

Settlement:

1. Theft: a big risk in the settlement process is theft. This could occur where the settlement process is intercepted by criminals or where staff involved in the process (including those writing or operating a computerised settlement system) divert part or all of the money to their own bank accounts.

2. Cost of recovery: even if there is no attempt to deliberately steal money, there may be a significant cost in recovering it, not to mention severe embarrassment, if the settlement process goes wrong and money is transferred to the wrong account; too much is transferred to the correct account; or the transfer is on the wrong day or at the wrong time.

3. Legal: settlement is a legal obligation arising from execution of a trade. A counterparty risks being sued by the wronged party if it fails to settle the right amount at the right time and according to the given settlement instructions.

The legal process, even if settled out of court, will be expensive and time consuming.

4. Reputation: any missed or erroneous settlement will cause damage to the reputation of the counterparty at fault. Trading works to a large extent on trust and poor settlement will quickly lead to trading lines being reduced or withdrawn. Trading is one of the main activities of investment banks and hedge funds, and settlement is the most visible face of the institution to its peers. So a failure to settle will arouse doubts as to the competence of the organisation concerned.

5. Unexpected charges: a party to a trade may be expecting a large receipt of money upon settlement. If the settlement is delayed for any reason, it will not have that money at its disposal. This could result in not being able to pay off a debt charged at a daily interest rate.

6. Other trades: a counterparty may have a trade with settlement expected on a given day. It may be planning to use that cash, financial instrument or commodity to execute a subsequent trade. A delay on the first settlement will affect other settlements that depend upon it.

Unsettled trades use up counterparty risk allocations and may prevent opportunities for more trading with the same counterparty.

7. Documentation: where securities are owned, there exists documentation risk. In order to receive coupons or dividends, the holder must ensure they are correctly registered (in the case of registered securities) or that they initiate the claim for payment process in a timely fashion (for bearer securities). There is also a risk that documentation may be lost or stolen.

8. Breaks: a major part of back office time is spent tracing "breaks", where a settlement has not been enacted. These breaks are very expensive in time and human resources. Sometimes huge numbers of unpaid settlements are built up because operations do not have time to chase them.

Payment systems:

Credit risk – risk that a counterparty has insufficient funds to settle its debt
Liquidity (timing) risk – risk of unavailability of funds at the requisite time

Straight Through Processing (STP): there are risks associated with STP. A fully automated system means that mistakes are fully automated. The machine cannot respond to potential or actual errors unless it has been programmed to do so. Due to the varied nature of trade booking errors, the design of the system cannot be relied upon to catch them all and, even when they are caught, the process requires human beings taking appropriate action. Also, some business functions are required to *merely* check trades in the STP. Since checking is a passive activity, it is easy for mistakes to slip through.

Provisional trades: the extent to which a provisional trade carries a legal responsibility must be clear and transparent to anyone acting upon or using that trade. Falsely assuming a provisional trade to be completely abstract could cause loss and is therefore a risk.

A clear risk exists if the provisional trade automatically becomes live when a counterparty does not withdraw by a given date. There may be a tendency to apply less stringency with the writing and checking of a provisional trade ticket, as it is not real. This bears risk because, in the event the trade is executed, it might be simply transferred to a live trading book with the falsely applied assumption of accuracy.

Orders: orders are instructions to trade but not trades themselves. A risk arises when orders are missed and clients or counterparties expect them to have been transacted. Another risk is caused by changes or deletions to orders not being reflected in the ensuing trades.

Exercise: there are risks, such as poor communication between traders and middle office, which lead to exercise being missed when it should have occurred, and being performed when it should not have occurred.

There is also a problem when market rates are very volatile and an option is at-the-money. A sudden swing could take the option into the money and make it worth exercising. Systems showing market data must be accurate and up to date – the timing of market data may be as crucial as its actual value.

Another issue arises from at-the-money options with volatile market data. When a trader expects an inflow of assets, he takes steps to hedge his position and reduce his risks. The problem of last minute decisions about option exercise is that the asset changes cannot be managed so effectively. This can result in greater hedging costs or greater exposure.

HUMAN RISKS

Inevitably a trading organisation relying on human beings is going to be subject to human risk. Here we list some of the common risks.

Too much knowledge in one person: if an individual is particularly good at his job because of his greater knowledge, experience or application, it is often tempting to give him more responsibility and a greater share of the overall burden of work. Other people do not study his area of expertise, because they know he can be relied upon. This causes a knowledge risk, where an area of the trading lifecycle is left solely in the hands of one individual. If that individual should leave the firm or become ill, there will be nobody to replace him. Although it may seem like a waste of resources, it is always important that every area has sufficient back-up. Too many organisations have failed to recognise their reliance on one person until it is too late and he has departed.

Not enough knowledge: this is one of the greatest risks to any organisation. Sometimes the management of a particular trading area becomes convinced that a type of trade or trading strategy is foolproof and certain to bring in risk-free profits. Trading commences and suddenly the lack of proper understanding is exposed to great cost. It may seem absurd that financial entities specialising in financial products with strict internal and external controls should be able to engage in trading that is misunderstood, but it happens surprisingly frequently. Even if controls and procedures are in place, they will be of little benefit if the fundamental behaviour of the product is not known.

It is not just in trading that a lack of knowledge can be risky; the trade lifecycle is a chain of processes and is therefore only as strong as its weakest point.

Although training is provided, particularly to junior staff, there is a tendency to consider a new product as a modification of existing products or to borrow techniques from one asset class to use in another – these assumptions can lead to incorrect processing and added risk.

Wrong people: each business function has its particular demands and responsibilities. Personality and outlook play a part in how well an individual suits his business function. Since large amounts of money are at risk, a trading environment can be very stressful. Stress leads to mistakes, increasing the risks to the firm.

Not enough investment in people: there is sometimes a tendency to believe that computers can solve all the problems and only minimal staffing levels are required in some business functions. If things are going well, this may well be the case. But for the unusual, the unplanned or the unlikely, computers will not be able to step in and sort out the problem. The balance between humans and machines is hard to gauge, but broadly speaking, computers should deal with the ordinary and expected; human beings the more specialist or unusual circumstances.

Whenever computers are running processes, it should never be assumed that they have performed the task correctly on every occasion. Even if a process has run successfully 200 times in succession, there is always a chance of a problem on the next run.

Reliance on short-term planning: there are obvious risks in working to short-term timescales. Trades are often designed to post profit quickly, while long-term negative effects are overlooked.

Longer term trading could be safer and more profitable, but it is often not considered because nobody will be around to draw bonuses from it.

Conflicts and tensions: in any commercial environment there are bound to be tensions and the stress of investment banking can accentuate them. However, some tensions arise from the very nature of the business functions and these are important to ensure trading is conducted with an appropriate level of control. When one or other side gains too much power, there could be risk to the business.

Trading versus control functions: the most obvious tension is between traders and the control functions. Counterparty and market risk control departments are responsible for reducing risks. If they refused all trading there would be no risk, but of course then there would be no business and no one to pay their salaries. Since traders are the revenue generators for everybody, there may be a tendency to allow traders more freedom than would be the case if the control functions were financially supported from elsewhere. Similarly if a member of product control objects to the trader's view of the current market price, he may be afraid to raise an objection because his career and bonus depend on keeping the traders happy.

On the other hand, in a cautious environment genuine trading under reasonable controls can be thwarted by over zealous control functions.

Communication: mistakes are very common where communication is missing or inadequate.

Panic: processes may be well designed, implemented and tested, but there may still exist a risk due to panic in the face of extreme conditions. Rehearsing emergency drills and making the emergency processes intuitive and user-friendly can mitigate this risk.

MARKET RISK CONTROL

There is a risk associated in relying too much on the market risk control department to avert risk from market forces. Staff in this department do not prevent disasters from occurring: the expectation is that should something unusual happen, they will be able to provide the necessary data on the risk profile of the organisation at various macro and micro levels so that the extent of the damage can be assessed.

Also, they cannot possibly measure every conceivable disaster. Nobody can determine how much or in what way the future replicates the past. Market risk control lives in the world of the unknown, but uses probability to give some feel for exposure to risk. Understanding the limitations of market risk controllers is very important in order to assess the credibility of their measurements.

Everything correlated: market risk allocates risk on an asset-by-asset basis. Interest rate traders are given so much interest rate risk, commodity traders commodity risk and so on. Most of the measurements of risk (with the exception of scenario testing) also consider each risk type separately. This means there is an implicit assumption that one type of market risk is not connected to other types. This assumption is not always correct: we have observed several episodes in the recent and distant past that have caused markets to react in concert across the range of asset classes. This means that in times of crisis markets are ultimately correlated to each other.

The tails: when we reach an extreme case of market data performance – known mathematically as the tail of the curve – different factors come into play and cause the standard model to become less reliable. Predicting behaviour at the tails is very difficult and as a result enhances the size of market risk.

The human factor: risk analysis is a mathematical exercise – valuations do not have emotions. However, an important point to bear in mind is that the driver for the valuations is the various input data. This comes from prices set by human beings reacting emotionally as well as intellectually to events around them. Although the human factor in market risk cannot be precisely quantified, it should be taken into consideration and studies on past crises can reveal trends in human and hence market behaviour.

COUNTERPARTY RISK CONTROL

Correlation between counterparties: even if a company has correctly gathered its counterparty data and understands the links between the various parent and child companies, there is still a hidden risk that once one counterparty fails, it will pull down others with it. For example, a hedge fund might require the support of a major investment bank for its funding. The counterparty risk department will have to decide how far to investigate the funding of its counterparties and decide if the cost of the extra research work outweighs the cost of not knowing the information.

Added complication of credit risk: counterparty risk is often a separate operation from the department trading credit products. In reality, the trade on a credit product has dual credit risk: the risk the trade refers to and the risk to the counterparty. To get a true picture of counterparty risk, knowledge should be shared between the two departments.

Insufficient consideration of counterparty risk: even if the counterparty risk control department is functioning correctly and setting sensible limits, its success at containing risk is contingent on the attitude and support of management. Managers are under pressure to deliver profits by promoting trading. Until there is a major reverse, they may not strictly enforce the reports and recommendations of the counterparty risk function, because they see them as being overly cautious or anti-trade.

Sudden counterparty changes: a limit may be set according to current counterparty rating information or by any other means. If that limit becomes fully or nearly fully utilised, there is very little room for manoeuvre should the counterparty suffer a reverse and the limit needs to be revised downwards. New trading with that counterparty can be restricted, but closing down existing trades might be expensive. If a credit-trading desk exists in the organisation, it will sometimes be asked to cover the exposure by buying credit protection on the counterparty.

There are occasions when a counterparty fails suddenly and spectacularly, such as Lehman Brothers in 2008. The whole market was caught by surprise, but a good counterparty risk department should be able to identify the outstanding exposures and perform a damage limitation exercise.

CASHFLOW

When trades, cashflows and asset holdings do not match up there are problems. Either the systems are not reporting what is going on or the processes are not being properly executed – both sources of major operational risk. Since these activities and measures are so intrinsic to the whole trading process, it is important that proper systems and controls are in place for managing them.

DATA

Putting too much faith in data: everybody involved in the trade lifecycle is using and working with the effects of input data. Key management strategies, day-to-day tasks and split second trading decisions are all based on input data – either directly or through reports and calculations. It is easy to assume that data is correct – we have been receiving it for many years, the supplier is authentic and other people use the same data.

Due diligence would surely require the question to be raised as to what happens if the data is wrong and perhaps more worryingly, what if it is wrong sometimes, but not always.

Not reacting to data: the other extreme is too little notice taken of input data. If the data is an accurate reflection of the state of the market, warning signs, such as larger than usual changes, should be detected quickly and reported to the people who can make decisions. It is of little use if a junior clerk in the back office spots an irregular pattern but by the time the news filters through to the management, it is too late to react.

Coping when data is not there: a good test of the resilience of an organisation is to switch off its market data supply for one day and see how it copes. Are there back-up procedures in place, can data be obtained or inferred from other sources? As data is so important these scenarios should be taken into consideration.

Ensuring authentic data: obviously to be a trusted source, data must be authentic. This may be easy to verify in the case of a daily feed from a vendor's ftp site or by a secure delivery mechanism, but other types of data can be potentially insecure. Live data arriving at users' machines or directly entering the database can be hazardous and difficult to monitor. The recipient of such data needs to balance the benefit of this information being available so easily, with the security risk involved.

REPORTING

Security: sensitive information falling into the wrong hands is a risk associated with the generation and transmission of reports.

Inaccuracy: decisions are often made based on information in reports. If these reports are inaccurate or incomplete, the firm could make the wrong decisions. Even correctly produced reports may be misinterpreted, if the readers are not fully educated about their limitations and scope.

Lack of support for readership: once a report has been distributed, there is a risk if nobody can interpret the results or explain how they were derived. The production team might have gone home, it may be another time zone or the producers themselves are not able to answer the queries. An unexpected result might indicate a major problem requiring urgent action or it may be a false alarm. Either way, prompt dialogue can avert many problems but it requires people of sufficient knowledge to be available.

Poor distribution: lack of coordination in report production or distribution might lead to mixed signals being transmitted which confuse or mislead the readership. Inaccurate translation can also carry risks in multiple language environments.

If a report requires retraction or correction, it is important to act fast. Generally, once something is in writing, it is hard to erase its effects, whether they are benign or malign. A written or electronic report always has the potential to be quoted or reused.

NEW PRODUCTS

New products carry additional risks because they are relatively untested. Fewer people have knowledge and experience and so there is a heightened human risk. Processes may treat the new risk type as an exception, excluding it from some of the standard operational risk controls and increasing processing risk.

Early participants in the new trade may misunderstand how to trade it and lose money. The trade may be too illiquid to get out of positions, causing losses when market conditions reverse. Assumptions underlying the initial trade development may turn out to be unfounded or wrong.

A costly infrastructure may be developed for the new trade, but it is wasted if the trade fails to reach its projected market volumes.

LEGAL AND REGULATORY

Closure: if a firm fails to fulfil its regulatory responsibilities, it could have part or all of its activities closed down.

Penalties and prosecution: depending on the nature of the breach, companies or individuals who have broken the laws or regulations governing their conduct may be subject to significant fines, criminal prosecution or both.

Litigation: a company that breaches its legal and regulatory obligations may also be liable to civil litigation brought by any party that has suffered as a result. If the entity fails to perform its activities with sufficient care, it could be liable to a claim of negligence. The standard of care owed by the entity will depend on the sophistication of the particular investor – with professional institutions viewed as requiring less protection than members of the public. Courts will look to standards mandated by regulation and applied by other firms in determining whether the requisite standard has been met.

Costs: the resolution of proceedings initiated by a regulator, or the defence of a lawsuit, can be very costly. They will typically require significant management time in addition to legal costs.

Reputational risk: in any case of personal or corporate malpractice, the company may suffer reputational risk. Potential clients may steer clear of companies that have breached legal or regulatory requirements. Counterparties may also be wary of trading with a company that does not play by the rules.

Advisory risk: legal risk does not rest solely on actual trading activities. There is also a considerable legal responsibility when advising clients on financial services. Thus advisory activities must be policed to the same degree as those of trading.

TESTING

Here we summarise the business and operational risks related to testing.

Too little testing: processes may not run correctly leading to extra costs for the business. Misleading results may have several undesirable consequences. The investment in developing or purchasing software is wasted if the software fails to perform correctly.

Too much testing: resources are wasted carrying out superfluous testing and improving software more than is necessary.

Poor testing: staff may be lulled into a false sense of security if they assume a system has been tested, when in fact it has either not been tested at all or not been tested effectively. This might lead to unexpected delays, faults or false results being taken as accurate.

Over-reliance on testing: testing a system thoroughly improves its quality and robustness, but does not make it more efficient. Underlying flaws in design or implementation may cause it to be harder to extend in the future or hinder its performance. A well-tested system is not necessarily a good system.

Poor communication: testing is a collaborative activity involving managers, developers, users and specialist testers. For testing to be effective, the results must be communicated to all interested parties. Developers must know and understand the faults, users must be aware of any shortcomings and managers need to build testing and fault fixing into their planning. Overall confidence in the system very much depends on good, effective testing.

BUSINESS CONTINUITY PLANNING (BCP)

An untested BCP plan can jeopardise the business by inducing a false sense of confidence.

Linked to this risk is the tendency of many people to undervalue the purpose of BCP. The BCP staff are dependent on IT and business professionals to tell them what is required – if the exercise is not taken seriously key components or activities might be missed.

Another risk is that the BCP is thorough, but cannot cope with a double or extensive disaster.

VALUATION AND MODEL APPROVAL

Most of the risks connected to the valuation process arise through insufficient testing and documentation. By documentation, we also mean communication of how and when to use the valuation.

In addition, the valuation must only be used in the scenarios for which it was built. There is often a temptation to take a model designed for one class of trades and apply it to other trades that appear similar. Insufficient appreciation of the subtlety and limitations of the model can lead to erroneous results in this situation.

A common risk associated with the process of approving valuation and risk management models is that the validation asserts the model does what it is supposed to do, but nobody checks that the model is appropriate for the business problem it attempts to solve. This can lead to the risk of valuation results being falsely relied upon.

MANAGEMENT

Decision making: a poor decision as well as lack of judgement, communication or information between management and staff increases the risk to an organisation.

Lack of empowerment: if staff see a potential risk or problem, but they do not have the authority to take action to avert it, the organisation will suffer.

Structural risk: a poorly designed organisational structure can lead to responsibility being given to the wrong people or not allocated to anyone. Whenever a manager lacks the ability to control a risk, the risk can grow.

DOCUMENTATION

Insufficient or inaccurate documentation: insufficient or inaccurate documentation might lead to false assumptions about the way a process, model or system is supposed to work or to it being operated incorrectly.

Unread documentation: there is no point producing a correct and thorough piece of documentation if the people who need to read it do not. Staff must be given the time to study documents that affect their work.

Out of date documentation: there is a risk if documentation is not kept up to date as the process, model or system changes it describes develop over time.

FRONT OFFICE

Apart from risks already mentioned, there are some that are specific to the front office trading and sales desks.

Sales: there is a risk in selling something that cannot be delivered. This can lead to legal costs or damage to reputation.

Trading: taking on too much market risk, being over-leveraged or violating trading limits can endanger the entire firm. Working without support and control functions also hampers the ability to book and manage the trading process. A lack of understanding of the complexities of a product might cause severe trading losses.

Liquidity: liquidity risk is present whenever a lack of market activity prevents trading out of held positions.

Funding: committing to a trade where insufficient funding is available is a source of risk to the firm.

RESEARCH

If not enough research was carried out to make proper decisions or the research was wrong, trading might be impaired or poor decisions taken.

IT AND SYSTEMS

We have already described data and reporting risks, but here we list some other risks associated with systems and IT.

Systems not working as expected and documented: most IT systems involve significant cost and time to complete. If they fail to fulfil their objectives then resources have been wasted and one or many business processes are left poorly implemented enhancing operational risk.

False reporting: either success is reported as failure or failure as success. This is always going to add some level of risk to the operation.

Project: projects overrunning can lead to trading opportunities being missed or an increase in operational risk. The same applies when projects do not deliver the functionality that was required.

System operation: whenever the operation of a system is wrong, a process may fail and operational risk is increased.

Diagnostic: when an error has occurred but is not detected or reported, a risk is created. Conversely, if a benign situation is falsely reported as an error, this can lead to much time being wasted tracking down a problem that does not exist.

EFFECTIVE CONTROL AND SUPPORT

As explained in Chapter 15, the financial entity has revenue generators together with people who support and control them. When these three divisions are not acting properly there may be risk.

Not enough support: revenue generation is impaired because the systems and resources required for making money are not available.

Not enough control: revenue generators, in particular traders, may take on too much risk or fail to think through the consequences of their trading positions.

Not enough revenue generation: restricting revenue generation by imposing too many controls will mean everyone in the firm loses their source of income. It is therefore essential that senior management set a strategy that gives each of the three divisions (revenue generation, support and control) the ability to carry out their business function with an appropriate balance to reflect the requirements of all stakeholders in the control of risk and generation of profit.

Recommended Reading

Frederick P. Brooks, Jr, *The Mythical Man-month*, Addison Wesley, 1995.

Geoff Chaplin, *Credit Derivatives: Risk Management, Trading & Investing*, Wiley Finance, 2010.

J. Davidson Frame, *Managing Projects in Organizations*, Jossey-Bass Inc., 1995.

Frank J. Fabozzi, *Bond Markets, Analysis and Strategies*, Prentice Hall, 1996.

G. R. Grimmett and D. R. Stirzaker, *Probability and Random Processes*, Oxford Science Publications, 1982.

John C. Hull, *Options, Futures and Other Derivatives*, Prentice Hall, 2008.

Peter Jäckel, *Monte Carlo Methods in Finance*, Wiley Finance, 2002.

Michael Simmons, *Securities Operations*, Wiley Finance, 2002.

Index

30/360 date calculation 242

accounting 131
  balance sheet 131–3
  financial reports 137–8
  profit and loss account 133–7
accrual dates 83, 90
  accrual convention 241
  and accrued P&L 134–5
aggregation of trades 54, 70, 79, 140, 234–5
agricultural commodities 27
AIG bailout 265–6
alerts 53
American options 35, 87, 88
application programming interface (API) 187
architecture, IT systems
  business logic 191–2
  data repository 192
  systems architects 155–6
  user interface 191
asset-backed securities (ABSs) 21–2, 265–6
asset classes 15
  bonds and credit 20–7
  commodities 27–30
  equities 19–20
  foreign exchange 17–19
  interest rates 15–17
  trade matrix 39
  trading across 30
asset holdings see holdings
asset managers 8
  reports for 137–8
'at-the-money', options 35, 88
audits, internal 160
average trades, exotic options 36

back book trading 7, 107
back office 152, 215
back testing 216
back-to-back trades 123

backup of data 256
bad data, dealing with 216–18
balance sheet 131–3
banks
  impact of credit crisis on 265
  reasons for trading 7–8
  traders' internal accounts 98
barrier options 36, 84, 238
Basel II 117–18
baskets, FX trades 18, 36
bearer securities 98–9
Bermudan options 35, 87, 88
bespoke deals 54
bid/offer spread 210–11
binary options 36
bond basis deltas 142
bonds 20–2
  coupon payments 22, 23
  government 20
  identification of 27
  proof of ownership 98–9
  tradeflow issues 22, 24
booking of a trade 66, 71–2
bootstrapping 240–1
breaks, settlement 79
brokers 4–5, 8, 59
buckets (time intervals) 120, 121–2, 123
business continuity planning (BCP) 255–6
  risks associated with 257, 278
business functions 9–10

calculation process 231–6
  bootstrapping 240–1
  calibration to market 242
  dates 241–2
  net present value (NPV) 236–40
  risks associated with 243
  tests for valuations 242–3
calibration process, valuation 53–4, 242
call options 31–2, 33–4

capital adequacy ratio (CAR) 118
cash 93
    balance sheet item 131–2, 133
    'cash CDOs' 44–5
    exchange dates 67
    exercise 87
    settlements 77, 84
cashflows 37–8, 75
    and asset holdings 93
        bank within a bank 98
        consolidated reporting 97
        custody of securities 98–9
        diversification 97
        holdings 93–5
        realised and unrealised P&L 97
        reconciliation 96–7
        risks 99, 275
        value of holding 95–6
    date calculations 241–2
    operational risk 275
    unknown, options valuation 238
    waterfalls, CDOs 55
change
    coping with 170
    resistance to 173–4
    to a trade 82–6
change management, IT systems 189–90
collateral 15, 84, 98, 124–5, 126–7, 266
collateralised debt obligations (CDOs) 43–4
    balance sheet 268
    data relating to 48–9
    future of 268
    gearing and rating terms 47–8
    management of 49–53
    pricing methodology 46–7
    reference pools 44–5
    static and managed 45–6
    valuation of 53–4
commodities 27–30, 77
communication 157, 165–6, 207, 278
competitive advantage 8, 175, 195
compliance officers 160–1, 251–2
compliance rules, CDOs 45–6
composition measures, CDOs 50
conduits see structured investment vehicles
    (SIVs)
confirmation of a trade 72–4, 251, 271
conflicts and tensions 164–5
consolidated reporting 97
control
    see also counterparty risk control; market risk
        control
    people involved in 158–66
    of report generation 229
    risks associated with 280
conversion, currency 237–8

correlation risk 106
cost-benefit analysis, IT systems 181
counterparty risk control 119, 159, 275
    as a function of time 120
    activities of department 125–7
    collateral 124–5
    consequences of counterparty default 119–20
    identifying the counterparty 67, 124
    imposing limits 123
    measurement of the risk 120–3
    payment systems 128–9
    reasons for non fulfilment of obligations 119
    risks involved in analysing credit risk 127–8
coupon payments, bonds 22, 23, 83
credit crisis (2007)
    background 261–3
    issues to be addressed 266–9
    mid-2007 events 263–6
credit default swap (CDS) 25–6, 34
    contracts 41–2
    deltas 143
credit derivatives 41, 54–6
    and the 2007 credit crisis 261–8
    collateralised debt obligations (CDOs) 43–54
    credit default swap (CDS) 41–2
    credit linked notes (CLNs) 42–3
'credit events' 41–2, 51
credit exposure 121–2
credit linked notes (CLNs) 42–3
credit rating agencies 26, 47
    need for a different process 266–7
    standardised nomenclature 267–8
credit risk 24
    see also credit default swap
    assets in the SIV 262
    bonds 20–4
    documentation 25
    insurance 24–5
    recovery rate 26–7
    risks involved in analysing 127–8
credit worthiness, measuring 26
currency
    conversion 237–8
    exposure to 3
    and foreign exchange 17–19
    and interest rates 15–17
    precious metals as 29
    sovereign debt 20
    and value of holding 95–6
current market data 213
current processes, understanding 171–3
curves, market data 211–13
custodians 76, 99, 152

data 209
    back testing 216

bad data 216–18
bid/offer spread 210–11
business risks of 221–2, 276
corrections to 219–20
curves and surfaces 211–13
integrity 220–1
market data 213–16
relating to CDOs 48–9
sources of 218–19
types of 209–10
data cleaning 218
data discovery 217–18
data engineering 217
databases 192, 209
dates
accrual 83, 90
calculation of 241–2
multiple settlement 78–9
overnight issues 79–80
relating to a trade 67–8
reporting dates 140–2
on trade tickets 79
day-count convention 22, 241
dedicated IT teams 182, 193, 194
default 25
see also credit default swap (CDS)
counterparty 119–20
risk 106
delivery versus payment (DvP) 76
delta hedging 108
delta risk 105, 113–14
deltas 142–3
deposits (loans) 15
derivatives 31
exotic options 36–7
linear 31
nonlinear 31–5
option terminology 35
option valuation 35–6
simpler products 38–9
structures and hybrids 37–8
designers, IT systems 183
digital options 36
directors, role of 162
disaster, types of 255–6
discounting, NPV calculation 236–7
distribution of reports 225, 229
diversification 97
diversity
and market liquidity 262–3
numerical measures of 46
dividends 19, 20, 82–3
documentation 25
models and systems 247
risks associated with 279
standardised legal 25, 66, 250–1

dreaming ahead 107
duties (fees) 75, 108, 137
DV01, risk measure 113

electronic systems 71
email 71
end of day roll 80
energy products 28
equities 19–20
errors
confirmation process 73–4
in data 216–18, 219–20
in reports 136, 228–9
European options 35, 87
exchange price 58
exchanges 5, 218
execution of a trade 71
booking 71–2
pre execution process 69–70
exercise, option trades 33, 87–8, 272
exotics 36–7, 85, 193, 238
expected loss (EL) 48, 121
exposure 3, 102–3
credit exposure 121–2
desirable vs. undesirable 101
external reports 224–5

face-to-face trading 71
fault logging 205–6
fees 75, 108, 137
finance department 159
accounting 131–8
financial reports 137–8
first-line support, IT 183–4
first loss piece (FLP) 43, 47–8
fixed and floating coupons 83
fixed bonds 21
fixed income 20, 103
fixings 83–4
float-for-fixed/float-for-float 16
floating rate notes (FRNs) 21
foreign exchange (FX) 17–19
forwards see futures and forwards
front book trading 7, 107
front-line support 155
front office
relationship with market risk control 116
risks associated with 279
FSA (Financial Services Authority) 161,
249
fugit 88
fund managers, financial reports for 137–8
futures and forwards 15, 17, 31, 32, 57
gold futures 212, 233
leverage 60
risks of 102

gamma risk 105, 113–14
gearing 47–8
government bonds 20
'the Greeks' 105–6, 114
grid computing 197

hedge funds 8, 128–9, 264
    financial reports fo 137–8
hedging strategies 108
hedging trades 103–4
historical market data 214
    back testing 216
    market risk control 215
    VaR calculation 113
holdings 93–5
    consolidated reporting 97
    proof of ownership 98
    realised P&L 97
    reconciliation 96–7
    value of 95–6
human risks 117, 162–6, 273–4, 275
hybrid and structured trades 37–8

illiquid prices 58, 59
illiquid products 115
illiquid trades 133, 233
implied data 220
implied volatility 213
'in-the-money', options 35, 105, 213
incentives 163–4
independent IT division 182, 193–4
index (synthetic equities) 19
industrial metals 28
inertia, obstacle to change 173–4
information technology (IT)
    application programming interface 187
    change management 189–90
    dependency on 170
    generic vs. specific solutions 188–9
    the IT divide 185–6
    performance issues 197
    procurement 182
    programmer creativity 187–8
    project estimation 197–8
    project management 185
    prototypes 186–7
    risks associated with 190, 279–80
    staff 154–7, 183–4
    timeline of a project 184
    types of development 193–4
    vendor vs. in-house solutions 195
    vendor vs. financial entity perspective 196
infrastructure, IT 155
in-house development, IT systems 195
inputs and outputs, IT systems 181–2
insider trading 252

instantaneous measures of risk 113–14
insurance 24–5, 42, 61
integrity of data 220–1
inter-bank market 211, 212
interest rates 15–17
    futures curves 211
    and option valuation 35
    rho risk 105
interfaces
    between systems 181–2
    user 186–7, 191, 192
internal audit 160
interpolation techniques 217, 231
investment banks 7–8
investors, impact of credit crisis 264–5
ISDA (International Swaps and Derivatives
        Association) 25, 250–1

knock-in/knock-out, barrier options 36, 85
knowledge
    and insider trading 252
    of project managers 156
    risks of 162–3

legacy IT systems 169
legal department 158
    compliance officer 160–1, 251–2
    documentation 25, 66, 250–1
    use of market data 216
legal risks 252–3, 277
    insurance 24–5
    litigation 158, 252, 277
    settlements 78, 271
legislation, compliance with 160–1, 177,
        251–2
Lehman Brothers, failure of 265–6
leverage 33–5, 60–2
libraries, programming 153–4
lifecycle of a trade see trade lifecycle
limit orders 105
limits 78
    on CDOs 45–6, 52–3
    controlling 115
    imposing 123
linear derivatives 31
liquidity 57–8, 262–3, 267, 279
litigation 252, 277
loans 15, 45, 133
    bootstrapping 240–1
    subprime mortgages 263–4

managed CDOs 45–6
management
    see also risk management
    approval for new products 177
    of CDOs 49–53

of changes 86
of new system releases 189–90
of projects 156–7, 183, 185, 198
responsibilities of 162
risks associated with 278
mark-to-market (MTM)
  input data for npv calculations 235
  investor losses 265
  mitigating negative impact of 269
  over reliance on 136–7
  undesirable uses of 232–4
  values 132, 136–7, 232
market data 49, 210, 213–14
  business usage of 214–16
  changes as a result of 83–4
  for credit derivatives 54–5
  for VarR calculation 112–13
market makers 4, 107, 210–11
market participants 3–4
market risk control 111, 159
  allocation of risk 114
  controlling the risk 115–16
  limitations of 116–17
  methodologies 111–14
  monitoring of market risk 115
  need for risk 114
  regulatory requirements 117–18
  responsibilities of 116
  risk in relying on 274–5
  usage of market data 215
market sentiment, factors affecting 233
master agreements 66, 250–1
matching of records 73
mathematical models 46, 117, 236, 243
  quantitative analyst role 152–4
  validation of 158–9, 178, 245
    implementation & documentation
      247
    testing process 245–7
maturity of a trade 7, 88–9, 133
mezzanine debt 43
middle office (product control) 149–52
  compiling daily P&L 136
  new products 178
  pre overnight checks 81
  usage of market data 215
millennium bug , legacy systems 169
missing data 53, 216, 217
models see mathematical models
money laundering 251
Monte Carlo technique 239
mortgage backed securities (MBSs) 21, 263–4,
    266
mortgages, subprime 263–4
multiple dimensions, report constraints 228
mythical man month 198

net present value (NPV) 232
  calculation of 235, 236–9
  sensitivity analysis 239–40
netting 122–3
new products 175
  checklist for 177–8
  evolution of 178–9
  origin of 175
  risks involved in 179, 277
  trial basis for 176–7
night-time processes 79–82
nonlinear derivatives 31–5
nostro accounts 77, 96
NPV see net present value

official market data 214
offsetting risks 8, 34, 102–3, 108
operational risk 262, 271–3
operations department 152, 215
operators, IT 157
options
  terminology 35
  valuation 35–6
  volatility risk 103, 114
orders 70, 272
'out-of-the-money', options 35, 105, 213
over-the-counter (OTC) trading 5
  commodities 28
  date properties 241
  forwards 17
  price 58
overnight processes 79–82

payment systems 128–9
  risks associated with 272
  settlement instructions 76
people involved in trade lifecycle 147
  back office (operations) 152
  compliance 160–1
  counterparty risk control department
    159
  finance department 159
  human risks 162–6
  information technology 154–7
  internal audit 160
  legal team 158
  management 162
  market risk control department 159
  middle office (product control) 149–52
  model validation team 158–9
  and origin of new products 175
  quantitative analyst 152–4
  researchers 149
  structurers and sales 148–9
  traders and assistants 147–8
  trading manager 161

performance
  fees 137
  of IT systems 196–7
  reports 138
physical commodities, settlement 29, 76–7
planning
  business continuity 255–7
  of processes 169–70
post booking processes 74–5
postal trades 71
potential future exposure (PFE) 122
pre-execution of trade 69–70
precious metals 28, 29, 77, 227
predictions 51, 107, 121, 122, 211
present value (PV) see net present value (NPV)
price 58–60
pricing methods, CDOs 46–7
process development/improvement 167
  coping with change 170
  current processes, understanding 171–3
  evolution of processes 167–9
  improving the situation 171–3
  inertia as obstacle to 173–4
  inventory of current systems 169–70
procurement of systems 182
producers 4
product appetite 3
product control 149–52
product development see new products
profit and loss (P&L)
  accounts 133–42
    individual trades 135
    responsibility for producing 136
    risk associated with reporting 136–7
    worked example 134–5
  accrued and incidental 134
  attribution reports 139
    benefits of 139–40
    example 142–3
    process of 140–2
  end of day 151
  realised and unrealised 97, 134
programmers, creativity of 187–8
project estimation 197–8
project management 185
project managers 156–7, 183
prototypes, IT projects 186–7
provisional trades 69–70
put options 31, 32–3, 34
pyramid of trade objects 188

quality control see testing
quantitative analysts 152–4

random market data 214
rapid application development (RAD) 193, 194

ratchet options (Cliquet) 36
ratings 47, 50
  agencies 120–1, 266–8
raw data 220
raw reporting 226
readership of reports 223, 224–5, 229
reconciliation 96–7, 139
recovery rates 46, 49, 106
  CDO pricing 46, 49, 106
  credit risk products 26
  default losses 121
redundancy
  processes 169
  reports 229
  resources 172
reference pool, CDOs 43, 44–5, 48, 50
registered securities 98
registration with financial regulator 249–50
regulation
  external 161
  market risk control 117–18
  registration 249–50
  risks associated with 277
release process, IT systems 189–90
repo (repurchase) market 15
reports 223
  CDO management system 52
  control issues 229
  enhancements 230
  errors in 228–9
  for fund and asset managers 137–8
  redundancy of 229
  requirements of 223–8
  risks associated with 230, 276
  role of middle office 150
  security issues 230, 276
reputation 78, 271–2
  reputational risk 253, 277
research 149, 279
resettable strike, exotic options 36
revenue generation
  people involved in 147–9
  risks associated with 280
rho risk 105
risk 11
  see also market risk control
  appetite for 3
  dealing with 12–13
  inevitability of 11
  managing 13
  quantifying 11–12
  unforeseen 13, 271
risk management 13, 101
  in absence of trader 104–5
  of actively managed trades 102–3
  hedging strategies 108

hedging trades 103–4
impact on managers 102
impact on traders 101
trading strategies 107
types of risk 105–7
risk summary
    business continuity planning 257, 278
    cashflows and asset holdings 99, 275
    changes to a trade 86
    counterparty risk control 275
    credit risk analysis 127–8
    data 221–2, 276
    documentation 279
    exercise 88, 272
    front office 279
    human 117, 162–6, 273–4, 275
    IT and systems 279–80
    liquidity 58, 129, 262, 279
    market risk control 274–5
    new products 179, 277
    orders 70, 272
    payment systems 128–9, 272
    provisional trades 69–70, 272
    regulatory and legal 252–3, 277
    reporting 136–7, 230, 276
    settlement 77–8, 271–2
    of SIVs 262
    STP systems 72, 272
    trade lifecycle 271–3
    valuation process 243, 278
robustness of IT systems 181
rogue trading 137

sales department 66, 149
    risks 279
    usage of market data 214
scenario analysis 55, 111–12, 234
scrutiny of trades 74
second-line support, IT 184
securities, custody of 98–9
security issues, reports 230, 276
semi-static data 48–9, 210
senior managers 102, 162
sensitivity analysis 113–14, 239–40
settlement 75–6
    breaks 79
    commodities 29, 77
    date s 67–8, 78–9
    of fixings 84
    non fulfilment of counterparty obligations 119
    nostro accounts 77
    risks involved in 77–8, 271–2
shares 19–20
short-term lending 15, 261–2
short-term pricing 153
short-term thinking 164, 273–4

simple products, importance of 38
SIVs see structured investment vehicles
software vendors 182, 196
sovereign debt 20
specification of IT systems, importance of 185–6
speculators 4
spot prices 35
    and exotic options 36–7
    leverage 60–1
spot trades 7, 17, 38, 102
spread of bid/offer 210–11
spreadsheets 153
    pros and cons 194
staff see people involved in trade lifecycle
stakeholders, IT systems 182–3
stale data 53, 82, 216
standardisation, documentation 25, 250–1
static CDOs 45
static data 48–9, 55, 210
stop-loss hedging 108
stop orders 70, 104
storage of data 192, 209, 210
straight through processing (STP) 72, 272
strike price, options 35, 36
structured assets 47
structured investment vehicles (SIVs) 261–2
    back-stop facilities financing 268
    hedge funds 264–5
    risks associated with 262
structured trades 37–8
structurers, role of 148
subprime mortgages 263–4
substitutions 45, 48, 51–2, 53
support activities
    IT system 183–4
    people involved in 149–57
    risks associated with 280
surfaces, market data 213
swaps
    credit default 34–5, 41–2
    foreign exchange 17–18
    interest rate 15–16
swaption 35
'synthetic CDOs' 45
synthetic equities (index) 19
systems 181
    see also information technology (IT)
    amalgamation 81
    architects 155–6
    architecture 191–2
    buying vs. building 195
    elements of good 181–2
    performance 196–7
    project estimation 197–8
    project management 185
    risks associated with 279–80

systems (*Cont.*)
　software vendors 196
　stakeholders 182–3
　timeline of a project 184
　types of development 193–4

tail behaviour, predicting 117, 274
technical authors 184
telephone transactions 71
tenors (durations) 26, 211
tensions and conflicts 164–5
testing 201
　back testing 216
　fault logging 205–6
　importance of 201–2
　mathematical models 246–7
　　tests for calculations 242–3
　responsibility of 202–3
　risks related to 206–7, 277–8
　stages and types of 203–5
　testers 157, 183
　when to perform 203
theft, risk of 77–8, 271
theta risk 106, 140
third-party managed CDOs 45–6
time for end of day, deciding 80
time decay, theta 106, 113
time horizon 112
time intervals (buckets) 120, 121–2, 123
time series analysis 218
time zones 80
timeline of a trade 67–8
timing of reports 225–6
trade lifecycle
　see also reports
　changes during lifetime 82–6
　confirmation 72–4
　and equity trades 19–20
　example trade 89–91
　execution and booking 71–2
　exercise 87–8
　maturity 88–9
　overnight 79–82
　post booking 74–5
　pre execution 69–70
　settlement 75–9
trade ticket, components of 65–8
trade/trading
　see also trade lifecycle
　anatomy 65–8
　business functions 9–10
　consequences of 6
　defining 9
　factors affecting 3
　policies 7
　reasons for 3, 7–8, 103

transactions 4–5
tradeflow issues
　bonds 22, 24
　commodities 29
　foreign exchange 18
　interest rates 17
traders 147–8
　impact of risk management on 101
　risk management in absence of 104–5
　usage of market data 215
trading at settlement (TAS) rules 29
trading assistants 148
trading disputes 158
trading exchanges 5, 218
trading lines (limits) 78
trading managers 161
　controlling the risk 115–16
　impact of risk management on 102
tranche correlation 54, 106
tranches, CDO 43–5, 54, 264–5
treasury desk 38
trials for new products 176–7
trigger event 24–5
trust issues 165

underlying 65
　effect on trade of changes in 85–6
underwriting process 263–4
'unexplained', PV differences 142
unforeseen risk 13, 271
unknown cashflows, options 238
unwinding a trade, cost of 59
user interface 191
utilitarian value of commodities 29

validation of models 158–9, 178, 245–7
valuation process
　credit derivatives 55
　non-financial example 231–2
　NVP calculation 232, 236–9
　risks associated with 243, 278
　testing 242–3
Value at Risk (VaR) 234
　calculation of 112–13
vega (kappa) risk 105
vendors
　data services 218
　IT solutions 195, 196
volatility 36
　implied 213
　vega risk 105
volume of a trade, effect on price 59

weighted average scores 46, 50

zero coupon bonds 21